Intelligent Design 101

Intelligent Design 101

Leading Experts Explain the Key Issues

H. WAYNE HOUSE

GENERAL EDITOR

Intelligent Design 101: Leading Experts Explain the Key Issues

© 2008 by H. Wayne House

Published by Kregel Publications, a division of Kregel, Inc., P.O. Box 2607, Grand Rapids, MI 49501.

All rights reserved. No part of this book may be reproduced, stored in a retrieval system, or transmitted in any form or by any means—electronic, mechanical, photocopy, recording, or otherwise—without written permission of the publisher, except for brief quotations in printed reviews.

Scripture taken from the *Holy Bible, New International Version*®. Copyright © 1973, 1978, 1984 by International Bible Society. Used by permission of Zondervan. All rights reserved.

Library of Congress Cataloging-in-Publication Data
    Intelligent design 101: leading experts explain the key issues / by H. Wayne House, general editor.
        p.   cm.
    Includes bibliographical references and indexes.
    1. Intelligent design (Teleology) 2. Creationism. I. House, H. Wayne. II. Title: Intelligent design one hundred and one. III. Title: Intelligent design one hundred one.
BS651.I575   2008   215—dc22   2007048374

ISBN 978-0-8254-2781-7

Printed in the United States of America

08 09 10 11 12 / 5 4 3 2 1

To the scholars and scientists of the intelligent design movement who have stood for the academic freedom to follow the evidence wherever it may lead, doing so even when facing significant personal and career costs.

Contents

List of Illustrations

Contributors

Michael J. Behe graduated in 1974 from Drexel University in Philadelphia, with a Bachelor of Science degree in chemistry. He did his graduate studies in biochemistry at the University of Pennsylvania and was awarded a Ph.D. in 1978 for his dissertation research on sickle cell disease. From 1978 to 1982, he did postdoctoral work on DNA structure at the National Institutes of Health. From 1982 to 1985, he was assistant professor of chemistry at Queens College in New York City, where he met his wife. In 1985 he moved to Lehigh University, where he is currently professor of biochemistry. He has written more than forty technical papers and two books, *Darwin's Black Box: The Biochemical Challenge to Evolution* (London: Free Press, 1996) and *The Edge of Evolution* (London: Free Press, 2007), which argue that living systems at the molecular level are best explained as being the result of deliberate intelligent design. *Darwin's Black Box* has been reviewed by the *New York Times, Nature, Philosophy of Science, Christianity Today*, and more than one hundred other periodicals. He and his wife reside near Bethlehem, Pennsylvania, with their nine children.

Eddie N. Colanter is director of bioethics and culture at the Newport Institute for Ethics, Law, and Public Policy. He is visiting lecturer of philosophy of religion and of bioethics at Faith Evangelical Seminary, and is cofounder of the Intelligent Design and Evolution Awareness (IDEA) Center. Colanter is currently working on a Ph.D. in theology, ethics, and culture at Claremont Graduate University. He holds an M.A., cum laude, in bioethics from Trinity Graduate School; an M.A. in faith and culture, cum laude, from Trinity Graduate School; an M.A. in Christian apologetics, summa cum laude, Simon Greenleaf University; and a B.A. in philosophy (minor in biology) from the University of California, San Diego.

Logan Paul Gage is a policy analyst with Discovery Institute, working out of the Washington DC office, serving as a liaison to policy makers on Darwinism and intelligent design. He received his B.A., summa cum laude, from Whitworth College in Spokane, Washington, where he majored in philosophy, history, and American studies. At Whitworth he studied philosophy under the direction of Stephen Meyer.

H. Wayne House is distinguished research professor of biblical and theological studies at Faith Evangelical Seminary, Tacoma, Washington, and a professor of law at Trinity Law School, California campus, of Trinity International University. He holds a J.D. from Regent University School of Law; a Th.D. from Concordia Seminary, St. Louis; an M.Div. and Th.M. from Western Seminary; an M.A. from Abilene Christian University; and a B.A. from Hardin-Simmons University. He has authored, coauthored, or edited more than thirty books and scores of articles in the subjects of theology, law, and ethics.

Phillip Johnson was born and raised in Aurora, Illinois, and graduated from Harvard and the University of Chicago Law School. After law school, Johnson clerked for Chief Justice Roger Traynor of the California Supreme Court and Chief Justice Earl Warren of the U.S. Supreme Court. He joined the faculty of the Boalt School of Law at the University of California at Berkeley in 1967 and has been a professor emeritus since 2000. Johnson has served as deputy district attorney while on leave from his teaching duties and has held visiting professorships at Emory University and at University College, London. With the publication of his book *Darwin on Trial* (InterVarsity Press, 1991), he began a second career as one of the foremost critics of Darwin's theory of evolution and its wider sociological and cultural implications. Johnson is one of the leading participants in the intelligent design movement and has done much to help these ideas gain acceptance and a wider hearing worldwide. Johnson is the author of several books on evolution, philosophical naturalism, and other cultural issues and speaks extensively around the United States. His "Leading Edge" column appears regularly in *Touchstone Magazine*.

Casey Luskin holds bachelor's and master's degrees in earth sciences from the University of California, San Diego, and a Juris Doctorate from the University of San Diego. He has published in science and legal journals, including *Geochemistry, Geophysics, and Geosystems*; *Progress in Complexity, Information, and Design*; and *Journal of Church and State*. He cofounded the Intelligent Design and Evolution Awareness (IDEA) Center, a nonprofit organization helping students start "IDEA Clubs" on university and high school campuses. Luskin conducted scientific research at Scripps Institution for Oceanography from

1992–2002, and is now an attorney working in public policy at the Discovery Institute in Seattle, Washington.

J. P. Moreland is distinguished professor of philosophy at Talbot School of Theology, La Mirada, California. He earned his Ph.D. in philosophy from the University of Southern California. He has written, edited, or contributed to thirty books, including *Does God Exist?* (Prometheus, 1993); *Philosophy of Religion: Selected Readings* (Oxford, 1996); *Naturalism: A Critical Analysis* (Routledge, 2000); *Universals* (McGill-Queens, 2001); and *Philosophy of Religion: A Reader and Guide* (Edinburgh University Press, 2002). He has also published more than sixty articles in professional journals, including *American Philosophical Quarterly, Australasian Journal of Philosophy, MetaPhilosophy, Philosophy and Phenomenological Research, Religious Studies*, and *Faith and Philosophy*. Besides teaching, he served for eight years as a bioethicist with PersonaCare, Inc., headquartered in Baltimore, Maryland.

Jay W. Richards is research fellow and director of Acton Media at the Acton Institute in Grand Rapids, Michigan. He has a Ph.D. in philosophy and theology from Princeton Theological Seminary, where he has been a teaching fellow; a Th.M. from Calvin Theological Seminary; and an M.Div. from Union Theological Seminary. He is the author of many scholarly and popular articles. His most recent books are *The Untamed God: A Philosophical Exploration of Divine Perfection, Immutability and Simplicity* (InterVarsity Press, 2003) and *The Privileged Planet: How Our Place in the Cosmos Is Designed for Discovery*, with astronomer Guillermo Gonzalez (Regnery, 2004). *The Privileged Planet* is the basis for the popular documentary "The Privileged Planet: The Search for Purpose in the Universe," which has aired on many PBS affiliates in the United States.

Foreword

Imagine you just won the state lottery. Suppose the pot for this lottery was up to several hundred million dollars. The pot had gotten that big because no one had won the lottery for such a long time —until you got lucky! Out come the reporters to interview you about how it feels to win this vast amount of money. You say the usual things: "I really don't know what to say. . . . I'm overwhelmed. . . . This is the happiest day of my life. . . . The first thing I'm going to do is buy my parents a new home."

But then, along comes a reporter from the Eccentric Broadcasting Network (EBN), and he asks you the following question: "You know, it was an incredible long shot that you should win this lottery. What's your secret? How did you pull it off? Where did you get the skill set to win that lottery?" You stare at this reporter in disbelief. This is a lottery after all. Eventually someone was bound to win it. You don't need any special skill set (read "intelligent design") to win the lottery. You just have to buy a ticket and get lucky. Case closed.

Many scientists, when confronted with the possibility that life and the universe were designed, react in the same way you did when confronted with the possibility that you somehow engineered winning the lottery. According to them, there is no evidence of design in the universe. Rather, the best evidence is that everything proceeds by unbroken natural laws. Accordingly, nature at bottom is nothing more than matter, energy, and the forces by which these interact. In short, nature works out its destiny purely by chance and necessity and not by design.

But even though you would be right to dismiss a reporter who suggested that you had somehow "designed" winning the lottery, you would be wrong to side with materialistic scientists who regard the universe as exhibiting no evidence of design. In the last forty years, advances in our understanding of cosmology and biology, especially molecular biology, have shown just how inadequate materialistic theories are in accounting for the appearance of design throughout the universe.

In reply, scientists committed to materialism say that the appearance of design in the universe is *only* an appearance, and that when we really understand the underlying science, we'll see that there is no actual design. Such a dismissal of design, however, rings untrue. When Oxford biologist Richard Dawkins, in *River Out of Eden*, writes, "The illusion of purpose is so powerful that biologists themselves use the assumption of good design as a working tool,"[1] one is right to start wondering if the appearance of design in nature is really only an appearance.

In fact, the best scientific evidence now confirms that design in the universe is real. This volume will help you sort through that evidence. But it does more. It situates the scientific debate over theories of intelligent design and unintelligent evolution within a broader philosophical and cultural conversation. The list of contributors is superb, the scope of the contributions is comprehensive, and the topic is absolutely central to understanding the struggle for people's hearts and minds. If you want to know what's driving the culture war, read this book.

—WILLIAM DEMBSKI
Research professor in philosophy at
Southwestern Baptist Theological Seminary, Ft. Worth, TX;
and senior fellow with Discovery Institute's Center for
Science and Culture, Seattle, WA

Preface

Since 1859 there has been a struggle between two ways of looking at the world, one in which blind, random, and unguided material forces brought about all forms of life, and another in which an intelligent agent designed life intentionally and with purpose. This complex debate involves many religious, philosophical, and scientific questions and arguments. Contrary to popular belief, this struggle is not simply between science and religion, or even between science and philosophy. It is about competing scientific explanations of the data.

The controversy over biological and cosmological origins is ancient. Natural philosophers, such as Plato and Xenophon of ancient Greece, debated whether mindless matter or some intelligent mind is the primary cause of our world. This was centuries before the time of Christ and thousands of miles from the epicenter of the Jewish religion. Darwinists and the media characterize the modern debate as between unsophisticated fundamentalist Christians and infallible scientists. Yet many skeptics of Darwin and proponents of intelligent design are well-credentialed scientists and other scholars with legitimate scientific and philosophical theses. Through February 2007, more than seven hundred scientists signed a statement of dissent from neo-Darwinian evolution.[1]

But what is evolution? What is popularly called evolution more accurately should be called neo-Darwinian macroevolution. Macroevolutionary theory is founded upon the view that all life shares its inception in a common organism, and became diversified via an unguided process of DNA mutation and natural selection. Charles Darwin's original theory of change through macroevolutionary processes initially had a difficult time winning converts. Most scientists of Darwin's day found his theory to be unsupportable.[2] The dominant view of leading scientists was that species are immutable, the opposite of what Darwin proposed. Indeed, Darwin's book, *The Origin of Species*, never really explained the *origin* of species, but merely provided a supposed mechanism for biological change within species. As did Darwin himself, many modern Darwinian scientists expect the public to accept, without question, their grand claims. Most evidence offered cites meager examples of small-scale change within a species. Change within a species is called *microevolution*. Most people should have the good sense to know when a viewpoint is being forced due to lack of evidence.

One fascinating aspect of the current debate is that many leading Darwinists behave more like the stereotypical "fundamentalists" than do the religious "fundamentalists" they oppose. They imagine zealots who seek to censor the teaching of evolution on purely religious grounds. In the secular academy, questioning of the neo-Darwinian creation account usually is not tolerated. Establishment opposition to any alternative supposition to neo-Darwinian evolution is as voracious as that encountered by Galileo Galilei (1564–1642) when he published his arguments for a Copernican, sun-centered solar system. People on all sides of the macroevolution debate see the important worldview implications in the balance.

Because of its intolerance to dissent, academia generally has a "pro-Darwin-only" approach to origins. Wearing philosophical blinders, Darwinists commonly proclaim in a self-contradictory fashion that intelligent design is both false and unfalsifiable.[3] Evolution, they say, is the only possible answer, and thus is infallible fact.[4]

Those with an open mind see the issue differently. Intelligent design is a fresh, and compelling, alternative to the tired arguments of Darwinism. In the pages of this book, experts in science, philosophy, and law provide reasons to embrace intelligent design as the reasonable alternative to neo-Darwinian macroevolution.

Acknowledgments

My thanks to the people at Kregel who have worked on this project: Dennis Hillman, publisher; Stephen Barclift, managing editor; Paul Ingram and Paulette Zubel, editors; and Miranda Gardner, assistant editor.

Thank you, too, Dennis Wagner and Access Research Network for the use of the graphic of the flagellum in chapter 3.

Special thanks to Dr. Michael Bauman, as well as to research colleague Dr. William Grover, who read through the initial draft of the manuscript and made many helpful suggestions.

One

Bringing Balance to
a Fiery Debate

PHILLIP JOHNSON

Fifteen years ago I published a book that I thought might add a few ounces of balance to the debate over Darwin's theory of evolution. The main thrust of that book, *Darwin on Trial*, was that evolution is propped up more by naturalistic philosophy than by the scientific evidence. Much to my pleasant surprise, this book turned out to be the match that lit the tinder beneath a stockpile of dry logs. This is not to my credit; the logs had been piled high, and the tinder gathered. Darwinian naturalists had accumulated a large stock of public discontent.

Darwinists long expected the average fair-minded American to accept a meaningless universe on paltry evidence. For example, the same Stephen Jay Gould who told us that "[B]iology took away our status as paragons created in the image of God. . . ."[1] also acknowledged that "the extreme rarity of transitional forms in the fossil record persists as the trade secret of paleontology. The evolutionary trees that adorn our textbooks have data only at the tips and nodes of their branches; the rest is inference, however reasonable, not the evidence of fossils."[2] Such reasoning could not be, and had not been, swallowed by most Americans who were not already committed to an atheistic world.[3] This stockpile of discontent was not my doing.

Indeed, when I wrote *Darwin on Trial*, I didn't even realize that there was a pile of logs to be lit. I could not see that millions of Americans had figured out the truth about evolution long before I had. Yet *Darwin on Trial* became a uniting force around which many like-minded individuals— scholars of many stripes, churchgoers, students, and even open-minded agnostics who dared extend their skepticism to Darwin—could rally. For many, that rallying cry ultimately became "Intelligent Design!" Like any good story, however, the journey is much more important than the destination.

The 1980s was a tumultuous time for the creation-evolution debate. Evolutionists of all stripes rejoiced as creationists battled one another over questions like whether the tectonic plates moved during the flood or which peak of the Ararat mountains held Noah's ark. Interesting though these debates may be, it became clear to me that creationists were gaining little ground against the monolith of evolutionary "science," which had united to take control of education and the media.

Today, the landscape of the debate looks very different. I cannot take credit for the subsequent shifts in antievolutionary thought, for it seems that endless debates over alleged ark-sightings left the skeptical public yearning for a better approach. First, the pathway must be traced back to the more primordial origins of this debate.

Gathering the Firewood

The modern chapter of this story opened in 1959. That was the high point for Darwinism in the United States and the world. Darwin's masterpiece, *The Origin of Species*, was published in 1859 and rapidly swept the scientific world. Yet there remained much cultural opposition to the Darwinian way of thinking, especially in the United States. Many attribute this to American religiosity, but I believe it had more to do with the American spirit of free, independent thought that drove this country to its current status as the world's leader in science. Regardless, as 1959 approached, evolutionary scientists thought that the midcentury would be an ideal time to hold a triumphant celebration. A professor at the University of Chicago organized the Darwin Centennial Celebration and landed the most prominent Darwinian speaker, Sir Julian Huxley, to keynote the event.

> In the evolutionary pattern of thought there is no longer either need or room for the supernatural. The earth was not created: it evolved. . . . So did religion.
>
> —Sir Julian Huxley, 1959 address

Huxley was the grandson of Thomas Henry Huxley, the British naturalist who pushed for public debates in favor of Darwinism in the early years. Grandfather Huxley became known as "Darwin's bulldog," because of his spirited advocacy for Darwin's theory. Grandson Huxley was a prominent zoologist in his own right and one of the founders of what would later come to be called the *neo-Darwinian synthesis*, the modern version of Darwinism. He was also an international statesman, a founding father of the United Nations Educational Scientific and Cultural Organization (UNESCO). Huxley was also the would-be founder of a new religion of evolutionary humanism. He wrote a book called *Religion Without Revelation* (Harper, 1957) that attempted to found a religion upon the scientific way of thinking. Science replaced revelation as the source of knowledge, and humanity, rather than God, sat at the top of Huxley's *scala naturae*.

This centennial was held at the University of Chicago on Thanksgiving weekend, 1959. It attracted so much press attention that it seemed to signify to the world, as intended, that Darwinism was triumphant everywhere. Huxley, in his keynote address, made it clear that this was a triumph in science and in religion. He said that there is now no room for a divinized father figure, an imaginary god who is really just a projection of our human father. Huxley was branding a new religion in which "[i]n the evolutionary pattern of thought there is no longer either need or room for the supernatural. The earth was not created: it evolved. So did all the animals and plants that inhabit it, including our human selves, mind and soul as well as brain and body. So did religion."[4] Essentially, then, one religion is replaced by another—triumphant evolutionary science explains everything.

At that point, many scientific authorities had the view that only a minor "mop-up" operation was necessary in the cultural war against theistic religion. Christianity, in particular, had been beaten. Science, the new religion, would replace it, with evolution as the creator.

In the years approaching 1959, events seemed to herald the arrival of evolution triumphant. In 1953, a young graduate student, Stanley Miller, appeared to have solved the chemical origin of life quandary. In the Miller-Urey experiment, pulses of electric energy were sent through a mixture of gasses thought to represent the atmosphere of the early earth, producing a mixture of chemicals that included some amino acids. Amino acids are the building blocks of proteins, and proteins are the building blocks of life. Thus the Miller-Urey experiment was represented to the world at that time as proof of the origin of life. Even Carl Sagan's *Cosmos* television series used the experiment to show how scientists have created life in a test tube. Finally, the beginning of the Darwinian narrative was completed—the origin of life itself was validated through the Miller-Urey experiment. Today we know that Miller chose his gasses in his experiment for no other reason than that they were useful in producing various organic molecules. Geochemists reject Miller's reducing atmosphere of methane and ammonia, rendering the experiment moot.[5]

Another famous buttress of evolution was the peppered moth. Scientists observed that more dark-colored moths appeared in England in some years, and more light-colored moths appeared in other years. This disparity in color was claimed to show the creative power of natural selection, as evidence that it could create moths and trees and birds and people. The peppered moth story was presented to the world in 1959 as Darwin's missing evidence—the evidence of natural selection operating in the wild and not just in domestic animal breeding like dog breeding. (Today it is known that many of the moths were glued to tree trunks where they would not normally rest, calling into question the very basis of the experiment, namely, that birds eat moths on tree trunks.)[6]

Another event that had enormous impact on the public as well as the scientific community occurred in 1957. The Soviets launched the first space satellite, Sputnik, which successfully orbited the earth. The American scientific elite were worried about this development because if the Soviets conquered space, they could set up rockets in space or on the moon. This Soviet accomplishment led to an enormous push in America to make the United States preeminent in science and remove worries over the growing scientific achievements of Communism. A large part of the educational arm of this effort entailed producing textbooks. The government went into the business of producing biology textbooks that emphasized evolution with an end to overcoming superstitions such as Christianity—although they didn't put it quite so boldly.[7] Nonetheless, the idea was to train thinking—all good citizens are to have an aptitude toward naturalism. The elites thought of naturalism as a scientific way of thinking: rely on nature and science, not on God.

Each of these events were said to make the case for the triumph of scientific materialism and Darwinism. That triumph fell apart, however, once people started scrutinizing the evidence.

The Creationist Counter-Reformation

At the time of the Darwin Centennial Celebration, various conservative Christians from the scientific community organized opposition to this assault upon theism. Theologian John Whitcomb and engineer Henry Morris published *The Genesis Flood* (Presbyterian & Reformed, 1960), which birthed the modern creation science movement. The modern creation science movement can also be traced to dissenting scientists who broke off from the American Scientific Affiliation in 1963 to found the Creation Research Society. In 1970, Morris and biochemist Duane Gish founded the Institute for Creation Research. Most of those affiliated with this "creation science" movement believed in a young earth, Genesis-based view of earth history and biological origins. They claimed that the fossil record supported a recent worldwide flood and that modern big bang cosmology had many deficiencies.

The creation-science movement was very successful in spreading its message and won political support in certain "red states" around the United States. This led to some famous court battles. In 1982, "Scopes II," *McLean v. Arkansas Board of Education*, a federal judge canonized into law the view that science only refers to "natural law." In a 1987 case, *Edwards v. Aguillard*, the U.S. Supreme Court declared creationism unconstitutional because it dared to postulate a supernatural creator. Those of the elites could never convince the public, but they managed to find seven Supreme Court justices who wanted to keep God on the other side of the "wall of separation."

That God may have been declared unconstitutional did not deter other innovative thinkers. In 1986, just before the *Edwards* decision, an astronomer, Hugh Ross, founded the creationist organization Reasons to Believe. The organization's view was that the universe and earth are billions of years old, but that God specially created life and did not use the evolutionary process. Ross developed arguments for the divine creation of the universe that accepted the big bang theory of cosmology and conventional physics. This gained many followers.

Two camps developed—young earth and old earth creationism. Sadly, they fought one another bitterly. Various books were fired back and forth, leveling all sorts of charges on both sides, from heresy to ignorance to deception. Needless to say, the Darwinists looked upon this debate with glee, realizing that the general public—who largely didn't care if Noah rode a dinosaur or a camel onto the ark—was theirs for the taking.

Uniting the Divided

Somewhere along the line, I stumbled into this debate. Despite long-standing infighting between the factions of creationists, a sizable segment of the U.S. public remained highly skeptical of neo-Darwinian evolution.

It was apparent that much of the public and creationists of all stripes shared one thing in common: They doubted naturalism and believed that ultimately there was a mind behind everything. For a majority of people, it was a creator god. No amount of Darwinian dogma or creationist infighting changed the public's perception that our universe was not chance-based, but came from a purposeful creator. Gallup Poll results through recent decades have consistently shown that only 10–15 percent of North Americans view life as having an atheistic origin. Well over 40 percent believe they were directly created by God. The other 40 percent still believe that God guided evolution. Some theists may have been duped by the naturalists into thinking there is overwhelming evidence for naturalistic evolution, while others may have principled reasons for accepting some version of evolution theory while nonetheless often rejecting much of the evolutionary story. What could possibly unite this very broad group of viewpoints—the 80 percent who did not accept a naturalistic view? What united them was the scientifically based theory of intelligent design.

Intelligent design developed in the early 1990s among some scientist colleagues of mine who fell into various viewpoints. If the public were the logs, then these scientists were the tinder. They agreed that there is fundamental evidence that a mind lies behind the origin of life and the universe. This theory does not identify the mind. That is left to theologians. What the theory does say is that science is capable of telling us that the universe and life bear detectable fingerprints of an intelligent designing agent. Intelligent design thus united into one movement people of many viewpoints who were once divided on side issues.

Lighting the Right Match

The strike that lit the match was the recognition that at the heart of evolution lies a philosophy of naturalism. Many of my fellow travelers in the wedge movement (more on that later) have exposed the deficiencies of naturalism. I'll take credit for one thing: *Darwin on Trial* lit the match. The culture as a whole was ready to realize that the core question in the debate over origins was whether there was some role played by a Creator. It doesn't matter to much of the public whether life began ten thousand years ago or 4.5 billion years ago. They reject the central claim that evolution took place in a random, unguided, and unsupervised manner. People need to know: *Is there evidence that God had a role?*

What is the right question? Like most things in life, people err by going too far to one extreme or the other. One of the most uninteresting and unimportant questions I can imagine is, "Could God have used evolution to create?" The answer is uninteresting because questions that begin with the words "Could God have . . . ?" invariably yield an answer of yes. God is omnipotent, omniscient, and omnipresent, and therefore can do anything He wants. The more interesting question is, "Did God use evolution to create?" This question is the one that addresses reality.

It doesn't matter to much of the public whether life began ten thousand years ago or 4.6 billion years ago. They reject the central claim that evolution took place in a random, unguided, and unsupervised manner.

There is one other problem with the question "Could God have used evolution to create?" Most people who say yes accept a definition for macroevolution that is quite different from the one promoted by evolutionary biologists. God-guided evolution isn't *evolution* as the scientific profession uses that term. Most evolutionists only recognize naturalistic evolution— unguided and purposeless, with no god playing a part. According to a statement issued in 1996 by the National Association of Biology Teachers, evolution means that higher forms of life (including humans) arose via an "unsupervised, impersonal, unpredictable, and natural process." Another widely used college text on evolutionary biology explains the necessary materialism of Darwinism:

> Darwin showed that material causes are a sufficient explanation not only for physical phenomena, as Descartes and Newton had shown, but also for biological phenomena with all their seeming evidence of design and purpose. By coupling undirected, purposeless variation to the blind, uncaring process of natural selection, Darwin made theological or spiritual explanations of the life processes superfluous. Together with Marx's materialistic theory of history and society and Freud's attribution of human behavior to influences over which we have little control, Darwin's theory of evolution was a crucial plank in the platform of mechanism and materialism.[8]

Macroevolutionary biology propositions directly conflict with the religious tenets of theists who believe that some nonmaterial, personal, and intelligent cause supervised or intervened at points in the history of life. In the view of most evolutionists, there is no such thing as a truly God-guided evolution because that would be slow creationism, which is not evolution at all.

At the other end of the spectrum are those who believe that the "right question" entails figuring out precise details about how and when God created. For this mind-set, there is only total victory or total surrender.

Football analogies explain this strategy well. As a San Francisco 49ers football fan, I recall times during the 1979–92 seasons when Joe Montana would come in as quarterback, down by six, with only two minutes left and his team on the twenty-yard line. Fans knew that only one touchdown was needed to win, but some drunk in the stands always shouted, "Joe, throw the bomb!" Of course, Joe would not throw the bomb. He didn't go for a touchdown in one play. He went up field five and ten yards at a time, and eventually the team scored. This is similar to how Charles Lyell, the famous uniformitarian geologist, argued that the Grand Canyon was cut an inch at a time by the Colorado River. Similarly, Julian Huxley and his midcentury evolutionist colleagues who wanted to overthrow theism didn't throw the bomb. They chipped away a bit at a time.

In the view of most evolutionists, there is no such thing as a truly God-guided evolution because that would be slow creationism, which is not evolution at all.

Today's skeptics of evolution must do the same to materialism. When I first entered this debate, naturalism was taken in most education circles as self-evident fact. There could be no answer other than "naturalistic evolution" because anything else would insert "God into the gaps." But that's the point: By defining the rules of science so as to exclude God, evolution fills every hole with naturalism. This is true whether what is in view is the evidence or the faith-based naturalistic philosophy. The first move in the game had to show the empirical deficiency of evolution, rather than simply attacking the philosophy behind it. Whether the earth is young or old is an extraneous issue, debated by those interested in throwing the bomb. What people need to know is whether this theory of evolution is the monolithic fact they are being told it is.

The original plan of attack was to find the weakest point in the materialist's power structure. Without a mechanism to build greater complexity, evolution is just a story. There were evolutionists before Charles Darwin, but they didn't have a mechanism that could explain biological change. Darwin provided the necessary mechanism, which is why evolution is always associated with his name. By attacking Darwin's mechanism—natural selection—it is possible to take down scientific materialism.

Natural selection is a real, identifiable force in nature, but it is no more powerful than is a dead man when it comes to producing offspring. Natural selection's great deficiency is that it cannot create new biological information. Some critical biologists have quipped that Darwin's theory looks at the "survival of the fittest" without accounting for the "arrival of the fittest."

Moreover, Darwin's prediction that proof would come, showing common descent for all living species, has yielded questionable results. The Darwinist community forgot that they should not *assume* common descent when they interpreted morphological and molecular homology to *prove* common descent. The stated assumption of course became a dogmatic conclusion. Meanwhile, molecular DNA evidence leaves no record of evolutionary transitions. Evolutionary "trees" built off of DNA often yield conflicting answers.

Finally, for the Darwinist, the fossil record turned out to be either quite boring or quite scary. Species appear abruptly and then remain unchanged for eons, only to disappear just as suddenly. This left Darwinian gradualists yawning about incompleteness. Punctuated equilibrium disciples of Stephen Jay Gould took the record seriously.[9] They bent over backward, however, to cram all evolutionary change into geological instants that would leave no traces of evolutionary transitions. All of this strained credulity regarding Darwin's theory.

The flaws of evolution require a whole book to expose. Other contributors to this volume will have more to say about these points. As a strategist, it is my role to explain why it was important to point out the empirical deficiencies of Darwinism.

Dividing or Uniting?

The second major strategic point is that you want to have as many allies as possible. My goal has been to unite the divided theists and open-minded skeptics of religion and divide the united evolutionist community. The neatest way to divide Darwinists is to point out the line that separates philosophical naturalists from those who are actually open to looking at the evidence carefully. This division is inevitable. Consider what evolutionist philosopher Michael Ruse recently wrote to the outspoken atheistic proponents of Darwinism, Daniel Dennett and Richard Dawkins:

> I think that you [Daniel Dennett] and Richard [Dawkins] are absolute disasters in the fight against intelligent design—we are losing this battle, not the least of which is the two new supreme court justices who are certainly going to vote to let it into classrooms— what we need is not knee-jerk atheism but serious grappling with the issues—neither of you are willing to study Christianity seriously and to engage with the ideas—it is just plain silly and grotesquely immoral to claim that Christianity is simply a force for evil, as Richard claims—more than this, we are in a fight, and we need to make allies in the fight, not simply alienate everyone of good will.[10]

Materialists recognize that they have to cover their tracks if evolution is to be accepted. By making inroads into their unstudied presuppositions at secular universities, one can create division between the hardcore philosophical materialists and those who would actually follow the evidence where it leads. It was vital that a collection of scholars realize the fundamental point that Darwinism is no stronger than the naturalistic philosophy that protects it from scrutiny. Given this cracked pedestal of evidence, what was propping Darwin up on his throne? It turned out that the naturalistic paradigm was not supported by evidence but by philosophy.

The tables turned. Darwinists had to deal with infighting over rates and modes. "Evolution happened," we were all reassured. However, no one could tell us precisely why, how, and even when. More important, the wedge movement mounted an organized attack, recognizing that what Darwinism lacks in empirical support, must be buttressed through philosophy.

But while I have helped unite many people to challenge the orthodoxy of evolution and materialism, I have also been accused of causing division.

I have received much criticism over the years from people in the Christian community, particularly professors at Christian colleges and seminaries. They feel that, insofar as I am able to influence Christians to challenge Darwinism, I am leading them to disaster, since evolutionary science cannot be beaten. I have never felt that way, and I certainly do not now, but it is a question to consider. Can Christians who are willing to dissent from Darwinism possibly win? The answer to that question can be found in the motivation behind many Christian "theistic evolutionists."

I have observed that many Christian colleges embrace Darwinism with an inordinate amount of passion. This is what we call "secular envy," when Christians feel they must swear allegiance to Darwin and prove their sincerity by becoming as dogmatically Darwinian as possible. What is really driving their angle on the debate is a desire for secular acceptance.

I'll let the reader decide if questioning Darwin is a losing strategy for Christians. Just remember that, in the end, it is the evidence that drives skepticism of Darwin.

The Triumph of Reason

Fast-forward to Kansas in 1999, where there was a resurgence of opposition to Darwinism. The State Board of Education in Kansas announced that they had rejected science teaching guidelines presented by various science organizations that demanded emphasis only on macroevolution. The pervasive attitude of these science organizations was that no questions were to be asked that brought evolution into question. Darwin said it. They believe it. That settles it.

The Kansas Board recognized this as unscientific dogmatism. The only thing that science has really demonstrated about evolution is that small-scale variations evolve within a species. For example, the classic peppered moth story, the textbook case of natural selection, only demonstrates that after many years you have more dark moths than light moths. The moths are still moths. There isn't any evidence that support for macroevolutionary change can be extrapolated from these observations. Kansas decided to test students on microevolution, but leave off unproven assertions about macroevolution—the big story of how a molecule becomes a man.

This bold act in Kansas became the shot heard round the world. The facts have been misrepresented in newspapers and magazines, which are typically influenced by the evolutionary scientific establishment and report whatever that establishment says as fact. Because of their lopsided reporting, the myth grew that the Kansas Board took evolution out of the curriculum and replaced it with the Bible. The scientific authorities were quoted on the Kansas action, and they pretended in all their quotes that they had never heard of any differentiation between microevolution and macroevolution. Yet these distinctions have been discussed for years in the scientific community.[11] But when a school board recognizes these debates and adjusts their curriculum accordingly, these ideological scientists pretend they never heard of it.

The response from the press was intriguing. Journalists panicked, and one received the impression that editors of the major newspapers in New York, Washington, Boston, and London spend most of their time worrying about the details of secondary education in the state of Kansas. Why were they so worried? It was because they encountered a serious resurgence of opposition to Darwinism, just when they thought the war was over. If the war was over, how did Kansas achieve this victory?

This drama was replayed in 2001 in Ohio.[12] There, science educators demanded the Ohio State Board of Education accept what was essentially a campaign of propaganda to teach evolutionary humanism under the guise of science and never allow students to question any of it. Our side desired a more objective treatment of the issue, one that recognized the scientific controversy over the claims of Darwinism. In particular, we found that even in the scientific literature there is much discussion disputing the claim that unguided material processes, random mutation, and natural selection can do all the work of biological creation. The science educators, of course, were furious at the very suggestion that evolution had any scientific deficiencies. They didn't want to "teach the controversy."

There has been an uproar over this suggestion that schools "teach the controversy" over evolution. Indeed, one Darwinist wrote a book attacking me, saying that Phillip Johnson is like the Japanese soldier who, in 1960, emerged from a jungle on the Philippines shouting "Bonsai," intending to wage war for the emperor. The soldier didn't realize that the war, World War II, was over. In this analogy, there is no controversy, and Phillip Johnson doesn't know that the war is over and his side lost. But what if that Japanese soldier had emerged with a small army and fought a battle with the U.S. occupation troops in the Philippines and won even a small victory? The history books would then have to be rewritten. That's precisely what has happened. In the end, the Ohio State Board of Education passed a standard for science education that allowed them to learn about scientific disagreement over neo-Darwinism. This was a small victory, protecting Ohio teachers who decide to teach students about the problems of Darwinism.[13]

As we all know, history sometimes repeats itself. After Ohio chose to teach evolution nondogmatically, the Darwinists struck back in Kansas and repealed the criticisms of evolution. But they didn't stop there. They actually redefined science as the search for purely natural explanations. Students were told to put the philosophical blinders over their eyes and pretend that only matter and energy influenced all of life's history. Even though these Darwinists claimed there was "no controversy" over evolution, they still felt the need to protect evolution by redefining science so that, under their terms, the only possible explanation is evolution.

This science-limiting language did not last. In 2005, a new Kansas Board of Education voted to reinstate critical analysis of neo-Darwinism. The Darwinists, predictably, started pouting as soon as the new science standards were introduced, and they haven't stopped. They have tried to equate teaching mere scientific criticisms of evolution with teaching religion. Just read one of the silly quotes we have from people like evolution professor Patricia Princehouse, saying "Critical analysis is just another name for creationism."[14] If this is Princehouse's best argument against informing students about the full range of scientific evidence regarding evolution, then perhaps she is projecting her fears about the religious consequences of evolution. But that was the point all along: Darwinism needs to recognize its own inherent naturalistic bias. Professor Princehouse and other Darwinist advocates of censorship in science education can say what they want, but they still haven't explained how evolution by natural selection explains the complexity of life.

Giving Darwinism a Wedgie

Critics of our movement today often proclaim with glee that they have exposed our "wedge strategy." *Creationism's Trojan Horse* is a book dedicated to explaining our evil strategy to take over the world.[15] I always find these conspiracy theories amusing because our strategy has been transparent from the beginning. After all, I titled my fifth book *The Wedge of Truth: Splitting the Foundations of Naturalism* (InterVarsity Press, 2002) and devoted my fourth to the wealthy Christian philanthropists Roberta and Howard Ahmanson because they "understood 'the Wedge'" and "love the Truth."

Regardless, the Darwinists are good and scared by this wicked "wedge strategy," as they call it. But when these conspiracy theorists write their books and articles attacking the wedge strategy, they never refer to my books. They refer to a fund-raising letter that was stolen from the Discovery Institute. This so-called wedge document outlined a proposed strategy for how to forge real research into intelligent design and also shape public opinion. They call the wedge document a secret strategy of wicked conspirators, as if we had something to hide. Yet everything in the wedge document was supposed to be based upon scientific research.[16] How could that be so objectionable? If they wanted to know about our strategy, all they had to do was read my books. How could we have been any more upfront? And everything we've been saying all along has been based upon science. What harm could there be in that?

The dangerousness of the wedge is that it threatens to split the pedestal of naturalism propping neo-Darwinism. Critics call the wedge movement simply a religiously motivated attack on naturalism, and not a bona fide scientific project. In fact, I predicted that critics would ignore the scientific problems with evolution and become obsessed with attacking the motives of the wedge:

> If we in the Wedge have an enemy, it is not those in open and honest opposition to our proposals but rather the obfuscators—those who resist any clear definition of terms or issues, who insist that the ruling scientific organizations be obeyed without question and who are content to paper over logical contradictions with superficial compromises.[17]

The enemies of the wedge are those who fixate upon the religious beliefs and motivations of Darwin critics rather than desiring to follow the scientific evidence where it leads. It gives me reassurance to realize that the Darwinists' current obsession with the wedge strategy is proof that my prediction was right. But in the end, for our critics to pretend that this debate was always only about science is for them to deny the source of their power as Darwinists.

Darwinists gained cultural power using the momentum of the Scopes Trial of 1925, as they convinced the culture that religion was outdated, close-minded, and simply wrong (or worse, irrelevant). They perpetuate this stereotype to the next generations by showing movies like *Inherit the Wind* in public high schools. Moreover, Darwinism conquered its last cultural foe when prominent religious scientists and religious leaders conceded that religion was irrelevant to informing real thoughts about the facts of where we came from. In a bait-and-switch move, Darwinists made a deal with our culture based upon their false promise that religion would be safe from evolutionary science. Darwinists today purport to explain everything in evolutionary terms from consciousness, to morality (or the lack thereof), to human behavior and sexual mores. When Michael Ruse isn't preaching to the public about theism-friendly evolution, he tells us that "[m]orality, or more strictly our belief in morality, is merely an adaptation put in place to further our reproductive ends. . . . Ethics as we understand it is an illusion fobbed on us by our genes to get us to cooperate."[18] These core tenets of religion are not safe from what Daniel Dennett calls the "universal acid" of Darwinism. Darwinism promised peace with religion, and then moved in for the kill.

Evolution was never only about science. It was about replacing God with a grand naturalistic creation story that said that we are the result of an unguided purposeless process that did not have us in mind. So today when our critics tell us that we shouldn't be aiming for "cultural renewal," our reply should not be to deny the move for renewal, but to show why Darwinists have created this need in the first place.

All this having been said, there is real science in the midst of this debate. There is no question that we can look at *Archaeopteryx* and say that it looks like something that could have been an intermediate between dinosaurs and birds. There is also no question that when we look at the bacterial flagellum, we can see that it closely resembles rotary engines found in cars and outboard motors designed by humans, which require all of their irreducibly complex engine parts in order to propel a bacterium. This constitutes a genuine scientific debate. But when our critics put up the facade that intelligent design is all about religion, we should remind them that evolution is not all about science.

Both sides are fighting about who controls the power to educate the next generation. Science plays a major role in this debate, but I will not accept for an instant that "our side" is singularly guilty of bringing cultural and moral arguments into this debate. We were forced to do that when Darwinists like Steven Pinker started telling us that it was understandable why evolution would cause teenage mothers to throw their newborns in dumpsters at the prom.[19]

The more that Darwinists "expose" the wedge strategy, the further they drive the wedge into the naturalistic log. Darwinists may pretend that their arguments are based purely upon science, but this bluff cannot stand. The end issue is whether you can have a true scientific explanation of everything in the world by keeping intelligent design out of the picture and assuming that all there has ever been is matter and energy.

The conflict is because naturalistic philosophy has dominated science. Intelligent design threatens that power structure, and the materialists are frightened. Yet despite grand proclamations of the death of intelligent design from the Darwinist camp, this debate is still going strong. Intelligent design proponents have done a very good job of bringing the scientific flaws in Darwinism to life. We've made powerful arguments, producing evidence in books and in peer-reviewed scientific publications. But the evidence and arguments are not going to be enough to carry the movement through to victory. Something else must happen that will help scientists—and the public upon which they rely for power—to realize that the scientific enterprise is fallible.

There was a time when many thought that the Roman Catholic Church was infallible. Similarly, today our culture thinks that individual scientists can make errors, but the scientific community as a whole is supposed to be self-correcting due to its processes of peer review, careful debate, and competition. These checks and balances are thought to ensure that no error can persist for long before being discovered and discarded. In that limited sense, our culture perceives the scientific community as infallible. The press treats them this way, perpetuating a rigid mind-set that is narrow-minded on an issue like evolution and troubling because the press outlets have so much cultural authority.

We are still quite a ways from anything that I can call a final victory or a decisive breakthrough. The other side still controls nearly all of the power, money, media sources, and educational authorities. Moreover, they use our tax money to wage this war. The problem they cannot overcome is that their story isn't true, and it is not difficult for the public to see this fact.

Endgame

The question now on everyone's mind is, "What is coming next?" I'm not sure I can answer that question, but I can take a cue from history. The Darwinists are scared by intelligent design. In 2002, the American Association for the Advancement of Science issued an edict condemning intelligent design.[20] Image that: The leading scientific organization in the United States took the unprecedented action of issuing a press release against an idea. The effect of this anti-intellectual proclamation is to tell all scientists and journals that "intelligent design is a disease for your mind, so you'd better close your mind or we'll see to it you are quarantined by the thought police." They started pouring money into evolution education seminars, and even used the threat of intelligent design in education for their fundraising campaign.

With a recent lower federal court decision calling intelligent design unconstitutional, Darwinists are on the move.[21] Their strategy is to link anything that questions evolution back to religious fundamentalism to discredit it. Moreover, witch hunts have taken place around the United States, trying to force skeptics of evolution or proponents of intelligent design out of the academy. In this political climate, untenured scientists are only safe if they keep their doubts about Darwin in the closet.

Amazingly, the new tactic of Darwinists is to wage a public relations campaign proclaiming to the masses that Darwinism is religion friendly. Never mind that macroevolution is used to explain everything from the origin of religion to morality to human sexuality. However, the poll data still suggest that the vast majority of the American public is skeptical of evolution. Meanwhile, Michael Ruse berates Richard Dawkins for talking openly about the religious implications of Darwinism.

Nonetheless, the Darwinists are proclaiming triumphant victory. In an amusing story at the end of 2005, the journal *Science* declared evolution to be the "breakthrough of the year," citing as proof, paltry microevolutionary evidence regarding viral evolution. It seems we're right back in 1959 again. We should remember that Darwin's centennial triumph fell quickly once people started scrutinizing the evidence, and such will happen again.

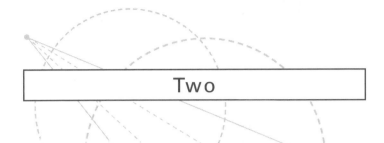

Two

Intelligent Design and the Nature of Science

J. P. MORELAND

The discussion in this book about the theory of intelligent design involves not simply science. At its root, it is a conversation about what science is, and what it is not. Michael Behe refers to this philosophical issue a number of times in chapter 4.

Dr. Behe and I participated in a conference on ID theory in Kansas City not long ago. Part of the conference was an eight-person panel debate in which Behe; Jonathan Wells; John Calvert, a lawyer from Kansas City; and I debated four world-class scholars. These were all professors at secular universities: Mano Singham, a theoretical physicist from Case Western Reserve; John Staver, past president of the Association of Science Educators in the state of Kansas and professor of science education at Kansas State University; Steven Gey, professor of law and a U.S. Constitution expert at Florida State University; and Dennis Lamoureux, a Canadian professor with doctorates in theology and dentistry. In addition to the debate, several seminars were held. I attended sessions with professors Singham and Staver to try to learn something about the more sophisticated arguments posed against intelligent design. I was profoundly disappointed by both speakers and found their talks deeply disturbing.

I went to hear thoughtful scientific arguments against intelligent design. Instead, at least two-thirds of both presentations consisted of philosophical arguments against intelligent design theory offered by men who obviously had never studied philosophy. They fell back on the same old bromides that have been repeatedly advanced and just as repeatedly refuted.

This situation is consistent with what I have found over the years: so much of the criticism of intelligent design is founded in extremely bad philosophy. Part of the problem is that classes in philosophy are not required in our educational system. From high school on, people are not trained to look at their disciplines with philosophical understanding. With such an erosion of philosophical training—and thus understanding—it is absolutely essential that those of us interested in this conversation understand its philosophical dimensions. As important as empirical facts and scientific thinking are to the debate, they are not enough.

The shift to Darwinism from a theism-centered view of biology in particular and science in general was largely a philosophical move to redefine the nature of science. In what may be one of the most authoritative books written on the Darwinian revolution, *Charles Darwin and the Problem of Creation*, Neal Gillespie makes the point that "Darwin's rejection of special creation was a part of the transformation of biology into a positive science. That is, one committed to a thoroughly naturalistic explanation of life based on material causes and the uniformity of nature."[1]

Gillespie's point is that the shift from creationist to Darwinist science was not primarily about discoveries of evidence. Indeed, the creationist model has remained more empirically supported than its Darwinist rival in such respects as the lack of transition forms in the fossil record. But the philosophical view of what science ought to look like changed to methodological naturalism. People are now shocked to hear that at the time of Darwin, the scientific establishment in the United States and Europe was populated mainly with creationists. They practiced their biology, geology, taxonomy, and other practices in light of a commitment to a creator and even to biblical teaching. These scientists did not think that they were importing religion into their science. Everyone recognized that they were practicing science. Even when scientists drifted from creationist ideas, no one initially thought that creationists were not doing science, even if they thought creationist theory was wrong.

But that is no longer the thinking. Today it is routinely argued that any form of intelligent design as an explanation for the origin of life ought to be, as a matter of principle, rejected. That is not a scientific assertion; it is a philosophical statement about science. More often than not, such claims are offered by those who have not done any reading in the philosophy of science.

The struggle about intelligent design continues on three fronts: One is the law and legal issues, discussed by Wayne House in this book. The other two relate to fundamental ideas that are at the very core of the conflict—the scientific discussion and the philosophical discussion. It is widely believed that *intelligent design science* is an oxymoronic term, like *jumbo shrimp*. The tactic of disqualifying an idea based upon its alleged religious implications was used against creationism in the 1980s. For example, twenty years ago, columnist Robert C. Cowen opined, "Creationists want public school biology classes to include the possibility of—and scientific evidence for—a creator as well. There is no such scientific evidence. The concept of a supernatural creator is inherently religious. It has no place in a science class."[2] Cowen's point is that science requires that its practitioners be committed to methodological naturalism. Consequently, when Behe and other scientists claim that evidence points to an intelligent designer—whether a creator god or not—their conclusion is taken to be a nonscientific personal choice. Supposedly such scientists have taken off their "science hat" and put on a "theology hat." Their religious inference cannot be a scientific one. Since their inference is religious, it has no place in the practice of science or in the teaching of science in the public schools. Here I will show what is wrong with this claim and give some useful ways of evaluating it in discussions with someone on the other side of the issue. I also want to argue that the commitment to methodological naturalism (a position I will define in detail) and to the claim that science can only appeal to natural causes and explanations is not religiously neutral. Such a commitment harms both religion and science.

I should say at the outset that ID theory does not attempt to identify the designer nor does it make explicit reference to God.[3] What I shall demonstrate is that even if ID theory did do these things, it would not thereby be disqualified as science.

I appeal to a handout that was distributed before the above mentioned debate by a group protesting our views. These persons represented a group called Kansans for Science Education. The handout attempted to show that what we are doing is not science. The first statement on this protest sheet says, "Intelligent Design is part of a movement disguised as science to allow supernatural causes into scientific explanations." Intelligent design is religious instead of scientific because the concept of God or an intelligent designer is a "supernatural" concept. I shall address this mistaken assertion, define and criticize methodological naturalism, explain why ID theory is scientific theory, and respond to two criticisms that are usually raised against ID.

To address the issue of whether an idea that has religious foundations or implications is inherently nonscientific, we need to take a look at the

---

Three Kinds of Theory Change in Science

TC_1: The old theory is simply abandoned (e.g., phlogiston to oxygen chemistry).

TC_2: Theory change is the occasion for rearranging goals, values, and procedures embraced by the scientific community (e.g., vitalism to mechanistic biology).

TC_3: The old theory is no longer regarded as a scientific theory (e.g., Darwinism as a shift from theistic science to methodological naturalism).

---

three kinds of theory change in the history of science. In the theory of science, it often happens that an old theory will be replaced by a new theory. This we might call *theory replacement*, in which an old theory is set aside and a new theory accepted. Historians and philosophers of science have identified three different kinds of theory change (hereafter referred to as "TC") in the history of science.

In the first kind, or TC_1, the old theory is simply abandoned in favor of the new theory, as science rejected phlogiston chemistry and accepted oxygen chemistry. A metal heated in the atmosphere gains weight. There was a time when people thought that this process was driving out an impurity of the metal, or phlogiston, which had "negative weight." The reason for the lost weight was the elimination of the phlogiston, the same as in other refining processes in which impurities in metal are removed. Antoine-Laurent Lavoisier (1743–1794), Joseph Priestley (1733–1804), and other scientists argued, however, that heating a metal in the atmosphere does not cause it to lose phlogiston, but rather to gain oxygen. This is the real reason for its gain in weight. Soon no phlogiston chemists were to be found in universities. A scientific theory was abandoned and a new scientific theory accepted. This is a category 1 theory change.

A category 2 theory change is more involved. A theory change of the TC_2 sort occasions a rearranging of goals, values, or procedures embraced by the scientific community. An example was the shift from vitalism to mechanistic biology. Each area of science is practiced in keeping with a commitment to a set of intellectual values. For example, an intellectual value might be "You ought to seek a simple explanation." The implication is that, if you have two explanations, prefer the simpler to the more complex.

"Seek a theory that is empirically accurate" is an intellectual value. Another is "Seek a theory that is predictably successful." One could have a theory that is accurate using empirical data, but it does not make any predictions. Or a theory could be predicatively accurate, but it does not harmonize very well with old empirical data. Other examples of values are "Prefer a theory that is repeatable" and "Prefer double-blind experiments to single-blind experiments."

Such values—preferring simpler explanations, preferring predictably successful theories, and the rest—are intellectual goals. A group of scientists who practice a certain craft have judged these to be desirable cognitive values. These goals are taken to regulate how science ought to be done.

Sometimes a theory change in science does not simply occur because a new theory replaces an old theory—a TC_1 change. Instead, the new theory replaces the old theory, which provides an occasion for adopting a new set of goals or values. An old set of goals or values is abandoned.

The shift from vitalism to mechanistic biology is a case in point. There was a time when scientists, especially in England and Germany, spoke of a vital fluid or a vital force behaving *teleologically* in a living organism. Over time, the organism develops in order to realize a certain function. I happen to believe that this is true, but the point is that, given a vitalistic view of organisms, one could explain what happened in an organism's development over time in terms of a final cause. A person could say that an eye develops so that the organism can see. That's the final cause explanation. In contrast, mechanistic biology only appeals to efficient causes, causes that actually produce an effect. *Why* the effect was produced is not considered. Thus, the change from vitalistic to mechanistic biology was not just a replacement of an old theory. Rather the change replaced an old value. This new theory sought to explain things by avoiding final causes and explaining things in terms of efficient causes only.

A TC_2 change involves a greater intellectual commitment than a TC_1 change. Additionally, philosophical reflection is a part of TC_2 changes. They are not, strictly speaking, scientific changes, because a preference of epistemic or cognitive value is partly philosophical rather than simply scientific.

TC_3 changes are even more dramatic. The old theory is no longer regarded as ever having been a scientific theory. A scientist does not abandon the old theory for the new theory simply because the old theory is regarded as an inaccurate one that ought to be discarded. Nor does the scientist merely adopt a new epistemic value as a replacement for an old one. The old theory is now regarded as having always been art, religion, or philosophy instead of science.

A TC_3 change occurred when a number of people abandoned the Marxist approach to biology because they came to regard it as nothing but political theory. It was not to be treated as a scientific theory at all. A TC_3 shift is almost entirely based on philosophical considerations, the reasoning of historians and philosophers of science. The process does not grow from scientific exploration itself. This is why, when a hundred Nobel prize-winning scientists took out a full-page ad in the *Los Angles Times*, and other U.S. papers, I read their statement with some irritation. They claimed to respect religion as long as it stays within its proper domain. They said they rejected creation or intelligent design theory (lumping together two ideas that aren't the same thing) as a mixture of science and religion. Science, they said, can explain things only as a result of natural causes.

When I noted which scientists signed the statement, I knew immediately that it was intellectually irresponsible. Philosophers, not scientists, have the intellectual training to make such judgments. It would be difficult to find philosophers of science, at least in North America, who would deny that intelligent design theory is science. Many of them consider ID theory to be false, though a growing number of them do not. Many would say it is not a good scientific theory. However, almost all recognize that it is a perfectly legitimate scientific theory. Most philosophers of science would regard the shift from ID theory to naturalistic Darwinism as either a TC_1 or TC_2 shift. They would not call it a TC_3 change, the kind of shift required if ID theory is to be rejected on the grounds that it is not science.

Two Observations About Moves Within Theories of Science

1. Burden of proof increases from TC_1 to TC_2 to TC_3.
2. TC_3 shifts are second-order philosophical debates about science and not first-order debates of science.

Why is it important for people to understand that philosophers of science do not reject intelligent design as a scientific theory? Officials, such as those behind the California Framework (a set of guidelines developed by the California Board of Education for teaching science in state public schools) define how science is to be taught. These officials do not understand the distinctions, so they will not allow intelligent design to be presented to our children.

Even if intelligent design science had serious flaws, there could be value in teaching about it as a bad scientific theory in a science class, but the current tendency is not even to allow that. The claim that a creationist or intelligent design theory is religion and not science means that there was a TC_3 change when evolution came on the scene. Thus, creationist theory did not pass from being acceptable to being unacceptable scientific theory. On the contrary, it passed from being a good scientific theory to no longer being a scientific theory. It came to be viewed as a religious idea. That is a philosophical claim, not a scientific one.

Before proceeding we need to understand the difference between a first order assertion and a second order assertion. A first order assertion is an assertion of fact regarding some process within a field that is made by those who work in that field. A first order assertion of organic chemists is that a methane molecule has four hydrogen atoms attached to it. A description of how magnetic fields work is a first order assertion of physicists.

A second order assertion is an assertion about the field itself, rather than what it studies. The claim that scientific study starts with observations, is not a claim *of* science. That is a claim *about* science. The claim that "in order for something to be scientific, a change has to explained by natural law" is a second order assertion. That is not a claim of science, but a claim about science. Likewise, the statement that "as a matter of principle, one ought to avoid intelligent design theory" is not a claim of science, but a claim about science. In fact, it is a philosophical claim about science. This distinction is so important because scientists who make such a claim are speaking outside their area of expertise. They are not trained in these matters. The vast majority of scientists who raise claims against intelligent design argue philosophically without even knowing it. Those who do have the expertise, true philosophers of science, seldom agree with the premises of this sort of argument against intelligent design.

At least two observations can be made about theory changes in science. The first is that the burden of proof increases as we move from TC_1

to TC_2 to TC_3 changes. The burden of proof increases because more is being claimed in successively higher level types of change. Let us suppose that I believe that a shift in science is a level 1 theory change. I am claiming that the old theory does not do a very good job of explaining things, and we ought to prefer the new theory. If I say that a change from an old theory to a new one is an example of a category 2 change, I am not just saying that the old theory should be abandoned in favor of the new one. I am claiming that we ought to get rid of an old set of values and adopt replacement goals and values.

But what about the theory 3 kind of change? In this change, I am not just saying that we ought to prefer a new theory. I am making the stronger claim that the old theory never should have been regarded as scientific. It is art or religion, a much bolder claim than simply saying that an old scientific theory should be disregarded, a level 1 change.

If, as we have related, the primary argument against the theory of intelligent design today is TC_3—that intelligent design is religion, not science—then the argumentation has been insufficient. To credibly show the necessity for such a change, a person must do more than only plead the need for a better theory of origins. The claim must show that intelligent design actually violates the very nature of science, that its assertions are religious instead of scientific. No one has sustained that huge burden of proof regarding ID theory. The shift to a strictly naturalistic practice of science—one that says intelligent design is religion—is a TC_3 shift and a second order philosophical debate about science. It is not significant that Nobel Prize-winning scientists say intelligent design is not science. Such a statement would be significant if it came from members of the academy of historians of science. This they are not doing. If philosophers of science across the United States determined that something about intelligent design theory disqualifies it as science—that would indeed be significant.

A couple of tests can enrich and further discussion by determining what level of change has occurred in this debate when someone says to you, "This is not science. I'm a scientist. Trust me when I say that this isn't science." These tests are two ways to demonstrate that debates regarding the scientific status of ID theory are philosophical and not scientific: (1) Ask what scientific experiment demonstrates the assertion. (2) Look at a university catalog to discover who is trained in these matters.

The first test comes when the scientist is asked, "What is the specific scientific theory or experiment that you can cite to prove that intelligent design is religion? I would like to evaluate the scientific evidence." Ask who the scientist was and in what journal the experiment was reported that provides the scientific evidence against ID theory as scientific.

The second test is really kind of fun. You have to do a little legwork for this. Find any university catalog and turn to the sections of chemistry, biology, physics, and geology. Read the course descriptions. Course syllabi would be even better. Observe what courses are listed as necessary for earning a B.S., M.S., or Ph.D. in biochemistry. Next, look for any class in biochemistry that discusses the definition of science and the difference between science and nonscience. No such course will be in the curriculum. Now, flip a few pages over to the philosophy curriculum and look for a course in the philosophy of science or one that attempts to define science. You will discover that you can get a Ph.D. in this discipline. I have perhaps thirty books in my personal library on the definition of biology and how it differs from chemistry or physics or religion. These books are not written by scientists; they are written by philosophers and historians.

Based on our answers to the two tests, we can evaluate methodological naturalism, what Gillespie called positive science.[4] Methodological naturalism is a definition of what science is. It says that, by its very nature, science is limited to providing strictly natural, especially physical, explanations for strictly natural, especially physical, phenomenon. Methodological naturalism usually appeals to natural law. Those who practice science are told that they must limit themselves to the rules of what "counts as science," naturalistic causes and natural laws. In the conference handout mentioned earlier, ID theorists are depicted as purposefully confusing people about this issue by replacing methodological naturalism (the fact that science studies only natural phenomenon) with ID theory. We are also accused of confusing people by equating methodological naturalism with philosophical naturalism, the view that only the natural world exists and there is no God. They would say, "One can believe in God as long as he is kept out of science."

Those who advocate that science studies only natural phenomenon have adopted methodological naturalism. This was the perspective of U.S. District Court Judge William Overton in *McClean v. Arkansas Board of Education* (1981), in which he ruled against the teaching of creationism in the public schools in the state of Arkansas.[5] The case did not involve intelligent design, but the same criteria would exclude it. Overton's decision was based upon his definition of science. First, to practice science, according to his opinion, one must only be guided by natural law. Second, a person can only explain natural phenomena by appealing to natural law. Third, a scientist's results must be empirically testable. Fourth, scientists must hold their views tentatively and not as the final word on a subject. Fifth, the theory must be falsifiable.

Now the truth of the matter is that methodological naturalism is simply false. First, there is no such thing as *a* definition of science. There have been attempts for at least twenty-four hundred years to define science and no one has been able to do so. There is no such thing as a definition of science. No line of demarcation applies to and specifies all and only science. Carefully note what I am and am not saying. I am saying that a line of demarcation would consist in a set of necessary and sufficient conditions that set apart something as scientific. They would be *necessary* in the sense that anyone practicing science would have to adhere to them. They are *sufficient* in that anyone adhering to those conditions is practicing science. A definition constructed around those necessary and sufficient conditions would clarify whether someone practices science or something other than science, such as religion, art, or politics.

There is no set of necessary and sufficient conditions by which to define science. There are good "rules of thumb" that help clarify what science is. You can say, generally speaking, that many scientists find certain elements fruitful when they practice their craft. Normally elements applying to one scientific area are peculiar to that area. They are not easily applied to another area. Working principles in particle physics have poor correlation to principles of psychology. But to tighten the definition of science to one set of elements and rule out everything else as nonscience is quickly discovered to be an impossible task. For every necessary condition, there are examples of obvious science that do not fulfill the condition. And for every sufficient condition, there are examples of nonscience that do fulfill the condition.

Let us apply this to the common perspective that something cannot be scientific unless it can be explained by natural law. This claim means that scientific systems can only be explained by natural laws. The big bang theory would not be scientific, because it is considered the beginning point of space, time, and matter. The big bang, in principle, is a boundary condition, for which there is allegedly no further explanation. Especially there is no explanation in terms of a law of nature. The rule is that something can only be counted as scientific if it can be explained by a natural law. Therefore, it is not scientific to try to describe characteristics of the big bang, place it at a point in the past at some temporal distance from the present, or establish its initial conditions. One cannot explain these things by an appeal to a law of nature. Similarly, constants of nature (e.g., the gravitational constant G; the rest mass of an electron) are brute facts for which there is no further explanation. These, in principle, are not explicable by natural law. Consequently, when a scientist attempts to describe the gravitational constant in the universe, he has stopped doing science. This is obviously false, so one can practice science without explaining something by an appeal to a law of nature.

What if one says that simply explaining things by appeal to a natural law is sufficient for one's act to be considered an exercise of science? This is not true either. Jeremy Bentham (1748–1832) developed a moral theory called hedonistic utilitarianism, a version of utilitarianism designed to be a moral theory. Bentham developed a series of natural laws that he took to be moral rules, and these natural laws correlated body movements with the amount of pleasure they produced in the greatest number of people. He developed a scale to measure the amount, intensity, and duration of pleasure given by eating a banana or telling the truth. A set of entirely natural laws were used to correlate actions with resulting pleasure. These natural laws he took to be moral rules that constituted ethical standards. Bentham was using natural law, but he wasn't practicing science. To explain why lying is wrong—answering a moral, not a scientific, question—he would have appealed only to an entirely natural law that lying diminishes pleasure. Such an explanation cannot get at the nature of "wrongness" or what lying is in relation to it. Relying only on natural law is not a sufficient condition for science. If it were, Bentham's theory would have been scientific instead of ethical.

What about holding one's theories tentatively? First, scientists do not always hold to a theory tentatively—nor should they. If I lectured to the medical faculty at the University of California at San Diego and told them that they needed to hold the circulation understanding of the blood as a tentative theory, would a single medical scientist be satisfied with my admonition? I hope not. Whether one is tentative has nothing to do with whether he or she is doing science. Tentativeness is a statement about scientists, not their theories. Maybe what Behe and other scientists who hold to intelligent design need to do is to get some emotional therapy, loosen up, and stop being so dogmatic. Maybe if they were more tentative about their views, they could publish in *Nature*. Second, there are theologians, artists, ethicists, and people in other disciplines who do hold to their theories in a tentative way. But that is not a sufficient basis for claiming that their tentativeness means they are practicing science.

There really is no such thing as a line of demarcation between science and nonscience. Although advocates of methodological naturalism have attempted to find that satisfactory line, all such attempts have failed.

Second, adopting methodological naturalism as a TC_3 theory change implies the implausible proposition that the work comprising 90 percent of the history of science was not science in the first place. Follow the argument carefully here. It's one thing to say that biologists at Harvard and Oxford in 1850 held biological theories to which we no longer subscribe. That's a perfectly legitimate thing to say. It is something entirely different to say that 90 percent of the practicing scientists in the 1850s weren't doing real scientific research. They were doing creationist science or ID science, and that's religion. This is an outlandish statement. Those who claim that one must do science, if it is being done at all, within a naturalistic methodological framework render as nonscience 80 percent of the work done in the history of the disciplines. Such a radical interpretation is terribly wrong-headed. This commitment to methodological naturalism is not consistent with the history of science. It is a revisionist's understanding of the nature of scientific exploration.

The third thing to understand about methodological naturalism is that it is not a neutral intellectual commitment. Its principles really do undercut theistic religion. This needs to be said because critics of ID theory employ the NOMA principle (standing for "nonoverlapping magisterial"), to argue against ID theory. This principle says that science is one thing and religion is another; they are totally separate spheres of life, science having to do with facts and reality, while religion concerns itself with matters of meaning and values. Now the NOMA principle is usually associated with an epistemological standpoint that limits the knowledge of reality to the hard sciences. Claims made in other fields, such as philosophy, ethics, or theology, are expressions of private belief that do not rise to the level that their findings can be counted as knowledge. According to NOMA, there is no such thing as nonscientific knowledge. The postmodernist and the scientific naturalist agree that you can't know something outside science.

What you have to understand is that the struggle regarding ID theory is ultimately about the nature of knowledge, not just the search for truth. It isn't about whether intelligent design theory is true. After all, you could simply assert that "there is an intelligent designer." According to the NOMA principle and the epistemology behind it, the response would be that even if your assertion is true, you couldn't know that it is true.

A few summers ago, *Time Magazine* published a cover story on how the universe will end. One of the article's premises was that for centuries humankind has tried to figure this out. Unfortunately, the only way people could approach this question was through religion and philosophy, which amounted to nothing but idle speculation. Now, said the article's writers, science has moved into this topic. For the first time in human history, we have actually gained knowledge and answers to our questions. The theory of knowledge presupposed in the article is this epistemology of scientism that is at the center of the debate.

We aren't arguing just about what is true fact. The struggle is about who has a right to say what we can know.[6] Postmodernists and naturalists do not believe there is knowledge outside the hard sciences, and this explains why evolution is embraced with a confidence that extends far beyond its justification. Methodological naturalism is responsible for the marginalization of religion in public discourse.

In my view, the arguments usually raised against ID theory are weak, and Darwinism is adopted with a degree of certainty that goes beyond the evidence. In light of the insights we have gained about the broad epistemological issues behind the ID debate, we are in a position to understand this dialectical situation. Suppose we had two rival theories competing for allegiance. Suppose we abandoned one of these scientific theories. Would we have stopped doing science? Would we have abandoned science? Clearly we would not. We would merely adopt one scientific theory and reject the other one.

Consider a second scenario. What if there is a scientific theory that is competing with something called a "religious theory"? And what if the culture has identified reason and knowledge with science, and religion with feeling and superstition? Now, if you give up the scientific theory in favor of the religious theory, you have abandoned reason itself in favor of superstition and feeling. This is what is really going on in debates between ID and naturalistic evolutionary theory proponents. This explains the hostility found among ID opponents.

Its commitment to methodological naturalism is why theistic evolution is inadequate to address the nonempirical problems relating to the possibility of religious knowledge and the overall marginalization of religion. Theistic evolutionary theory is based on the view that there may be a god, but the history of the cosmos and the development of life provide no scientific evidence for an intelligent designer, that it is purely describable by naturalistic processes. This perspective is what is addressed in the protest sheet at the conference I spoke of at the beginning of the chapter. It reads: "Support the role of science in seeking natural explanations for the physical world and support your choice of religion as it addresses your spiritual needs."

Listen to the cognitive label given to science. What does science give us? Explanations. What is religion? A choice. It is completely separate from any cognitive considerations or any evidentiary considerations. Theistic evolution plays into the hands of the secularists by making peace, not with evolution, but with the theory of knowledge at the root of the conflict: The only kind of knowledge allowed is scientific. If you try to appeal to a designer, you're not really explaining anything. That is the danger of this intellectual pacifist approach to harmonizing science and religion. By adopting theistic evolution and methodological naturalism, one implicitly affirms scientism and its limits on knowledge and thereby contributes, even if unintentionally, to the marginalization of Christianity in the culture.

So much for philosophical responses to critics of ID debate. I want to turn to a positive defense of the scientific credibility of ID theory by discussing two considerations.

Intelligent Design and the Use of Hypothesis in Research

Intelligent design can provide a conceptualization of what some entities are and how they were generated. For example, an intelligent design theorist can look at a kidney and say, "Because I theorize that this organ was designed intelligently, I believe that it will exhibit irreducible complexity. I believe that there is information behind this and it has a function."

If we have an intelligent design approach, we can theorize that a bacterial flagellum has a function. We may observe that it is irreducibly complex. Consequently there may be information or marks of information behind it. From this we could make positive and negative predictions. A positive prediction would be, for example, that we would find evidence of coadaptation of parts in light of a function as we research this organ. Negatively the prediction is that if a part is removed, it will not function any longer. Let's apply this to the discussion that Behe mentioned in his presentation of Russell Doolittle's quote in reference to the clotting of blood. Doolittle said that this function isn't, in fact, irreducibly complex. An intelligent design theorist might say that it is irreducibly complex and that if we were to take one of these parts away, it really will be demonstrated to be dysfunctional.

Suppose we are shown to be wrong in this case; our theory about the irreducible complexity of blood clotting has been falsified. That would not invalidate an intelligent design view, rendering it unscientific. Just the opposite; it would be a scientific theory—a falsified scientific theory. It is not merely a religious doctrine because it actually generated a prediction that was falsified. In actual fact, the ID prediction wasn't proven wrong; actually the blood clotting has been shown to be irreducibly complex. But even if it had been falsified, my point would not change: ID is, in fact, a theory that generates testable results, either positive or negative. This should be adequate reason to teach the viewpoint in the public schools. By trying to falsify the theory, Doolittle demonstrated that the theory is scientific. If the theory is not scientific, Doolittle could not have generated falsifiable test results. This can't be done with an aesthetic theory.

Intelligent Design and Scientific Explanation

The most important thing about a scientific theory is not that it makes predictions, though this can be important. Its most important contribution is that it explains things. Scientists sometimes explain things by appealing to an intelligent agent and not to a law of nature. An example is the SETI (Search for Extra-Terrestrial Life) program, which searches for signs of a conscious being who has thoughts, motives, and intentions.

Psychology, sociology, forensic science, archaeology, and similar branches of science do not attempt merely to explain phenomena in terms of a law of nature. An archaeologist does not suggest that a discovered artifact can be explained by a natural law. A scientific explanation of the artifact would seek to discover the purpose that the item played in a culture. The archaeologist would look for the intentions, motives, and values of those who made it. In doing so, the archaeologist has not stopped doing science. Science seeks explanations and the explanations in some branches of science do not appeal to any law of nature. These branches study conscious agents and their mental states along with their resultant causal products.

A person might respond that this is okay in archaeology and SETI, but it's not okay in a hard science such as biology. My response would be, "Who says?" Other branches of science give precedent for an intelligent design-based theory. If the facts in biology also show marks of intelligence, why can we not draw conclusions based on that evidence? Why do I have to take off my scientific hat and put on my religious hat in biology but not in archaeology? One might say, "You must, because the intelligent designer can be human in the other branches, but any designer posed in biology must be really big. He also would have to be unseen." Does the size or composition of the proposed intelligent designer change the nature of the inference so that it is nonscience? It is hard to see how that reasoning can be justified. As far as I can see, only by begging the question can we limit inferences to intelligent design to some branches of science. We should allow the evidence and adequacy of the explanation to justify including or excluding an inference to a designer. The exclusion should not be based on application of a set of arbitrary rules.

Intelligent design theory may also receive scientific confirmation. Theories explain facts. If ID explanations of facts can, indeed, be scientific, conversely, facts can confirm ID theories. Scientists are looking for confirmation for their theories. Can scientific data confirm the presence of an intelligent designer? Yes it can, and this can be seen in the design filter described by William Dembski. The design filter provides a way in which scientists can show that certain data may well confirm an intelligent design theory.

In view of all this, intelligent design theory can be used to guide research—because it makes positive and negative predictions. Intelligent design theory does, in fact, explain the observed data. Moreover, there are times that scientific data have no other reasonable explanation. There is nothing nonscientific about this.

Another element of a scientific theory is its adequacy in solving problems within its proper domain. It would be useful to examine intelligent design theory as it relates to problem solving in science. A scientific theory generally has two sorts of problems to answer: empirical and conceptual. Empirical problems are those that do not harmonize well with empirical data. Suppose the theory predicts that planets move in a certain way and the empirical data shows that they don't all move in the predicted way. This would be an empirical problem for the theory.

A scientific theory can also have two types of conceptual problems: external and internal. External conceptual problems occur when the implications of a scientific theory conflict with a rationally established belief from some field outside of science. If, for example, good philosophical arguments could be presented for the reality of free will or the finitude of the past, and a scientific theory implied the denial of these, the philosophical arguments would present an external conceptual problem for the scientific theory. The idea behind external conceptual problems is that science does not exhaust what it is rational to believe, and scientific theories must harmonize with what there is good reason to believe from sources outside of science. If, for example, good reasons can be presented to believe that the Bible is true (and there are, in fact, such reasons), and a scientific theory conflicts with a teaching of the Bible, that teaching would amount to an external conceptual problem for that scientific theory.

Internal conceptual problems occur when the very concepts of the theory are troublesome, such as, for example, when the concepts of a theory constitute circular reasoning. An example of an internal conceptual problem that has been repeatedly raised is the notion that evolution advances through the "survival of the fittest," or the survival of the reproductively advantageous. Thus, evolutionary change is defined as change in light of the survival of the fittest. And what are the fittest? Those organisms or structures that survive evolutionary change. Fitness, then, is defined in terms of survival, and survival is defined in terms of fitness. These definitions are arrived at through circular reasoning. Homologous structures is another example of arriving at a definition through circular reasoning. A homologous structure is a structure that allegedly results from common ancestry. How, though, can it be determined which structures result from common ancestry? They are the ones that are homologous.

I am not saying that these problems can't be solved, though I think they are very difficult to work around. Whether or not circularity problems can be solved, when scientists try to bring a theory in line with logic, they are not worried about empirical facts. They are troubled about conceptual issues inside their theory. Intelligent design is not chained by these problems of circular definition because it is not committed to the idea that homologous structures resulting from common ancestry drive the development of life.

Let us look another example of an internal conceptual problem, in contrast to an empirical problem. This one surfaces due to the implausibility of hypothetical evolutionary pathways regarding the transition from reptilian scales to bird feathers. An absence of fossil evidence for such a transition is an empirical problem. But it is perfectly legitimate for a scientist to admit that we don't have empirical evidence for this transition, but that there is a plausible hypothetical pathway for the transition in question. In this case, the scientist has not solved an empirical problem for his theory, but he has solved a conceptual problem. In providing such a hypothetical pathway for evolutionary transitions, a scientist needs to try to figure out what function a structure would serve if the animal had, say, 90 percent scales and 10 percent feathers. By way of analogy, consider Behe's famous mousetrap example of irreducible complexity. One response to the mousetrap example is to create a plausible hypothetical pathway from the slap to a full-blown mousetrap, in which each structure that develops serves either to trap mice or has some other function. Such attempted solution would try to use a theory to solve an internal conceptual problem in another theory.

While I cannot develop the point here, it can be argued that intelligent design theory replaces the need to postulate these implausible naturalistic pathways. There is a more plausible solution, that an intelligent designer with forethought was a participant. ID theory shows itself to be scientific because it solves an internal conceptual problem that plagues naturalistic evolutionary theory. It is a virtue of a good scientific theory that it solves conceptual problems that its rival doesn't solve. Again, intelligent design theory is scientific in that it provides a solution to internal conceptual difficulties that evolutionary theory doesn't solve very well.

What I have tried to demonstrate thus far is that the debate between intelligent design and evolution is not just about facts. It is also a debate about whether intelligent design is science. Along the way, I have tried to explain why I think methodological naturalism is not true. To summarize, intelligent design theory really is science because (1) it generates positive and negative test results; (2) it actually explains facts in scientifically standard ways; (3) it can be confirmed by facts; and (4) it solves internal conceptual problems that evolution doesn't solve. These are four things that a scientific theory ought to do, and intelligent design does all four. Thus, intelligent design exhibits what a scientific theory ought to exhibit and should be counted as a scientific theory and not simply a religious belief.

Three criticisms are frequently raised against intelligent design theory. The first is that intelligent design theory is a "god of the gaps" argument. This argument is used, say critics, when a person is ignorant of a natural explanation for a scientific phenomenon. If someone, for example, is ignorant about the cause of lightning, that person would say that the gods or a god did it. The charge is that ID appeals to a god to explain the things we don't yet understand. By contrast, the correct approach, it is argued, is not to say that God did it but to keep looking for a natural cause. An appeal to a designer to explain things of which we are ignorant impedes the growth of science.

Let me offer two quick responses to this criticism against intelligent design. The first is that ID does not appeal to a god (or some other designer) only in the face of unknowns. We have learned a lot from studying a flagellum. It is because we know so much about it that intelligent design becomes the best explanation for its existence. Our positive information about its irreducible complexity show marks of intelligence. Mousetraps and other types of structures are irreducibly complex. When I find evidence of irreducible complexity, I have an explanation, for irreducible complexity is a mark of intelligence. I have a positive reason for inferring intelligence in a biological organism. Such an inference is not just a way of covering up for our ignorance of a natural cause of irreducible complexity. The information in a DNA molecule is a legitimate basis for inferring an intelligent designer if information only comes from a mind. Such an inference stands at the heart of the SETI program. A scientist who discovers an information-rich signal naturally would infer that there are intelligent beings in space and look for a mind behind the information. So if I find information in a biological system, I appeal to a mind behind it, not because I don't have another explanation. There's a positive reason for my appeal. So the first reason the "god of the gaps" argument is faulty is that it misrepresents the theory of intelligent design. Intelligent design theory does not infer a designer to cover our ignorance of what caused a phenomenon; there are positive reasons for making the inference.

Second, it can be said that our opponents have a "naturalism of the gaps" argument. They always hold out for a naturalistic explanation. Let us suppose that I did that in trying to explain your behavior. There is a problem of our knowledge of other minds. Suppose you punch me in the nose and somebody said of you, "That person is really angry." Suppose I protested this explanation of your behavior on the grounds that one cannot appeal to mental states in such an explanation because they are invisible personal causes. Instead, I argued, we must hold out for a purely naturalistic explanation of your hand motion. There must be a solely naturalistic explanation, I claim, for why you punched me. Maybe the moon was too close, or there are some kinds of waves that we don't yet know about. Given enough time, however, science will describe a perfectly naturalistic explanation of that body movement that won't require me to attribute consciousness, agency, motives, intentions, or anything to the physical object called the body of the person who hit me.

To follow such a process would be ridiculous. It would forever keep me from finding the real cause of your behavior—it was intelligently designed, it was done intentionally to harm me, perhaps due to your dislike of philosophers. This would be a case of naturalism of the gaps, and it shows how inappropriate such a stance can be if evidence exists for a personal explanation. In a similar way, those who accuse ID proponents of advancing a god of the gaps argument have such an unflinching commitment to naturalistic explanations that their ability to deal fairly with ID theory is thereby undermined. They can fairly be accused of proffering naturalism of the gaps. Proponents of ID are not, then, the only ones who could be guilty of inappropriately handling gaps.

Here's the second criticism: intelligent design theory opens the door to Hindu, Mormon, and other religious versions of science. My response is, *So what?* ID does not try to address questions about the identity of the designer. Consider the bacterial flagellum, for example. The encoded information that forms the blueprint of the flagellum is irreducibly complex, showing that it was designed. But the DNA does not bear a label that says "made by God" or "made by Allah" or "made by Yoda." While I am a Christian and believe the designer is God, the genetic evidence alone does not allow me to identify the designer.

Members of the Church of Jesus Christ of Latter-Day Saints tend to support ID theory, but suppose the Mormons had their own clear model of the origin of life. If that model could be distinguished from others and had implications that could be tested, then Mormons should be given the chance to make their case. The Latter-Day Saints have generated an entire research program in archaeology based on views contained in *The Book of Mormon*. In doing that, they are practicing science. Such a Mormon research program might be falsified, but that's not the point. It would be a perfectly legitimate theory. Latter-Day Saints' views are distinct enough from those of Jehovah's Witnesses or Hindus or Orthodox Christians to generate their own scientifically testable implications.

If there were a distinctively Hindu view or a distinctively Mormon view of the origin of life, one that could be differentiated from the general theistic view and could be tested, I don't see the problem in considering those views. The problem relative to ID is, of course, the alleged slippery slope—an unwieldy number of rival religious "theories" will be generated, with which science simply cannot deal. The arguments go something like this: "Once the Christian nose is under the tent, one cannot stop other unwelcome views from entering." But, as I have just pointed out, this argument is a straw man.

Also, a piece of scientific evidence can sometimes be consistent with multiple theories. Suppose a discovery is made that falsifies one theory. There might still be two or three other theories that are consistent with this evidence. The evidence doesn't rule out all competing theories, but it still falsifies one of them. Intelligent design theory tends to show naturalistic evolutionary theories to be false, even if it leaves three or four other competitors on the map.

The third criticism that some people give is that intelligent design theory doesn't really explain things. It doesn't take us beyond the assertion that a designer "did it." How should we respond to this?

First, as noted, ID does not try to name the designer. But, does saying that my wife set the dining room table explain why the dining room table is set? Yes it does, but it leaves out important details about *how* she set the table. I might not explain that she put the plates first and the napkins last. In fact, I might not know the order in which she laid out the arrangement. But does it not explain *something* to say that my wife set the dining room table, even if I don't know the mechanism she used to accomplish this? I think it does. For example, it would explain the fact that the table setting didn't happen by chance or necessity. An intelligent mind did it. Also, the arrangement might show that my wife did it and not one of my kids. The assumption underlying this criticism is that if you don't cite a naturalistic mechanism, you haven't explained it. But this assumption is false.

The organization SETI became more familiar through the movie *Contact*. In that movie, the character played by Jodi Foster finds the first twenty-five prime numbers in a row and she argues that this means that intelligent life is communicating with us. Did this SETI observer know how that intelligent life produced the signal? She had no clue whatsoever. She didn't know what the signaling agents used on their planet to generate the first twenty-five prime numbers. Because she couldn't cite a mechanism that generated the signal, does that mean that what she said about her discovery was explanatorily superfluous? No. She was explaining something with it, even if she didn't have a "how" in her explanation.

To summarize, in addition to ID's need for further empirical work, which is absolutely critical and very important, ID proponents must remember the philosophical component to the ID debate. Critics have wished to disallow the ID movement from its inception by saying that it is not a scientific movement at all, that intelligent design is just religion masquerading as science. I've tried to say that such a claim involves, among other things, a TC_3 view of the shift from creationism to evolution and a demarcationist understanding of science. Neither claims can be justified. I have also tried to show that methodological naturalism is wrongheaded and, in fact, that intelligent design theory bears the features of good scientific theories and ought to be treated as scientific work even if one does not agree that its conclusions are true. It is still science nonetheless, as is evidenced by our critics' claim that they have derived from ID theory testable results that they think falsify ID theory. If they can falsify ID, why can't

ID be verified? I have tried to address this issue. Finally, I have responded to three objections against ID theory.

At the end of the day, remember, the yeoman's work here is scientific, but we have to keep in mind that people are trying to cut the legs out from underneath us by arguing philosophically, and when they do, we need to have a response.

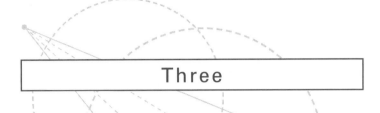

Three

Finding Intelligent Design in Nature

CASEY LUSKIN

How did the universe and life on earth come to exist in their present forms? This is perhaps the most fascinating, controversial, and timeless question faced by humanity. This origins question can be studied through many academic disciplines, including philosophy, theology, and science. This chapter will survey how science in particular informs us about questions of origins, as well as highlight some of the scientific data and arguments that lend support to the scientific hypothesis that various aspects of the natural world were designed by intelligence.

What Is Intelligent Design?

The theory of intelligent design (ID) states that some natural phenomena are best explained by an intelligent cause because, in our experience, intelligence is the cause of their informational properties. Intelligent design thus begins with observations about the kinds of information that are produced when intelligent agents act. The type of information generally known to come about by the action of intelligent agents is called specified complexity.[1] An intelligent agent is any personal being with the ability to think with will, forethought, and intentionality in order to achieve some predetermined goal it has conceived.[2] Design theorists look for objects in nature with informational properties known to derive from the action of intelligence. From these properties, we can infer that an intelligent agent was at work in the origin of that object.

Intelligent design scientists invoke explanations that are based upon our observational experience of what intelligent agents produce when they act. Our observations of human intelligence first establish a cause-and-effect relationship between mind and the origin of information (see fig. 3.1). After finding information in natural objects, a scientist is then justified in inferring that an intelligent agent was at work. Intelligent design is thus based upon our present empirical understanding of the cause-and-effect relationship between intelligent agents and the production of new information.

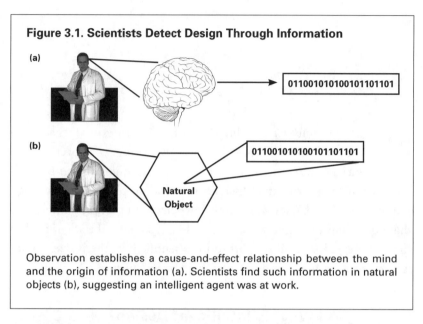

Figure 3.1. Scientists Detect Design Through Information

(a)

011001010100101101101

(b)

011001010100101101101

Natural
Object

Observation establishes a cause-and-effect relationship between the mind and the origin of information (a). Scientists find such information in natural objects (b), suggesting an intelligent agent was at work.

ID reasoning is used to discriminate between natural causes and intelligent causes in such existing scientific fields as archaeology, forensic science, and the search for extraterrestrial intelligence (SETI). For example, archaeologists discriminate between naturally occurring rock formations and those shaped by human intelligence. An archaeologist may repeatedly come across rocks with a semitriangular shape. One point invariably is sharp, with an acute angle and notches at the other points and along the opposite side of the triangle. The archaeologist realizes that the natural forces of erosion, such as water or wind, would not repeatedly produce this shape. Moreover, the archaeologist realizes that this specific shape would be ideal for piercing and wounding a large animal. Like a detective, the archaeologist examines these rocks and finds them associated with the remains of dead animals. She is justified in thinking that the complex and specified shape of these rocks is the result of an intelligent cause. These rocks were not shaped by the unguided forces of nature. She concludes they are intelligently designed projectile points, commonly called arrowheads.

Design theorists simply ask, "If we can detect design in fields like archaeology with projectile points, why can't we detect design in fields like biology, where our DNA contains incredible amounts of complex and specified information?" (see fig. 3.2). Specifically, design theorists ask, "If we can identify properties that in our experience come only from intelligence, then why can't we infer design when natural objects contain those same properties?"

Design proponents think that this same kind of reasoning can be used to detect design in such natural sciences as biology, physics, and cosmology.[3]

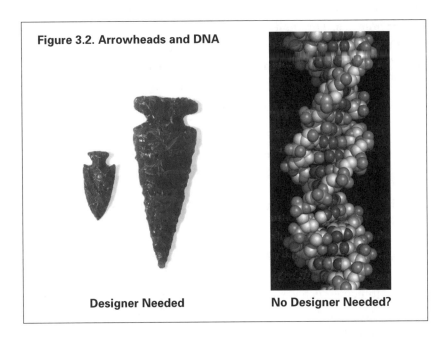

Figure 3.2. Arrowheads and DNA

Designer Needed   **No Designer Needed?**

A Case Study in Intelligent Design

As noted, the theory of intelligent design begins with observations about how intelligent agents act when they design objects. Scientists observe that when intelligent agents act, they are capable of using foresight, will, and intentionality to solve complex problems. Design theorist William Dembski has observed, "The principal characteristic of intelligent agency is directed contingency, or what we call choice."[4] By observing the sorts of choices that intelligent agents commonly make when designing systems, we can make a positive case for intelligent design, using predictable, reliable indicators of design.

For example, consider a hunter who sees that large bison live in herds in the middle of expansive, open plains. The hunter needs to kill bison so his family can eat and have clothing. The bison are difficult to kill, however, because they are keenly alert to their surroundings and easily startled. What is more, these plain environments provide little cover for hunters, and bison herds cannot be approached at a close range or they will stampede, endangering the hunter and making close-range hunting nearly impossible. The hunter knows that the only way to stop and kill one of these animals is to hunt it from afar. This hunter must choose a solution to his problem.

The need to immobilize a large quadruped from a considerable distance represents a complex problem. Being an intelligent agent, the hunter is capable of looking at this problem and thinking about ways to solve it. The hunter knows that there are fundamental design constraints that must be met in any solution:

1. The solution must seriously wound the bison.
2. The solution must work from a distance.

Either of these basic constraints may be further broken down, based upon what the hunter knows about bison:

1. Bison are large animals that can be immobilized by a wound in a vulnerable place.
2. Inflicting such a wound will require an object traveling with great momentum. Roughly speaking, great momentum can be achieved via a small object moving at a high speed, or a larger object moving at a slower speed.
3. Large objects are not easily flung over long distances. The object used to wound the bison must be small and travel at a high speed.
4. Bison have tough hides, so the object must be capable of easily piercing the skin of the bison.
5. Bison stampede when startled, meaning that there may only be one chance to use the hunting technique. This will require success (accuracy) on one of the first tries.

The solution chosen by the hunter must be capable of flinging a small, sharp object at a high speed over a great distance with considerable accuracy in order to wound the bison so it can then be killed.

There are innumerable things that the hunter could build, but in order to survive he must find a specific and complex solution that meets the design constraints. The hunter can solve this problem because he is an intelligent agent who can think with the end goal in mind, and imagine ways to solve the problem that would be highly unlikely to arise via natural processes.

Design theorist Stephen C. Meyer explains that this is precisely how intelligent agents act. They think with the end goal in mind to produce unlikely configurations of matter to solve a problem: "Agents can arrange matter with distant goals in mind. In their use of language, they routinely 'find' highly isolated and improbable functional sequences amid vast spaces of combinatorial possibilities."[5]

Design theorists have thus observed that when intelligent agents act they produce high levels of complex and specified information. Something is complex if it is unlikely, and it is specified if it matches a preexisting pattern. Meyer explains that language, machines, and computer codes are prime examples of designed objects with large quantities of complex and specified information:

> [W]e have repeated experience of rational and conscious agents—in particular ourselves—generating or causing increases in complex specified information, both in the form of sequence-specific lines of code and in the form of hierarchically arranged systems of parts. Our experience-based knowledge of information-flow confirms that systems with large amounts of specified complexity (especially codes and languages) invariably originate from an intelligent source from a mind or personal agent.[6]

Thus language, machines, and codes are examples of things that in our experience come only from intelligence.

A solution to the hunter's problem could be a bow-and-arrow apparatus. This is a complex machine because it requires a number of parts that must be configured properly in order to function:

1. There must be a semirigid bow with some elasticity so as to put tension on the string to make it tight.
2. There must be a string attached to the ends of the bow.
3. There must be arrows capable of flying accurately and puncturing the skin of the bison.

This apparatus represents a complex and specified solution to the hunter's problem—it is complex because it is an unlikely configuration of many parts, and it is specified because it meets the design constraints to solve the hunter's problem and successfully immobilize bison. The bow-and-arrow apparatus contains complex and specified information.

Each of the three objects, or subparts of the bow-and-arrow apparatus, the bow, the string, and the arrow, are necessary if there is to be a functional hunting device. If any of the three subparts are missing, the bison cannot be killed. A string by itself could not kill a bison. A lone arrow without any launching and aiming apparatus also could not be easily used to kill bison. A bow lacking a string or arrow would be useless against a large bison. Any combination of these parts is useless to kill a bison unless all three are present. The complexity of the bow and arrow is *irreducible* because if it were reduced (i.e., if any part were taken away), then it would cease to function properly. Thus irreducible complexity is a special type of specified complexity.[7]

Irreducible complexity is found in any "single system composed of several well-matched, interacting parts that contribute to the basic function, wherein the removal of any one of the parts causes the system to effectively cease functioning."[8] The bow and arrow is irreducibly complex because if you remove any of its parts, it ceases to function. Irreducible complexity is easy to detect by taking a functional machine and individually removing parts to determine if it stops working properly when its parts are removed.[9]

Using the example of the hunter and the bow, it can be seen that intelligent design theorists have a valid rationale for detecting design in nature by finding specified or irreducible complexity, a hallmark that an intelligent agent has been at work. There are many situations where informational complexity in nature indicates that an intelligent agent was at work. In this chapter, we will look at

- physics and cosmology;
- DNA and the information in life;
- the information processing machinery in life;
- function for "junk" DNA;
- micromolecular machines;
- the relationships between organisms (systematics); and
- the fossil record and the history of life.

Though intelligent design may be compatible with the teachings of various religions, the theory itself is not a "faith-based" explanation. Intelligent design is an empirically based theory that uses the scientific method to make its claims. The scientific method is commonly described as a four-step process, involving (1) observations, (2) hypothesis, (3) experiments, and (4) conclusion. As noted, intelligent design begins with the observation that intelligent agents produce complex and specified information (CSI). Design theorists hypothesize that a natural object that is designed must contain high levels of CSI. Pro-ID scientists perform experimental tests upon natural objects to determine if they contain complex and specified information.

We have seen that one easily testable form of CSI is irreducible complexity, in which reverse-engineering experiments on biological structures show whether they require all of their parts to function. When ID researchers find irreducible complexity in biology, they conclude that what is irreducibly complex must have been designed. Even if some critics disagree with the conclusions of intelligent design, they cannot deny that the theory has an empirical basis.

Intelligent Design in Physics and Cosmology

Some of the most potent arguments for design in nature come from physics and cosmology. Ever since Einstein announced his theory of relativity in the early twentieth century, it has been recognized that the laws of the universe are finely tuned to permit the existence of advanced life.[10]

The atheist cosmologist Fred Hoyle writes, "A component has evidently been missing from cosmological studies. The origin of the Universe, like the solution of the Rubik cube, requires an intelligence."[11] Physicist Paul Davies gives the analogy of the universe as a machine whose physical parameters can be controlled by twiddling a set of knobs that must be "finely tuned" to permit for the existence of advanced life:

> [L]ife as we know it depends very sensitively on the form of the laws of physics, and on some seemingly fortuitous accidents in the actual values that nature has chosen for various particle masses, force strengths, and so on. If we could play God, and select values for these natural quantities at whim by twiddling a set of knobs, we would find that almost all knob settings would render the universe uninhabitable. Some knobs would have to be fine-tuned to enormous precision if life is to flourish in the universe.[12]

If the physical laws and constants of the universe must be just right in order to permit the existence of advanced forms of life, some of these finely tuned parameters include

- the masses of the electron, neutron, and proton;
- the strength of the strong and weak nuclear forces;
- the resonance levels of carbon and oxygen; and
- strength of polarity of the water molecule.

The fine-tuning of the laws of physics and chemistry to allow for advanced life turns out to be an extreme case of specified and complex information. The laws of the universe are complex because they are highly unlikely. Scientists have calculated the odds of our universe appearing by chance to be less than one part in 10^{123}.[13] The laws are specified in that they match the narrow band of parameters required for the existence of advanced life. As Hoyle argues, "[a] common sense interpretation of the facts suggests that a super intellect has monkeyed with physics, as well as with chemistry and biology."[14] The universe itself shows evidence of having been designed.

One rebuttal employed by ID critics to avoid the conclusion that the universe was designed is to postulate the existence of an unlimited number of alternate universes, wherein our universe won a cosmic lottery and got the correct parameters that can harbor life. Under this objection, if there are enough universes out there, chances are that eventually one will happen to get the right conditions for life. Critics say that universe happens to be ours. If it was not, we wouldn't be here to know about it.

Yet the multiverse hypothesis has multiple difficulties. Primarily, there is "no foreseeable way to detect other universes," meaning the possibility is purely philosophical, based upon a leap of faith. It is impossible to disprove.[15] Moreover the "multiverse" objection violates Occam's razor, a principle that cautions against making unnecessary assumptions.

Which is more likely, the untestable existence of infinite other universes (existing for no apparent reason), among which one might permit life, or the prior action of intelligence? We know from experience that intelligence is the likely cause of the high level of complex and specified information contained in our universe. Modern objections to cosmic design seem to stem from the same psychology that caused some early twentieth-century physicists to object to the scientific conclusion that the universe had a beginning. As Arthur Eddington wrote in *Nature* in 1931, "Philosophically, the notion of a beginning of the present order of Nature is repugnant to me. . . . I should like to find a genuine loophole."[16]

Design theorists are not interested in loopholes, and they see that the most simple and elegant answer emerging from modern physics and cosmology is that the universe was designed.

Intelligent Design in DNA and the Information in Life

Deoxyribonucleic acid, or DNA, forms the chemical blueprint for life. Living organisms contain anywhere from thousands to billions of bits of information in their respective genetic codes. The information in DNA is stored by the ordering of certain chemicals called nucleotide bases (see fig. 3.3). These nucleotides are adenine (A), cytosine (C), thymine (T), and guanine (G). In DNA, adenine only binds to thymine, and cytosine forms bonds only with guanine. These nucleotide bases thus come in pairs, called base pairs. Yet no known physical or chemical laws dictate the ordering of these base pairs, as each nucleotide base is equally likely to occur in the code.[17] Nonetheless, these four chemicals are ordered in such a way that they instruct the machinery of the cell to produce all the proteins

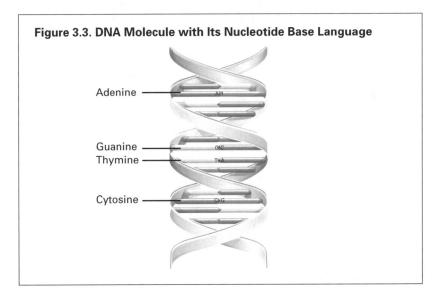

Figure 3.3. DNA Molecule with Its Nucleotide Base Language

Adenine

Guanine
Thymine

Cytosine

necessary for a living organism to survive. As Leslie Orgel, an evolutionist and authority on "chemical evolution," wrote in 1973, this specified complexity distinguishes life from nonlife:

> It is possible to make a more fundamental distinction between living and nonliving things by examining their molecular structure and molecular behavior. In brief, living organisms are distinguished by their specified complexity. Crystals are usually taken as the prototypes of simple, well-specified structures, because they consist of a very large number of identical molecules packed together in a uniform way. Lumps of granite or random mixtures of polymers are examples of structures which are complex but not specified. The crystals fail to qualify as living because they lack complexity; the mixtures of polymers fail to qualify because they lack specificity.[18]

The specified complexity in DNA conforms to a language that is understood and used by the cell. A 2004 article in *Cell Biology International*, coauthored by a theoretical biologist and an environmental biologist, explains that such a form of integrated complexity cannot arise by natural processes, regardless of how much time is allowed:

> New approaches to investigating the origin of the genetic code are required. The constraints of historical science are such that the origin of life may never be understood. Selection pressure cannot select nucleotides at the digital programming level where primary structures form. Genomes predetermine the phenotypes which natural selection only secondarily favors. Contentions that offer nothing more than long periods of time offer no mechanism of explanation for the derivation of genetic programming. No new information is provided by such tautologies. The argument simply says it happened. As such, it is nothing more than blind belief.[19]

Thus, before an organism can be produced, a functional genetic code must exist that can help the information in DNA to survive. Such a system would be unlikely to arise by natural processes.

Another paper by the same authors in *Physics of Life Reviews* challenges the ability of Darwinian mechanisms or self-organizational models to account for the origin of the language-based chemical code underlying life. They explain that "evolutionary algorithms, neural nets, and cellular automata have not been shown to self-organize spontaneously into non-trivial functions."[20] However, the organization found in life "typically contains large quantities of prescriptive information," and this prescriptive information "requires choice contingency rather than chance contingency or necessity."[21] The genetic code and the organism form a functionally integrated unit that cannot exist apart from one another. The foresight and "choice" of an intelligent agent would be necessary to produce the type of irreducible complexity inherent in the DNA-protein system.

The *Cell Biology International* article concludes that to explain the origin of the code, "new research approaches" must be found. But new scientific research approaches have already been found: we learned from the hunter and the bow that intelligent agents produce integrated systems that require multiple components in order to function. We already know from studying human intelligence that language and encoded information come from intelligent agents. The informational meaning in the DNA is not reducible to the physical matter from which it is made:

> As the arrangement of a printed page is extraneous to the chemistry of the printed page, so is the base sequence in a DNA molecule extraneous to the chemical forces at work in the DNA molecule. It is this physical indeterminacy of the sequence that produces the improbability of occurrence of any particular sequence and thereby enables it to have a meaning—a meaning that has a mathematically determinate information content equal to the numerical improbability of the arrangement.[22]

This "meaning" derived from the specified and complex information contained in DNA is precisely the type of code or language that, Stephen C. Meyer recognizes, "invariably originate from an intelligent source from a mind or personal agent."[23] Design proponents see the incredible amount of language-based specified and complex encoded information in DNA as testifying that a programmer was involved in the origin of life.

Intelligent Design in Biochemical Information Processing

The presence of information in the DNA alone is insufficient to produce a living organism. All living cells must be able to transform the encoded chemical message in our DNA into the proteins that are necessary for cellular functions. The conversion of DNA into protein relies upon a software-like system of commands and biochemical codes. This command-based information processing system is in many respects identical to the types of commands seen in computer software. Though not an ID-proponent, the computer software genius Bill Gates recognizes that the information processing capabilities of DNA are "like a computer program but far, far more advanced than any software ever created."[24]

The biochemical language of the genetic code has start commands, stop commands, and building instructions. The language uses three-string series of nucleotide bases (called codons) to specify commands. Within the language, most codons signify a particular amino acid, so a series of codons tells the cell which amino acids are to be strung in what order to build functional proteins. So similar is this to the function of a computer program that the staunch Darwinist, Oxford zoologist Richard Dawkins, agrees, "The machine code of the genes is uncannily computer-like. Apart from differences in jargon, the pages of a molecular biology journal might be interchanged with those of a computer engineering journal."[25]

A poignant example of intelligent design is found in the machinery cells use to convert the information in the genetic code into protein. As seen in figure 3.4, DNA in the cell nucleus is transcribed into mRNA, which is then transported out of the nucleus to the ribosome (a). Free-floating pieces of DNA, called tRNA, then bind to the mRNA at the ribosome (b). Amino acids are attached to tRNA. (Proteins are simply long chains of amino acids.) When the tRNA binds to the mRNA, the amino acids are linked into a protein that is being constructed at the ribosome. Figure 3.4c provides an expansion of the area in the red box of 3.4b. Each tRNA has a codon and each type of codon always carries a particular amino acid. The codon on the tRNA can only match specific codons on the mRNA. This forms the basis of the language in the DNA, allowing the amino acids to be strung together in the sequence specified by the DNA.

An irreducibly complex circuit can be understood from how tRNA molecules are assigned to the right amino acids. For the language of our genetic code to be translated properly, each tRNA codon must be attached to the correct amino acid. If this critical step in DNA translation is not functional, then the language of DNA breaks down and there is no way to properly order the amino acids in proteins.[26]

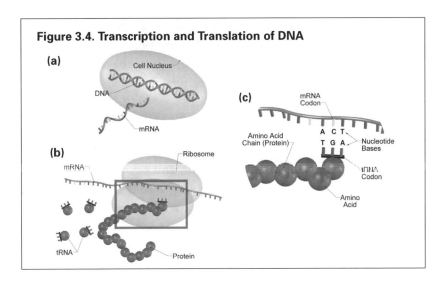

Figure 3.4. Transcription and Translation of DNA

The tRNA molecules are attached to the proper amino acid through special enzymes called aminoacyl—tRNA synthetases (aaRSs). These aaRSs ensure that the proper amino acid is attached to a tRNA with the correct codon through a chemical reaction called aminoacylation. Accurate translation requires not only that each tRNA be assigned the correct amino acid, but also that it not be aminoacylated by any of the aaRS molecules for the other nineteen amino acids. Yet these aaRSs themselves are encoded by the DNA. This forms the essence of a "chicken-egg problem": the aaRS enzymes themselves are necessary to perform the very task that constructs them (see fig. 3.5).

In order for the language of DNA to be translated accurately, a whole suite of proteins and cellular organelles must be present and functioning properly. As the article in *Cell Biology International* observes, "The letters of any alphabet used in words have no prescriptive function unless the destination reading those words first knows the language convention."[27] Without the hardware to convert the information in DNA into protein, the message is lost. Yet this hardware itself is generated by the very processes and functions they fulfill in the cell. The article explains:

> The nucleotide sequence is also meaningless without a conceptual translative scheme and physical "hardware" capabilities. Ribosomes, tRNAs, aminoacyl tRNA synthetases, and amino acids are all hardware components of the Shannon message "receiver". But the

instructions for this machinery is itself coded in DNA and executed by protein "workers" produced by that machinery. Without the machinery and protein workers, the message cannot be received and understood. And without genetic instruction, the machinery cannot be assembled.[28]

This integrated system forms a highly specified and irreducibly complex circuit, suggesting intelligent design. That all living cells use a similar irreducibly complex suite of DNA, enzyme, and organelle machinery to perform the fundamental biological task of converting DNA into protein is strong evidence that intelligence was involved in the origin and development of life on earth.

The system of DNA, cellular replication machinery, operating under a nonphysical language of chemical codes, must have originated from a source that was intelligent. Just like the hunter trying to solve the problem

Figure 3.5. The Origin of DNA and the Chicken and Egg Problem

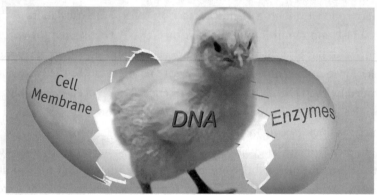

DNA is vital to the cell, and the origin of DNA presents an example of a "chicken-and-egg problem": Which came first—DNA or the cell membrane and enzymes? DNA needs enzymes (like aaRSs) to replicate and produce proteins in the cell, but the enzymes are encoded by DNA. Moreover, DNA needs protection provided by the cell membrane, but molecules of the cell membrane are also encoded by the DNA. The answer to this riddle is that none came "first," for all are required simultaneously in DNA-based life. These fundamental components form an irreducibly complex system in which all components must have been present from the start for a cell to survive. This presents a challenge to the step-by-step evolution required by Darwin's theory, and exhibits irreducible complexity—a hallmark of intelligent design.

of hunting bison, the solution to the origin of the information-processing capabilities in cells must be able to reach the "end goal" to produce a highly unlikely configuration of matter to solve a complex problem. As one scientist explained in a mainstream scientific journal, "chance and necessity cannot explain sign systems, meaning, purpose, and goals," and since "mind possesses other properties that do not have these limitations," it is "therefore very natural that many scientists believe that life is rather a subsystem of some Mind greater than humans."[29]

Intelligent Design in "Junk" DNA

Molecular biologists continue to discover how DNA works. Yet a common objection to intelligent design is the observation that some stretches of DNA do not code for proteins and have no known function, leading to the (often incorrect) assumption that they are undesigned genetic "junk." According to Dawkins, our DNA "consists of multiple copies of junk, 'tandem repeats', and other nonsense which may be useful for forensic detectives but which doesn't seem to be used in the body itself."[30] Making a wholesale argument against creationism, Dawkins contends that "creationists might spend some earnest time speculating on why the Creator should bother to litter genomes with untranslated pseudogenes and junk tandem repeat DNA."[31]

Design theorist Jonathan Wells explains that molecular biologists may wrongly assume that non-coding DNA is undersigned functionless junk: "Since non-coding regions do not produce proteins, Darwinian biologists have been dismissing them for decades as random evolutionary noise or 'junk DNA.' From an ID perspective, however, it is extremely unlikely that an organism would expend its resources on preserving and transmitting so much 'junk.'"[32]

Wells highlights the observation that intelligent agents tend to produce functional objects. Like the hunter and the bow, intelligent agents produce structures that have a purpose. It seems unlikely that an intelligent agent would design something that does absolutely nothing. While a structure may have been initially designed but lost its function over time, we can hypothesize that any truly nonfunctional structure in biology came to that state via nonintelligent processes. This provides a clear testable and falsifiable prediction for intelligent design: if something was designed, then it will have been designed to perform some function. This testable prediction can be applied directly to DNA.

As molecular biologists learn more and more about DNA, they are continually testing—and refuting—the hypothesis that DNA is actually largely composed of useless genetic junk. They are finding that what they thought was "junk" DNA actually has function. For example, in 2006 the scientific journal *Nature* reported that scientists are using methods of code breaking to discern the hidden function in "junk" DNA, as they are "treating DNA as we used to treat problems in intelligence."[33] The article reported that our DNA contains many layers of encoded information beyond the mere language of codons:

> [R]esearchers now know that there are numerous other layers of biological information in DNA, interspersed between, or superimposed on, the passages written in the triplet code. Human DNA contains tissue-specific information that instructs brain or muscle cells to produce the suite of proteins that make them brain or muscle cells. Other signals in the sequence help decide at what points DNA should coil around its scaffolds of structural proteins. These are the codes that computer buffs such as Shepherd want to crack with raw processing power. . . . [M]any stretches of DNA in humans and other organisms manage to multi task: a sequence can code for a protein and still manage to guide the position of a nucleosome.[34]

DNA contains repetitive elements, which according to some neo-Darwinists, are like selfish parasites in the genome and therefore "inferred to be meaningless."[35] Yet in 2002, Richard Sternberg of the Smithsonian surveyed the literature and found extensive evidence for function of such repetitive elements and concluded, "the selfish DNA narrative and allied frameworks must join the other 'icons' of neo-Darwinian evolutionary theory that, despite their variance with empirical evidence, nevertheless persist in the literature."[36] Elsewhere Sternberg and leading geneticist James A. Shapiro conclude that "one day, we will think of what used to be called 'junk DNA' as a critical component of truly 'expert' cellular control regimes."[37] Genetics research published in leading scientific journals continues to uncover functions for allegedly functionless types of DNA including pseudogenes,[38] introns, SINE,[39] LINE,[40] and ALU elements.[41]

A striking admission of the false assumption that non-coding DNA is useless genetic junk was highlighted in an article titled, "The Unseen Genome: Gems Among the Junk," in *Scientific American* in 2003. Though written from a neo-Darwinian perspective, the article explains that non-coding DNA was "long ago written off" by molecular biologists using neo-Darwinian assumptions:

> The extent of this unseen genome is not yet clear, but at least two layers of information exist outside the traditionally recognized genes. One layer is woven throughout the vast "noncoding" sequences of DNA that interrupt and separate genes. Though *long ago written off as irrelevant because they yield no proteins*, many of these sections have been preserved mostly intact through millions of years of evolution. That suggests they do something indispensable. And indeed a large number are transcribed into varieties of RNA that perform a much wider range of functions than biologists had imagined possible. Some scientists now suspect that much of what makes one person, and one species, different from the next are variations in the gems hidden within our "junk" DNA.[42]

The article goes on to explain that these non-coding sequences, called introns, "were immediately assumed to be evolutionary junk."[43] However, in a stark admission, the article calls that Darwinian assumption "too hasty" and then quotes a molecular biologist explaining how Darwinian-based dogma stifled research, calling the failure to recognize introns as possibly "one of the biggest mistakes in the history of molecular biology."[44] Similarly, a paper from the *Annals of the New York Academy of Sciences* asserts that "neo-Darwinian 'narratives' have been the primary obstacle to elucidating the effects of these enigmatic components of chromosomes," and therefore, "a new conceptual framework is needed."[45] Yet design proponents predicted long ago that these non-coding stretches of DNA might have some function. Had more researchers considered intelligent design, the molecular biology community might have been encouraged to proactively investigate function for these types of DNA. This could have significantly advanced our understanding of the cell and led to advances in medicine.

Examples of DNA of unknown functions still persist, but design encourages researchers to investigate functions, whereas Darwinism has caused some scientists to wrongly assume that non-coding DNA is junk. Intelligent design makes powerfully accurate predictions regarding the functionality of DNA that could open up fruitful avenues of scientific research.

Intelligent Design in Micromolecular Machines

The irreducibly complex nature of the transcription–translation information processing machinery in living cells is not the extent of irreducible complexity in biology. In fact, the cell is full of miniature machines that even anti-ID biologists find bear a striking resemblance to human-designed machines. As former National Academy of Sciences president Bruce Alberts, a staunch critic of ID, writes,

> The entire cell can be viewed as a factory that contains an elaborate network of interlocking assembly lines, each of which is composed of a set of large protein machines. . . . Why do we call the large protein assemblies that underlie cell function protein *machines*? Precisely because, like machines invented by humans to deal efficiently with the macroscopic world, these protein assemblies contain highly coordinated moving parts.[46]

The bacterial flagellum has become a famous example of an irreducibly complex biological machine. The flagellum is a micromolecular rotary engine, functioning like an outboard motor on bacteria to propel it through some liquid medium to find food or a hospitable living environment. There are various types of flagella, but all function in a process very similar to that of a rotary engine made by humans, as found in some cars or boat motors. Moreover flagella contain many parts that are familiar to human engineers, including a rotor, a stator, a U-joint, and a propeller (see fig. 3.6). As one molecular biologist writes in the journal *Cell*, "More so than other motors, the flagellum resembles a machine designed by a human."[47]

Most important, the flagellum is irreducibly complex. It fails to assemble or function properly if one mutates or removes any one of its approximately thirty to fifty genes.[48] In this all-or-nothing game, mutations cannot produce the complexity needed to provide a functional fla-

Figure 3.6. Bacterial Flagellum

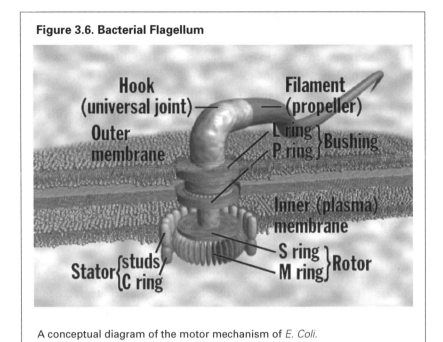

A conceptual diagram of the motor mechanism of *E. Coli.*

Copyright © 1998, Access Research Network, www.arn.org. All rights reserved. International copyright secured.

gellar rotary engine one incremental step at a time, and the odds are too daunting for it to assemble in one great leap. Yet the flagellum is a highly specified machine that bears the hallmarks of design. Just like the hunter and the bow, the flagellum meets the specific design requirements necessary in a motor that would efficiently propel a bacterium through liquid.

Some Darwinists have countered that parts can be "co-opted" from one job to another in the cell to build irreducible complexity. For example, the neo-Darwinian biologist Kenneth Miller argues that ability to find function for some subpart of the flagellum, such as the injection function of the Type III Secretory System (which contains approximately one-fourth of the genes of bacterial flagellum), refutes the irreducible complexity of the final flagellar system.[49]

But there's a problem with this explanation: Biological parts are not necessarily interchangeable. According to the emerging field of systems biology, biological structures are integrated wholes whose individual parts have complex interactions. Miller's explanation merely explains how proteins could become available to be borrowed, but in biology, "a system is not just an assembly of genes and proteins, its properties cannot be fully understood merely by drawing diagrams of their interconnections."[50] Comparing biological systems to an engineered airplane, a review paper in *Science* examines how complex assembly instructions are necessary to explain how precise biological parts will combine to interact with one another in a functional system:

> Identifying all the genes and proteins in an organism is like listing all the parts in an airplane. While such a list provides a catalog of the individual components, by itself it is not sufficient to understand the complexity underlying the engineered object. We need to know how these parts are assembled to form the structure of the airplane.[51]

Thus, merely having the parts available in the cell does not account for how the parts of an irreducibly complex system will suddenly assemble and then interact properly to perform some new function. The specific assembly and ordering of interacting parts in the cell can't be produced by chance, any more than an old truck will increase its horsepower merely by being kept in an auto shop full of brand-new Hemi engines. Miller's Darwinian explanation vastly oversimplifies the complexity of the cell.

To further understand why Miller's "co-option" explanation does not refute irreducible complexity, consider the example of a car engine and a bolt. Car engines use various kinds of bolts, and a bolt could be seen as a small "subpart" or "subsystem" of a car engine. Under Miller's logic, if a vital bolt in my car's engine might also perform some other function— perhaps as a lug nut—then it follows that my car's whole engine system is not irreducibly complex. Such an argument is obviously fallacious.

In assessing whether an engine is irreducibly complex, one must focus on the function of the engine itself, not on the possible function of some subpart that may operate elsewhere. Of course a bolt out of my engine could serve some other purpose in my car. Nonetheless, this observation does not explain how many complex parts such as pistons, cylinders, the camshaft, valves, the crankshaft, spark plugs, the distributor cap, and wiring came together in the appropriate configuration to make a functional car engine. Even if all of these parts could perform some other function in the car (which is doubtful), how were these parts assembled properly to construct an engine that runs? Their precise configuration requires intelligent design.

Intelligent Design in the Relationships Among Organisms

Systematics is the field of science that studies the relationships among living organisms. Neo-Darwinism predicts that all organisms share a common ancestor (or group of ancestors). Many evolutionary biologists have hoped to help construct a complete evolutionary "tree of life" in which all of the alleged family relationships among all of the organisms are explained.

It is important to realize that intelligent design is not necessarily incompatible with common ancestry. Even if all organisms on earth share a common ancestor pool, that would not necessarily mean that the primary mechanisms causing the differences between species are purely blind, unguided processes, such as natural selection. Intelligent agents are not constrained by the blind process of neo-Darwinism, so intelligent design can make its own contributions to systematics by providing a mechanism for understanding how characteristics, particularly genes, become distributed among living organisms.

For example, we know that intelligent agents use functional components that work in different systems. An everyday example might be the use of wheels on both cars and airplanes. This is explained by design theorists Jonathan Wells and Paul Nelson: "An intelligent cause may reuse or redeploy the same module in different systems, without there necessarily being any material or physical connection between those systems. Even more simply, intelligent causes can generate identical patterns independently."[52] To return to the example of the hunter, an intelligent agent can use a sharp-pointed tool on the end of an arrow shot by a bow to penetrate, and then use a similar sharp object for scraping and cutting by hand. Similarly, intelligent design may lead us to expect that functioning parts, such as genes, might appear in different organisms.

The implications of this observation can help us understand why certain organisms share similar genes. For example, Darwinists often tout a statistic that 98 percent of human DNA and chimpanzee DNA is the same, claiming this as conclusive evidence for common ancestry. Yet Wells and

Nelson note, designers often reuse part designs for different applications. If a designer wanted to generate a species similar to humans, it naturally follows that the designer would redeploy many of the same genes. In other words, genetic similarities between humans and chimpanzees could be the result of common design rather than common descent. It may be difficult to distinguish between common design and common descent, but that does not imply that we should rule out the possibility of common design.

One way to discriminate between common design and common descent is to observe that an intelligent agent is not constrained to use similar genes only in similar species. Intelligent design might, in fact, lead us to expect that similar gene patterns might appear in widely divergent organisms without turning to neo-Darwinian hypotheses about common ancestry. In many cases, this is precisely what we find.

Similar parts have been found in organisms that are thought to be distinctly related, when related species do not contain those parts. The same genes may control eye or limb growth in different organisms whose alleged common ancestors are not even thought to have had such forms of eyes,[53] wings,[54] or limbs.[55] A striking macromorphological[56] example is the skeletal similarity between marsupial and placental "wolves." Their common ancestor is allegedly to have been a small rodentlike mammal that lived over one hundred million years ago (see fig. 3.7). Darwinists would call this data unexpected extreme examples of "convergent evolution," but the data fits naturally when explained as common design.

Precisely what does neo-Darwinian evolution predict regarding the distribution of genes in organisms? Under neo-Darwinism, genes exist because they were inherited from an ancestor. Thus Darwinists expected that new genetic data will fit with developed hypotheses about the evolutionary relationships of living organisms (called phylogenetic trees). In 1965, Emile Zuckerlkandl, an evolutionary biologist, predicted that the coming flood of DNA sequence data would confirm evolutionist expectations of evolutionary history:

> It will be determined to what extent the phylogenic tree, as derived from molecular data in complete independence from the results of organismal biology, coincides with the phylogenic tree constructed on the basis of organismal biology. If the two phylogenic trees are mostly in agreement with respect to the topology of branching, the best avail-

able single proof of the reality of macro-evolution would be furnished. Indeed, only the theory of evolution, combined with the realization that events at any supramolecular level are consistent with molecular events, could reasonably account for such a congruence between lines of evidence obtained independently, namely amino acid sequences of homologous polypeptide chains on the one hand, and the finds of organismal taxonomy and paleontology on the other hand.[57]

What actually happened as evolutionary biologists compared the hypothetical evolutionary phylogenetic trees based upon genes with those based upon larger-scale characteristics of organisms was that they have found widespread discrepancies.

One early study in 1993 tried to fit together gene-based and morphology-based phylogenetic trees (comparing physical characteristics). The researchers expressed disappointment: "As morphologists with high hopes of molecular systematics, we end this survey with our hopes dampened. Congruence

Figure 3.7. Extreme "Convergence" of the Marsupial and Placental Wolf

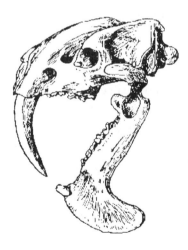 

The skulls of the marsupial *Thylacosmilus atrox* (left) and the placental *Eusmilus sicarius* (right) saber-toothed cats.

Schindewolf (1993), reproduced in John A. Davison, "A Prescribed Evolutionary Hypothesis," *Rivista di Biologia/Biology Forum* 98 (2005):155–66, fig. 1.

between molecular phylogenies is as elusive as it is in morphology and as it is between molecules and morphology."[58] Another study reports that, despite a vast increase in the amount of data since Darwin's time, "our ability to reconstruct accurately the tree of life may not have improved significantly over the last 100 years." The report analysis also said, "Despite increasing methodological sophistication, phylogenies derived from morphology, and those inferred from molecules, are not always converging on a consensus."[59]

As the "consensus" becomes harder and harder to reach, Darwinian systematists have tried to construct phylogenies in which data from many genes are averaged together to produce a single tree. In this approach, evolutionists construct phylogenies only after assuming common descent. They do not follow correct scientific method in trying to falsify the hypothesis by determining if trees based upon separate characteristics match one another.[60] If they were willing to test their hypothesis, their methods would be very different.

With the advent of the biotechnology revolution and DNA sequencing, it is now clear that conflicts exist not only between morphology-based trees and gene-based trees, but also between different types of gene-based trees (or "molecular" trees). For example, leading biologist Lynn Margulis, who rejects ID, explains in her article "The Phylogenetic Tree Topples" that "many biologists claim they know for sure that *random mutation* (purposeless chance) is the source of inherited variation that generates new species of life and that life evolved in a single-common-trunk, dichotomously branching-phylogenetic-tree pattern!"[61] But she dissents from that view and attacks the dogmatism of evolutionary systematists, noting, "Especially dogmatic are those molecular modelers of the 'tree of life' who, ignorant of alternative topologies (such as webs), don't study ancestors."[62] Yet Margulis herself ignores the possibility that intelligent design was involved in the history of life.

Despite the entrenched assumptions in this field, observed by Margulis, some evolutionary biologists are willing to acknowledge that the genetic data is not leading to a clear picture of evolutionary descent. Biologists Hervé Philippe and Maximilian J. Telford in the journal *Trends in Ecology and Evolution* recognized that the animal phylogeny has undergone "major reorganisations over the past few years"[63] as new genetic evidence is overturning former ideas about evolutionary ancestry that were based upon morphology. Their article recommends building the tree of life by comparing large numbers of genes, because phylogenetic trees based upon individual genes commonly are in conflict with trees based upon another gene. The hope is that incorporating more data will smooth out the inconsistencies between the conflicting phylogenetic trees.

A recent study in the journal *Science* tried such a technique of using large amounts of gene data to construct the phylogenetic tree for the major groups of multicellular animals (also called metazoa). Yet the study reports, "Despite the amount of data and breadth of taxa analyzed, relationships among most metazoan phyla remained unresolved."[64] Again, the problem is that the data simply do not neatly produce a Darwinian tree that clearly demonstrates evolutionary relationships.

Striking admission of troubles in constructing a tree of life came from a paper by two evolutionary biologists titled "Bushes in the Tree of Life." They acknowledge that "a large fraction of single genes produce phylogenies of poor quality," observing that one study "omitted 35 percent of single genes from their data matrix, because those genes produced phylogenies at odds with conventional wisdom."[65] Such a selective use of data does not inspire confidence in the methods evolutionary biologists use to construct their phylogenetic trees. But what about the proposed solution that inconsistencies will be resolved as data is added? The paper suggests that "certain critical parts of the [tree of life] may be difficult to resolve, regardless of the quantity of conventional data available."[66] This implies that the excuse that phylogenetic trees are difficult to construct because of insufficient data is no longer feasible. "The recurring discovery of persistently unresolved clades (bushes) should force a re-evaluation of several widely held assumptions of molecular systematics."[67]

The authors are both neo-Darwinists, so they do not reevaluate the assumption of a neo-Darwinian common ancestry. They suggest the problems can be fixed by analyzing less commonly studied types of molecular characteristics. They appeal to new and untried techniques, which they hope carry the true phylogenetic signal they seek:

> Although it may be heresy to say so, it could be argued that knowing that strikingly different groups form a clade and that the time spans between the branching of these groups must have been very short, makes the knowledge of the branching order among groups potentially a secondary concern.[68]

They recommend acceptance of the possibility that, contrary to the expectations of evolutionary systematists, widely different groups really do share similar gene sequences. They attempt to reconcile the genetic data with common descent by postulating rapid phases of evolution, during which there was insufficient time for differences in the DNA of different lineages to accumulate to allow modern biologists to resolve the evolutionary relationships. This is an exercise in explaining away the data, not explaining the data. Perhaps the inability to construct robust phylogenetic trees using molecular data stems from the fact that neo-Darwinian common descent is wrong.

The aforementioned prediction, made by Emil Zuckerkandl in 1965, that genetic data would confirm common ancestry seems to be failing. The fundamental problem for neo-Darwinism is that phylogenetic trees based upon one gene or characteristic will often conflict with trees based upon some other gene or characteristic. The father of molecular systematics, Carl Woese, found that conflicts in phylogenies are present not only at the base of the tree: "Phylogenetic incongruities [conflicts] can be seen everywhere in the universal tree, from its root to the major branchings within and among the various taxa to the makeup of the primary groupings themselves."[69] The implication is that genetic and morphological similarity is found in places where neo-Darwinism predicts that it should not exist. Neo-Darwinists try to explain these discrepancies by invoking such *ad hoc* explanations as horizontal gene transfer, rapid evolution, differing rates of evolution, convergence, and a lack of data. However, a simple solution to this quandary could be based upon the thought that an intelligent agent might reuse part designs that work in widely different and ultimately unrelated organisms. Perhaps common descent is challenged by the data because the data show the result of common design by an intelligence and not merely neo-Darwinian processes.

Intelligent Design in the Fossil Record and the History of Life

The theory of intelligent design can also be applied to the fossil record to detect where design has occurred in the history of life. As always, intelligent design is based upon an observed understanding of how intelligent agents act. Design theorists observe that intelligent agents are capable of rapidly infusing large amounts of information into a form that produces fully functioning machines. As four pro-ID scientists, Stephen C. Meyer, Marcus Ross, Paul Nelson, and Paul Chien, explain, "We know from experience that intelligent agents often conceive of plans prior to the material instantiation of the systems that conform to the plans—that is, the intelligent design of a blueprint often precedes the assembly of parts in accord with a blueprint or preconceived design plan."[70] This is precisely the type of reasoning that can be applied to the case of the hunter and the bow: A hunter will construct a fully functional bow before trying to kill an animal.

Intelligent agents can thus rapidly infuse large amounts of genetic information into the biosphere. This led some design theorists to conclude that "intelligent design provides a sufficient causal explanation for the origin of large amounts of information, since we have considerable experience of intelligent agents generating informational configurations of matter."[71]

This sort of reasoning can be applied to detect design in the history of life through analysis of the fossil record. Design may be inferred in the history of life when we see in the fossil record fully formed blueprints that appear suddenly, reflecting the rapid infusion of large amounts of biologically functional information into the biosphere. This could be reflected in the fossil record as the abrupt appearance of new types of organisms, without any directly similar precursors. When we find the rapid appearance of new fossil forms that lack similar precursors, we may infer intelligent design.

The history of life shows a pattern of explosions, in which new fossil forms come into existence without any clear evolutionary precursors. This is evidence in agreement with design theory, which predicts that species may appear abruptly. Charles Darwin explained that his theory led him to believe, "The number of intermediate varieties, which have formerly existed on the earth, [must] be truly enormous."[72] However, Darwin recognized that the fossil record in his day did not contain fossils of these "intermediate" forms of life: "Why then is not every geological formation and every stratum full of such intermediate links? Geology assuredly does not reveal any such finely graduated organic chain; and this, perhaps, is the most obvious and gravest objection which can be urged against my theory."[73]

Nearly 150 years later, only a small fraction of the thousands of known species are claimed to be candidates for Darwin's intermediate forms. Fossil evidence of evolutionary intermediates is generally absent, as paleontologist and committed evolutionist Stephen Jay Gould explains: "The absence of fossil evidence for intermediary stages between major transitions in organic design, indeed our inability, even in our imagination, to construct functional intermediates in many cases, has been a persistent and nagging problem for gradualistic accounts of evolution."[74]

Darwin saved his gradual theory of evolution by claiming that the reason intermediate fossils had not been found was "the extreme imperfection of the geological record."[75] It just happened that the intermediate links were not the ones fossilized. Even Gould noted that Darwin's argument that the fossil record is imperfect "still persists as the favored escape of most paleontologists from the embarrassment of a record that seems to show so little of evolution directly."[76]

In the last few decades, however, increasing number of scientists have recognized that, while the fossil record is imperfect, it may still be adequate to assess questions about evolution. One recent study reports that, "if scaled to the . . . taxonomic level of the family, the past 540 million years of the fossil record provide uniformly good documentation of the life of the past."[77] Paleontologists recognize that "jumps" between species without transitional forms, were not simply the result of an incomplete record. As Niles Eldredge and Ian Tattersal write, "The record jumps, and all the evidence shows that the record is real: the gaps we see reflect real events in life's history—not the artifact of a poor fossil record."[78]

Eventually many evolutionists accepted that the fossil record did not contain Darwin's predicted transitional forms. David S. Woodruff, an evolutionary biologist who studied under Gould, implored his colleagues, "Evolutionary biologists can no longer ignore the fossil record on the ground that it is imperfect."[79] Another article explains, "The fossil record in giving a clear account of evolutionary history has been questioned because of its incompleteness." Yet the writers say that this excuse is outdated. "New evidence suggests . . . that this is not an overwhelming problem."[80]

Rather than finding a record showing the slow evolution of organisms, the fossil record consistently shows a pattern where new fossil forms come into existence abruptly, which many have dubbed "explosions" in the history of life.

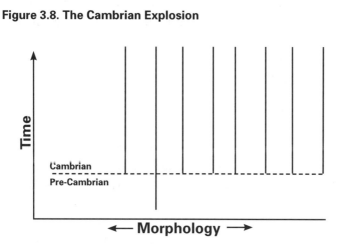

Figure 3.8. The Cambrian Explosion

The actual fossil record of the major animal phyla as documented in the Cambrian Explosion. Vertical lines indicate the actual fossil record of the phyla. The dotted line marks the Cambrian–Pre-Cambrian boundary. Richard Dawkins says the Cambrian Explosion fauna are, "already in an advanced state or evolution, the very first time they appear. It is as though they were just planted there, without any evolutionary history" (*The Blind Watchmaker: Why the Evidence of Evolution Reveals a Universe Without Design* [New York: W. W. Norton, 1996], 229).

According to paleontologists, almost all of the major living animal phyla appear in the fossil record during the Cambrian Period, about 530 million years ago (see fig. 3.8). This takes place within a 5–10 million-year period called the *Cambrian explosion.* Some biologists agree with Susumu Ohno that the rapid appearance of many biological features in one Cambrian explosion strains traditional evolutionary explanations:

> It follows that 6–10 million years in the evolutionary time scale is but a blink of an eye. The Cambrian explosion denoting the almost simultaneous emergence of nearly all the extant phyla of the Kingdom Animalia within the time span of 6–10 million years can't possibly be explained by mutational divergence of individual gene functions.[81]

Before the Cambrian, very few fossils having anything to do with modern phyla are found in the fossil record. According to R. S. K. Barnes, P. Calow, P. J. W. Olive, and D. W. Golding,

Most of the animal phyla that are represented in the fossil record first appear, "fully formed" and identifiable as to their phylum in the Cambrian some 500 million years ago. . . . The fossil record is therefore of no help with respect to the origin and early diversification of the various animal phyla.[82]

Though this quote is from a textbook on invertebrate zoology, it is now known that even vertebrates—fossil fish—appear in the Cambrian explosion.[83] Meyer et al. note, "The suddenness of the appearance of animal life in the Cambrian, 'the Cambrian explosion' has now earned titles such as 'The Big Bang of Animal Evolution' (*Scientific American*), 'Evolution's Big Bang' (Science), and the 'Biological Big Bang' (*Science News*)."[84]

There are many other examples of explosions in the history of life. One evolutionist concedes that, for the origin of fishes, "this is one count in the creationists' charge that can only evoke in unison from paleontologists a plea of *nolo contendere* [no contest]."[85] Plant biologists have called the origin of plants an explosion: "The Siluro-Devonian primary radiation of land biotas is the terrestrial equivalent of the much-debated Cambrian 'explosion' of marine faunas."[86] Vertebrate paleontologists believe there was a mammal explosion because of the few transitional forms between major mammal groups. Evolutionary paleontologist Niles Eldredge explains that "there are all sorts of gaps: absence of gradationally intermediate 'transitional' forms between species, but also between larger groups—between, say, families of carnivores, or the orders of mammals."[87]

Another study reported a bird explosion, as well as a mammal explosion, in the "Early Tertiary 'explosion'" because many bird and mammal groups appear in a short time period lacking immediately recognizable ancestral forms.[88] Finally, others have called the origin of our own genus *Homo*, a "genetic revolution,"[89] in which "no australopithecine [ape] species is obviously transitional."[90] This genetic revolution has been called a "big bang theory" of human evolution.[91]

The most common objection from evolutionists is to claim that the fossil record contains many transitional forms. To be sure, the fossil record does contain examples of possible transitional forms. But they are rare in a record that shows rapid explosions of biodiversity and the sudden, abrupt appearance of biological novelty. Moreover, a close examination of many of these alleged transitional fossils reveals they do not agree in significant ways with the evolutionary stories they are supposed to support.

Perhaps the most famous example of a possible transitional form is *Archaeopteryx*. This bird from the late Jurassic period had various reptilian features, such as teeth, claws, and a bony tail. Evolutionists have cited this mix of features as evidence that birds are descended from the dinosaurs.[92]

While there is no doubt that *Archaeopteryx* represents a bird species with a mosaic of reptilian and avian traits, these observations are not support for a transition unless the fossil fits a larger, coherent picture of evolution. *Archaeopteryx* was a true bird, capable of flight, but where did it come from? The theropod dinosaurs, from which *Archaeopteryx* is said to have descended, lived at least 20 million years after *Archaeopteryx*.[93] This does not bother evolutionists, who claim that the fossil record is merely imperfect; the fossils representing ancestors of *Archaeopteryx* may not be accessible. This, however, leaves us with a striking situation: *Archaeopteryx*, a true bird, has no real candidates for fossil ancestors whatsoever. Given that *Archaeopteryx* really is a bird, then from what, if anything, did birds evolve?

The theropod-to-bird hypothesis has bigger problems than fossil order. An evolutionary interpretation of the fossil data requires that many key features that allow birds to fly, including feathers, evolved for a purpose other than flight.[94] Feathers supposedly evolved from scales, but pennaceous feathers are so well suited for flight that it is difficult to imagine transitional stages between scales and fully functional flight feathers.[95] According to much prevailing evolutionary wisdom, natural selection is not the powerful force driving the evolution of traits necessary for flight. Rather, bird flight has become a mere accident and lucky by-product of a morphological coincidence. This does not make for a compelling evolutionary story.

Evolutionary paleontologists sometimes claim to have found "feathered dinosaurs" that make compelling evidence that birds are descended from dinosaurs. Expert and evolutionist Alan Feduccia observes, however, that these fossils are "replete with features of secondarily flightless" birds, meaning that they are true birds that have lost their ability to fly and are not evolutionary intermediates.[96] More directly, Feduccia explains that developmental biology strongly challenges the dinosaur-to-bird hypothesis. In all egg-laying vertebrates, the digits (i.e., fingers) on the hand develop out of a mass of cartilage. Bird digits develop out of digits 2, 3, and 4 from the cartilaginous array, but fossil evidence indicates that theropod dinosaurs develop their "fingers" from digits 1, 2, and 3. This strongly contradicts the cladistic methodology that evolutionists use to argue that birds must be descended from dinosaurs.[97]

But if birds didn't come from theropods, this leaves a large gap, for there are no nearby fossil candidates for the ancestor of birds. Feduccia concludes, "In spite of some paleontologists' desperate pleas for us to accept through faith the dinosaurian origin of avian flight, the details of the origin of birds remain elusive after more than a hundred and fifty years."[98] There is simply not a coherent picture of evolution through this transitional form. Perhaps a better explanation is that *Archaeopteryx* represents a mosaic form where an creative designer used creativity to play a variation upon a theme.

Transitional Forms and Retroactive Confessions of Evolutionist Ignorance

But what of all the constant media hype over newly discovered "missing links"? Most often, it is only when new supposed missing links are touted to the public that the evolutionary biology community admits how little evidence it previously held for the evolutionary transition in question. This phenomenon of evolutionists confessing their "retroactive ignorance" can be witnessed in media coverage of three missing link announcements in 2006. Not only do these fossils prove to be paltry examples of Darwin's missing transitional fossils, but they have been accompanied by stark Darwinist admissions of how little they knew about the evolutionary issue in question prior to making the find.

The first example came in early April of 2006, when scientists announced the discovery of *Tiktaalik roseae*, an alleged missing link between fish and four-legged or tetrapod animals. After making this find, evolutionists acknowledged the previous lack of fossil evidence for such a transition. Leading scientists Edward B. Daeschler, Neil H. Shubin, and Farish A. Jenkins wrote in the journal *Nature* that "the origin of major tetrapod features has remained *obscure* for lack of fossils that document the sequence of evolutionary changes."[99] But this admission came only after they announced the find.

That same month, paleoanthropologists reported discovering fossils of the hominid species *Australopithecus anamensis*. The find amounted to a couple of canine teeth of intermediate size,[100] but apparently the evolutionary biology community felt comfortable enough to finally admit that "until recently, the origins of *Australopithecus were obscured* by a sparse fossil record."[101]

In September 2006 scientists reported that they had discovered what may be the most complete australopithecine fossil specimen ever found. The specimen represented a baby from the well-known species *Australopithecus afarensis*. The media claimed it had "a mixture of ape-like and human-like features,"[102] which was "a critical missing link."[103] It was recognized that prior to finding this fossil there was a "developmental void"[104] or "important gap"[105] in the fossil record. Yet no one spoke publicly of these "gaps" or "voids" prior to finding this fossil.

This behavior is not new: evolutionists regularly confess their prior ignorance on some important point of evolutionary history only *after* they report an alleged big breakthrough. This behavior may be conscious or unplanned, and they might argue that it simply represents the progress of science. Regardless, it is predictable that the next time the public is told about some missing link, it will also hear about how precious little evolutionists had known previously. A reasonable person might wonder, "How strong is the evidence for Darwinism, really?"

Do these fossil finds really provide the evidence for large-scale evolutionary change that evolutionists claim? *Tiktaalik* was a fish with fins and does little to tell us how fins evolved into feet. In another confession of retroactive ignorance, Jennifer A. Clack and Per Erik Ahlberg wrote about *Tiktaalik* that the gap between fish and fins was previously "frustratingly wide."[106] The article went on, "There remains a large morphological gap between them and digits as seen in, for example, Acanthostega."[107] Yet as they admit, there are no fossils showing how fins turned into feet. The fin of *Tiktaalik* is completely different from the fingered limbs of real tetrapod feet in *Acanthostega* (see fig. 3.9).[108] Yet the *Nature* article places *Tiktaalik* as the closest known fish specimen to tetrapods, revealing the stark lack of fossils documenting any kind of a transition between fins and feet.

Some of the australopithecine fossils reported in April 2006 were called "intermediate" simply because of a couple canine teeth of intermediate

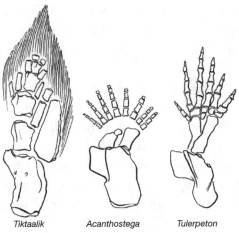

Figure 3.9. True Tetrapod Feet Versus Fish Fins

Tiktaalik   Acanthostega   Tulerpeton

Reprinted by permission from Macmillan Publishers Ltd. Neil H. Shubin, Edward B. Daeschler, and Farish A. Jenkins Jr., "The pectoral fin of Tiktaalik roseae and the origin of the tetrapod limb," *Nature* 440 (April 6, 2006): 764–71.

size and shape. The technical term used in the scientific paper reporting the find was intermediate "masticatory robusticity."[109] But a couple teeth that function well at chewing harder food does not a major evolutionary transition make.[110]

This "missing link," highlighted on a front page MSNBC article, was said to document human evolution. That is very misleading. Not only was the species *Australopithecus anamensis* already known from prior fossils, but it is said to have lived over 4 million years ago, far removed from the appearance of our own species and even from our own genus. Yet MSNBC called this "the most complete chain of human evolution so far."[111] If a couple of 4 million-year-old teeth of "intermediate size" makes "the most complete chain of human evolution so far," then the evidence for Darwinian evolution of the human species is quite limited indeed.

Finally, when reporting on the "baby ape" fossil specimen of *Australopithecus afarensis* reported in September 2006, the media called it an ape-man skeleton[112] that was "half ape" and "half human."[113] These descriptions are incredibly misleading, if not outright falsehoods. As previously noted, these apelike australopithecine fossils predated humans by millions of years. Moreover, a scientific study reported in the *Journal of Molecular Biology and Evolution* finds that *Homo* and *Australopithecus* differ dramatically: "We, like many others, interpret the anatomical evidence to show that early *H. sapiens* was significantly and dramatically different from . . . australopithecines in virtually every element of its skeleton and every remnant of its behavior."[114]

Noting these many changes, the study calls the evolutionary origin of humans "a real acceleration of evolutionary change from the more slowly changing pace of australopithecine evolution" and notes that this transformation must have included radical changes:

> The anatomy of the earliest *H. sapiens* sample indicates significant modifications of the ancestral genome and is not simply an extension of evolutionary trends in an earlier australopithecine lineage throughout the Pliocene. In fact, its combination of features never appears earlier.[115]

These rapid, unique, and genetically significant changes are termed a genetic revolution in which "no australopithecine species is obviously transitional." One commentator proposes this evidence implies a big bang theory[116] of human evolution. Now that *Homo habilis* is best recognized as an australopithecine, due to its apelike skeletal structure,[117] it is no wonder an article in *Nature* last year recognized the lack of a clear-cut immediate ancestor for genus *Homo*:

> *H. ergaster* marks such a radical departure from previous forms of *Homo* (such as *H. habilis*) in its height, reduced sexual dimorphism, long limbs and modern body proportions that it is *hard at present to identify its immediate ancestry* in east Africa. Not for nothing has it been described as a hominin "*without an ancestor*, without a clear past."[118]

Clearly these australopithecine finds are not half ape, half human, as the australopithecine apes were sharply distinct from our genus *Homo*, which is apparently without an ancestor or a clear past.[119]

Regardless of how the media spins these fascinating fossil finds, they will surely stir debate over biological origins. But anyone who thinks that each newly touted fossil is the "missing link" or even clear evidence of an evolutionary transition has either forgotten history or isn't looking very carefully at the evidence. The moral here is to take with a grain of salt media claims that scientists have discovered new proof of evolution or a missing link.

Evolutionist Damage Control

Many statements can be found from paleontologists discussing the lack of transitional forms in the fossil record. Yet sometimes evolutionists try to engage in damage control and disavow their statements that the fossil record lacks plausible transitional intermediates.

Stephen Jay Gould, for example, complained about being quoted on the lack of transitional forms in the fossil record, saying that "it is infuriating to be quoted again and again by creationists—whether through design or stupidity, I do not know—as admitting that the fossil record includes no transitional forms. Transitional forms are generally lacking at the species level, but they are abundant between larger groups."[120] This statement was written during the heat of political battles over teaching creationism, and it directly contradicts one of Gould's earlier statements, when he stated, that "transitions between major groups are characteristically abrupt."[121] In that quote, Gould plainly claimed that transitions are missing not only at the species level, but at higher taxonomic levels.

Moreover, Gould's scientific partner in promoting the punctuated equilibrium model of evolution, Niles Eldredge, states, "Most families, orders, classes, and phyla appear rather suddenly in the fossil record, often without anatomically intermediate forms smoothly interlinking evolutionarily derived descendant taxa with their presumed ancestors."[122] Elsewhere, Eldredge explains, "In fact, the higher up the Linnaean hierarchy you look, the fewer transitional forms there seem to be."[123] It appears that Gould's denial of what he previously admitted to be true—the general lack of transitional forms between higher taxa—was a politically motivated statement that is betrayed by his own more sober analyses, as well as the stark assessments from his colleague.

Finally, some evolutionists might claim that ideas about the lack of transitional forms in the fossil record are outdated, that new finds confirm that the fossil record is somehow loaded with transitional forms. Yet consider this 1995 statement of Eldredge:

No wonder paleontologists shied away from evolution for so long. It never seemed to happen. Assiduous collecting up cliff faces yields zig-zags, minor oscillations, and the very occasional slight accumulation of change—over millions of years, at a rate too slow to account for all the prodigious change that has occurred in evolutionary history. When we do see the introduction of evolutionary novelty, it usually shows up with a bang, and often with no firm evidence that the fossils did not evolve elsewhere![124]

In 1997, vertebrate paleontologist Robert Carroll wrote, "Fossils would be expected to show a continuous progression of slightly different forms linking all species and all major groups with one another in a nearly unbroken spectrum. In fact, most well-preserved fossils are as readily classified in a relatively small number of major groups as are living species."[125] Similarly, in 1999, Oxford zoologist Mark Pagel discussed the lack of transitional forms in the journal *Nature*:

> Paleobiologists flocked to these scientific visions of a world in a constant state of flux and admixture. But instead of finding the slow, smooth and progressive changes Lyell and Darwin had expected, they saw in the fossil records rapid bursts of change, new species appearing seemingly out of nowhere and then remaining unchanged for millions of years—patterns hauntingly reminiscent of creation.[126]

In 2001, leading evolutionary biologist Ernst Mayr wrote: "Wherever we look at the living biota . . . discontinuities are overwhelmingly frequent. . . . The discontinuities are even more striking in the fossil record. New species usually appear in the fossil record suddenly, not connected with their ancestors by a series of intermediates."[127] It can thus be confirmed that the fossil record does not contain the pattern of transitional forms predicted by Darwin. Paleontologists had to accept this fact in order to preserve evolutionary theory, and so they came up with new ideas about how evolution worked.

Punctuated Equilibrium

Because the fossil record did not exhibit Darwin's predicted slow and gradual evolution with transitional forms, some paleontologists sought to find a theory of evolution where "changes in populations might occur too rapidly to leave many transitional fossils" (see fig. 3.10).[128] In 1972, Gould and Eldredge proposed the theory of "punctuated equilibrium," in which most evolution takes place in small populations (called "reproductively isolated") over relatively rapid geological time periods, followed by long periods of stasis, during which populations remain largely unchanged. By reducing the numerical size of the transitional population and the number of years for which it exists, punctuated equilibrium greatly limits the number of organisms bearing transitional characteristics. This limited population decreases the likelihood that transitional forms would be fossilized.

The question must be asked if a punctuated equilibria model requires too much genetic change too fast. One glory of Darwin's theory was the long time periods available for the origin of biological complexity. Furthermore, Darwin imagined that evolving populations might be quite large, increasing the chances that favorable mutations would happen. As Darwin

---

Figure 3.10. Problems with Punctuated Equilibrium

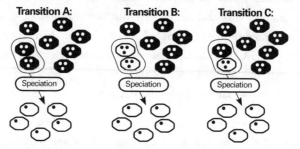

In each transition, the following occurs: (image) → (image) → (image) where some members of the initial parent (upper) population ultimately evolve into the descendant (lower) population of (image). An intermediate form is (image).

Explanation: This diagram illustrates difficulties faced by a punctuated equilibrium model. Three speciation events are shown where two members of the upper population (encircled) become reproductively isolated, and undergo allopatric speciation.

Transition A: There are no forms of (image) in the initial population, and thus it requires significant genetic change to go from (image) to (image) during speciation. This shows how punctuated equilibrium permits no transitional forms ((image)) to be found. Geneticists have complained this requires too much biological change during speciation. Gould and Eldredge replied that the transitional form ((image)) could have existed in the initial population ((image)), thus lessening the amount of change required during the speciation event.

argued: "For forms existing in larger numbers will always have a better chance, within any given period, of presenting further favourable variations for natural selection to seize on, than will the rarer forms which exist in lesser numbers."[129]

Yet punctuated equilibrium denies evolutionary change both of these advantages: it compresses the vast majority of evolutionary change into small populations that evolved during the vast minority of geological time.[130] Too few rolls of the dice are allowed for the variation to arise. Though some evolutionary biologists believe the rapid appearance of species could be accounted for by neo-Darwinian population genetics, they have been critical of punctuated equilibrium:

> [S]ome of the genetic mechanisms that have been proposed [by proponents of punctuated equilibrium] to explain the abrupt appearance and prolonged stasis of many species are conspicuously lacking in

Transition B: Transitional form ⊙ exists in the initial population, requiring smaller amounts of change during the speciation event. However, the paleontological argument for why no transitional forms were fossilized is weakened, because transitional morphology is required to preexist for long periods of time in the initial upper population.

Transition C: One might reply that this model represents a compromise, where transitional form ⊙ is rare in the initial population (rare enough to not be fossilized), but still exists. It luckily gets caught in the reproductively isolated segment of the initial population, so it contributes its genes during the speciation event. This might be possible, but illustrates the trade-off punctuated equilibrium faces: as transitional morphology gets rarer in the initial population (decreasing the probability the transitional form will be fossilized), the odds of the transitional form finding itself in the reproductively isolated population, and being able to pass on its genes to a new population, also decrease significantly. Thus, as punctuated equilibrium proponents argue that transitional forms are found in the initial population, chances are higher that it should have been fossilized, and punctuated equilibrium loses its argument for why transitional forms are not found in the first place.

Conclusion: Punctuated equilibrium must walk a fine line to allow for large morphological change at an extremely rapid rate, and yet keep the transitional population small enough so that its representatives are not fossilized. Can punctuated equilibrium have it both ways? Is it likely that this model of evolutionary change would predominate the history of life, as would be required by the lack of transitional forms in the fossil record? Perhaps punctuated equilibrium represents special pleading and requires an unlikely mechanism with many weaknesses.

empirical support. Thus, we do not feel logically compelled to abandon neo-Darwinism in favor of the theory of punctuated equilibria.[131]

There has been a recognition that speciation, which purports to explain the rapid and large morphological jumps in the fossil record, may require too much biological change in too little time, in the words of Gould and Eldredge: "Evolutionary biologists have raised a number of theoretical issues from their domain of microevolution . . . [and] continued unhappiness . . . focuses on claims that speciation causes significant morphological change."[132]

Gould and Eldredge counter that variation could exist in the larger population before reproductive isolation was achieved and speciation could take place: "[M]orphological change may accumulate anywhere along the geological trajectory of a species. But unless that change be 'locked up' by acquisition of reproductive isolation (that is speciation), it cannot persist or accumulate . . ."[133] But such a claim implies that transitional variation would long predate the speciation event. This negates the explanation punctuated equilibrium provides to attempt to explain why transitional forms did not fossilize in the first place (see fig. 3.10). If the transitional morphological variation existed in the larger population prior to the speciation event, why does the fossil record so rarely document evolutionary transitions?

Because fossils documenting the gradual change of neo-Darwinism are generally absent, some evolutionary biologists have sought genetic mechanisms for rapid change. They have hypothesized that small mutations in genes controlling the development of an organism, called *Hox* or *homeobox* genes, could allow for large, abrupt changes in morphology. But this explanation seems challenged by the complexity of organismal development. J. Madeleine Nash writes:

> The drawback for scientists is that nature's shrewd economy conceals enormous complexity. Researchers are finding evidence that the Hox genes and the non-Hox homeobox genes are not independent agents but members of vast genetic networks that connect hundreds, perhaps thousands, of other genes. Change one component, and myriad others will change as well—and not necessarily for the better. Thus

dreams of tinkering with nature's toolbox to bring to life what scientists call a "hopeful monster"—such as a fish with feet—are likely to remain elusive.[134]

Perhaps evolution is without a reasonable explanation for the lack of transitional forms in the fossil record. As molecular biologist Michael Denton writes, a punctuated equilibrium explanation essentially requires miracles:

> [M]ajor discontinuities simply could not, unless we are to believe in miracles, have been crossed in geologically short periods of time through one or two transitional species occupying restricted geographical areas. Surely such transitions must have involved long lineages including many collateral lines of hundreds or probably thousands of transitional species.[135]

The Best Explanation for Patterns in the Fossil Record?

Intelligent design does not invoke, as Denton put it, "miracles," but it does invoke intelligence. We know from experience that intelligence is a "sufficient causal explanation for the origin of large amounts of information." Moreover, intelligent agents tend to produce machines that are fully functional when they are introduced for usage. As four pro-ID scientists wrote when discussing the Cambrian explosion, "a blueprint or plan for the whole precedes and guides the assembly of parts in accord with that plan."[136] Thus, when the fossil record tells us that most of the animal phyla that are represented in the fossil record appear fully formed in the Cambrian explosion, we have positive evidence for design. Throughout the history of life we see large amounts of biological information appearing rapidly, often without any clear evolutionary precursors. The fossil record shows wholesale blueprints introduced fully formed with integrated parts already functioning within the body plan. Indeed some pro-ID scientists find that irreducible complexity predicts that biological life-forms should come into existence in an abrupt fashion:

> [G]ranted that there are indeed many systems and/or correlated sub-systems in biology, which have to be classified as irreducibly complex and that such systems are essentially involved in the formation of

morphological characters of organisms, this would explain both, the regular abrupt appearance of new forms in the fossil record as well as their constancy over enormous periods of time. For, if "several well-matched, interacting parts that contribute to the basic function" are necessary for biochemical and/or anatomical systems to exist as functioning systems at all (because "the removal of any one of the parts causes the system to effectively cease functioning") such systems have to (1) originate in a non-gradual manner and (2) must remain constant as long as they are reproduced and exist.[137]

The irreducible complexity characteristic predicted by intelligent design implies that the fossil record will exhibit a pattern of abrupt appearance of novel, fully functional, complex body plans, followed by stasis. This is precisely what we find in the fossil record. The rapid appearance, without precursors, of large amounts of biological information in the history of life, as witnessed in the numerous "explosions" of life detailed in the fossil record, provide powerful evidence for intelligent design.

Conclusion

Intelligent design remains controversial, despite the fact that there are lines of scientific evidence supporting it from many fields within science, including biochemistry, systematics, genetics, and paleontology. Many scientific organizations have rejected intelligent design for political reasons by purposefully mischaracterizing it as a supernatural explanation that is not testable.[138] The evidence briefly outlined here explains that intelligent design is a testable scientific hypothesis based upon our understanding of the type of information produced when intelligent agents act. Intelligent design does not necessarily appeal to the supernatural, but rather appeals to an explanatory cause with which we have much observational experience— intelligence.

Invoking a testable explanation like intelligent causation strains what many scientists feel is acceptable, because they are precommitted to explanations that invoke only unguided and blind material processes. Scientists would do well if they were willing to accept the words of physicist Leonard Susskind in the scientific journal *Nature*: "It would be very foolish to throw away the right answer on the basis that it doesn't conform to some criteria for what is or isn't science."[139] Ironically, *Nature* printed those words to defend the multiverse hypothesis, an alternative to design discussed earlier. Perhaps a fair-minded scientist will allow the same words to be used in defense of intelligent design, because the evidence and arguments outlined in this chapter show that intelligent design is a potent explanation of much scientific data.

Four

Darwin's Black Box

*Is Irreducible Complexity Still
a Conundrum for Darwinism?*

MICHAEL J. BEHE

Since this chapter concerns the topic of evolution, I begin by asking, *What is the fundamental nature of life?* Ammonium cyanate, when you heat it, produces urea. This reaction was first shown to occur by a German chemist, Friedrich Wöhler, in 1828.[1] He was astounded that urea was produced when he heated ammonium cyanate in the laboratory. Now, why was he astounded? Ammonium cyanate was known to be an inorganic material—that is, something that is not found in living things. But urea was known to be a biological waste product. This was the first demonstration that something nonliving could give rise to something from life. The result startled everybody, shattering the assumed distinction between living and nonliving things. More than that, it opened up for study by science all of life, because if living things are made up of ordinary matter, like rocks and gasses, then science can study them.

Moreover, in the approximately 175 years since Wöhler's experiment, science has learned a lot about life. We've discovered the shape of DNA, learned to read the genetic code, and learned to clone genes and cells and even whole organisms. What, though, has this scientific progress told us about the fundamental nature of life in the universe? This, of course, is a very large question. People give various answers, but I think these answers can be broken down into two broad categories. The first broad category is represented by Richard Dawkins, a biologist at Oxford University. He said, "The universe we observe has precisely the properties we should expect if there is, at bottom, no design, no purpose, no evil and no good, nothing but pointless indifference."[2]

> **An organism and a machine have many points in common. . . . Their functioning presupposes a precisely thought through and therefore reasonable design.**
>
> **—POPE BENEDICT XVI**

The second category is represented by Pope Benedict XVI (formerly Joseph Cardinal Ratzinger, an advisor to Pope John Paul II). During the mid 1980s, he wrote a little book titled *In the Beginning: A Catholic*

Understanding of the Story of Creation and the Fall. In the book, he wrote, "Let us go directly to the question of evolution and its mechanism. Microbiology and biochemistry have brought revolutionary insights here. . . . They have brought us to the awareness that an organism and a machine have many points in common. . . . Their functioning presupposes a precisely thought through and therefore reasonable design."[3] He continued,

> It is the affair of the natural sciences to explain how the tree of life, in particular, continues to grow and how new branches shoot out from it. This is not a matter for faith, but we must have the audacity to say that the great projects of the living creation are not the products of chance and error. They point to a creating reason and show us a creating intelligence, and they do so more luminously and radiantly today than ever before.[4]

Notice a couple of the points that Ratzinger made. The first is that, contrary to Professor Dawkins, he thinks that life is designed—that it shows signs of purpose. To support this contention, Ratzinger points to the great projects of a living creation (which point to a creating reason), to physical evidence, not to theological or philosophical or scriptural evidence, as important as those might be. The second is that, in particular, he thinks that the science of biochemistry has great importance in these questions—and biochemistry is the study of the foundation, the molecular foundation of life.

It is my purpose to show you why I think that Pope Benedict XVI has the better of this discussion and why I think that Professor Dawkins is whistling past the graveyard.

Much of this conversation started in 1859, in which Charles Darwin published his great book, *The Origin of Species*, where he proposed to explain what nobody else had ever been able to explain: how the great complexity and variety of living things might be explained simply by natural processes, without guidance from or help of an intelligence. His explanation was the theory of evolution by natural selection.

Darwin saw that there was variety in all sorts of organisms; for example, some organisms in a species are bigger than others, some were faster, and some were brighter in color. He also knew that not all members of a species are able to survive to reproduce, because there sometimes is not enough food to go around. So he reasoned that the ones whose chance variation gave them an edge in the struggle to survive would, on average, survive and leave offspring. If the variation could be inherited, then, over time, the characteristics of the species could change. Over long periods of time, great changes could occur. It was an elegant idea, and many biologists quickly saw that it could explain some things. Nonetheless, many biologists thought that, while it could explain some things, it didn't seem to explain everything. They knew that a number of very complicated structures in biological systems could not be explained by Darwin's gradual approach. One is the eye. Biologists of the nineteenth century knew that the eye is a very complicated structure: it has a number of different components. For example, it has a lens for focusing light, a retina for detecting light, eyelids, tear ducts, and ocular muscle tissue. Also, they knew that if an organism is so unfortunate as to be born without one of these components, the result is severely diminished vision or outright blindness. Consequently, while they thought that Darwin's theory could explain some things, they didn't think it could explain complicated systems like the eye.

Darwin knew about the eye, and he wrote about it in a chapter of *The Origin of Species*, appropriately titled "Organs of Extreme Perfection and Complication." In that chapter, Darwin said he did not know how evolution might have produced the eye. Nonetheless, he said, if you look at the eyes of different modern organisms, you see a lot of variety. In many modern simple creatures, there is not really an eye but a light-sensitive spot. These cells are sensitive to light, and light coming from various directions will stimulate the cells so the organism can tell that it is in the presence of light. But, with an arrangement like this, an organism can't tell where the source of the light is. Light coming from any direction stimulates the retina, so information about the directional source of the light is lost. But, Darwin continued, if you take an arrangement like this—a light-sensitive spot—and put it in a little depressed region, light coming from different directions will strike one side of the retina and the other side will be in shadow. In this manner, in theory, the organism would have a way to tell the direction of the light source.

Darwin continued that if you deepen that little depression and start to fill it with a gelatinous material, you have the beginnings of a crude lens, which would be a further improvement. By using arguments like this, Darwin was able to convince many of his contemporaries that a gradual evolutionary pathway existed from something as simple as a light-sensitive spot to something as complicated as the modern vertebrate eye. If evolution could explain the eye, what could it not explain?

But, there was a question left unanswered. Something was left hanging in the air. Where did the light-sensitive spot come from? It seems like an odd starting point. Most things aren't light sensitive. A podium from which I teach isn't light sensitive. The floor is not light sensitive. What does it take to make a light-sensitive spot? Darwin didn't even attempt to speculate about how such a thing might have come into existence. Darwin wrote in *The Origin of Species*, "How a nerve comes to be sensitive to light hardly concerns us more than how life itself originated."[5] This is fine, but in modern times science has become interested in the questions "How did life originate?" and "What does it take to make a nerve sensitive to light?" Nonetheless, I think Darwin was correct in not trying to address these questions. The science of his day didn't have the conceptual or physical tools to even begin to address such questions. Take, for example, atoms and molecules, which we know to be one of the fundamental levels of matter. In the nineteenth century, nobody actually knew whether such things really existed. Moreover, the cell, which we now know to be the fundamental basis of life, was thought to be a simple glob of protoplasm, similar to a microscopic bit of gelatin. We now know that this is untrue. Darwin and his contemporaries didn't have the tools to address many questions. Darwin hoped that future work would vindicate his theory. He left his unknowns as a black box for future science to work on.

The term *black box* is often used in science to indicate some system, machine, or something that does something intriguing, but you don't know how it works. You can't see inside the black box, or if you can see inside, you can't figure out what's going on. A good example of a black box for many people is a computer. A computer does really amazing things, and you can use it to play games or process words and for other tasks, but I haven't the foggiest idea how it does what it does. Even if somebody lifts off the cover of a computer to show me the insides, I still don't know how it does what it does.

To Darwin and his contemporaries, the cell was a black box. Like a computer, it did really fantastic and interesting things, but they did not have the slightest idea how it worked. Consequently, he left it as a black box, as he did the question of the origin of vision, for future work to explore.

When we see a black box in action, the tendency is to think that it must operate according to familiar principles that we haven't quite figured out how to apply. Whatever it's doing is relatively simple and involves nothing new.

An example of that tendency of overlooking the complexities of black boxes can be illustrated from the "Calvin and Hobbes" comic strip.[6] Calvin is always jumping in a box and flying off with Hobbs somewhere back in time or over to the next county. A little boy can easily imagine that he can jump in a box and fly off as if he's in an airplane because Calvin doesn't know how air- planes work. He thinks that if you get

Figure 4.1. Rhodopsin

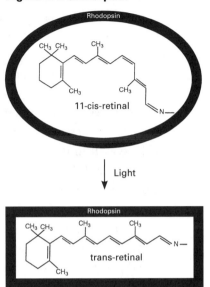

in something that has flaps that looks like wings, and a stiff wind comes along, maybe you'll take off. When Calvin grows up and becomes an engi- neer, he'll realize that airplanes are really complicated machines, and he'll no longer think he can just hop in a box and fly off.

Scientists aren't little boys like Calvin, but we all have the tendency, when we see some black box in action, to assume that it must be working because of familiar principles. This is not always the case.

Let us now look at that question that Darwin was not able to address, asking what modern science can contribute to the discussion of what makes a light-sensitive spot. What happens when a photon of light first registers on your retina?

Light striking the retina, it interacts with a small, organic molecule called 11-cis-retinal that is similar to a bent molecule, as when you bend your arm. When light hits this molecule, it isomerizes, snaps out, and turns into a linear molecule called trans-retinal (see fig. 4.1).

This is the switch that, as explained above, sets in motion a chain of events that results in vision. This process is a complex one, but I'll walk you through it. The retinal is actually bound to a protein called rhodop- sin. The retinal is about a third of the length of this molecule, rhodopsin.

119

Retinal changes forces the shape of the rhodopsin to alter, which then gets bound. When that happens, the change in the shape of the rhodopsin exposes a site, which allows it to interact with another protein molecule that is called transducin. So, rhodopsin and transducin interact with each other. When that happens, another binding site is exposed, allowing the rhodopsin-transducin complex to interact with another molecule called phosphodiesterase. This phosphodiesterase molecule is an enzyme that acts as a chemical scissors, turning a molecule cyclic GMP into something called 5'-GMP. In the cell, there is a lot of cyclic GMP. Some of it binds to a protein called an ion channelan ion channel, which normally allows calcium ions into the cell, and it normally binds cyclic GMP. But when the phosphodiesterase cuts the cyclic GMP in the cell, the cyclic G, which is attached onto the ion channel, falls off. That changes the shape of the ion channel. The channel shuts down, calcium ions can no longer enter the cell, and the voltage across the cell membrane changes. A signal is sent down the optic nerve to the brain. The interpretation by the brain is vision.

This is Darwin's simple light-sensitive spot. While this seems complicated, it is just a little overview of the chemistry of vision. Many more processes than this are necessary for this system to work. For example, how does the system get back to the starting point and reset for the next photon? What Darwin and his contemporaries hoped to be simple starting points have turned out to be considerably more complex than anyone in the nineteenth century could have imagined.

If it could be demonstrated that any complex organ existed which could not possibly have been formed by numerous, successive, slight modifications, my theory would absolutely break down.

—Charles Darwin

Regardless of its complexity, someone may ask how we can tell whether the complexity can be explained by Darwin's theory. Darwin himself gave a criterion by which to judge his theory.

Darwin wrote, in *The Origin of Species*, "If it could be demonstrated that any complex organ existed which could not possibly have been formed by numerous, successive, slight modifications, my theory would absolutely break down."[7] In this passage, Darwin emphasized that his was a theory of gradual change. Natural selection had to act in tiny steps, improving things very slowly. If things improved too quickly or in a leap, it would start to look suspiciously like something was involved other than natural selection.

Taking Darwin at his word, we might ask what sort of a system, organ, or cell couldn't be formed by numerous successive slight modifications. The answer is found in irreducible complexity. An irreducibly complex system has a number of parts that act with each other, so that if you take one of the parts away, the system no longer functions. A way to grasp the concept is by looking at an example of irreducible complexity from everyday life.

A mousetrap has a number of different parts. It has a wooden platform to which everything else is attached. A tightly wound spring has an extended end that pushes against the platform. The spring hooks over another metal part, the hammer, which squashes the mouse that trips the mechanism. The hammer has to be cocked and stabilized by the holding bar. The end of the holding bar has to be inserted into the catch. So, the mousetrap has a number of parts, all of which must work. When you take away the spring, or the catch, or the platform, the trap is broken, and it won't work at all. The mousetrap is irreducibly complex.

Figure 4.2. Mousetrap

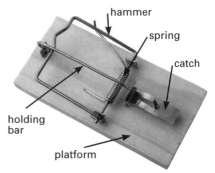

Irreducibly complex systems are real headaches for Darwinian theory because natural selection can only select something that is already working and improve it, step by tiny step. But if you wanted to evolve something like a mousetrap by something like a Darwinian process, how would you do it? What would you start with? Would you start with, say, the platform, and hope to catch mice inefficiently, as by tripping them? Subsequently, evolution might add the spring to improve efficiency. An unfortunate mouse might trip and be impaled on the exposed end of the spring. It doesn't seem likely that you could do it that way, because irreducibly complex systems only work when they are pretty much all assembled. Unassembled systems seem to be stumbling blocks for Darwin's theory of evolution by natural selection.

Well, mousetraps are very interesting, of course. I have spent a lot of time thinking about them. But what we really want to know is whether there are irreducibly complex biological, cellular, or biochemical systems. Yes, there are a great number of them.

One example is the bacterial flagellum (see fig. 3.6 on page 87). The bacterial flagellum is, quite literally, an outboard motor that bacteria use to swim. Like a mousetrap, it has a large number of parts. One part is the propeller. As the motor turns, this spins, which propels the bacterium forward by pushing against the liquid of the medium. The propeller is attached to the driveshaft at a "hook region," which acts as a universal joint, allowing freedom of rotation around both ends. The driveshaft is attached to a motor, which uses a flow of acid from outside the cell for power. While the motor is turning at up to around ten thousand revolutions a minute, it has to be kept stationary in the plane of the cell membrane, just as an outboard motor has to be attached firmly to the boat while the propeller is turning. And there are proteins that act as clamps to hold the structure in place as it spins, shown toward the bottom of the figure as the double ring made of lozenge-shaped parts. The driveshaft has to poke up through the cell membrane. Proteins act as bushing enclosure for this shaft to allow it to do so. While the bacterial flagellum is certainly complex, it doesn't do justice to the complete complexity of the flagellum. Genetic studies have shown that thirty to forty different protein parts are required for this apparatus to function in the cell. About half of those are actual components of the bacterial flagellum itself, and another twenty or so are required to build the flagellum in the cell, which is a rather large structure. It has to be built in stages, and components have to be added in the right sequence, and so on.

Like the mousetrap, the bacterial flagellum is irreducibly complex. If you take away the propeller, the hook, the driveshaft, the motor, or virtually any others of the thirty to forty different parts, you don't have a flagellum that spins half as fast as it used to, or a quarter as fast as it used to. You have either a broken flagellum that doesn't spin at all, or the structure doesn't even get built in the cell because the cell has a number of checkpoints at which it can look to see if the building is proceeding as planned. If it isn't, it shuts the process off in order to save resources. The bacterial flagellum is a major headache for the very gradual Darwinian evolution that is proposed for most biochemical systems.

What I've said up to this point is really not all that new. A number of scientists have pointed out that the complex systems at the foundation of life and in cells don't look amenable to a gradual development. Among a number of scientists, Stuart Kauffman at the Santa Fe Institute, Lynne Margolis at the University of Massachusetts, and Robert Shapiro at the University of Chicago have expressed skepticism that things like this can be put together gradually in the fashion that Darwin envisioned. Scientists have proposed various other solutions.

Where I differ from those other critics of Darwinian theory is in the alternative that I have proposed to explain these things. If you look at such systems as the bacterial flagellum, the intracellular transport system, the blood clotting cascade, or any of a number of biochemical systems, you quickly notice that each looks like the product of design. They look like they were constructed for a specific purpose by an intelligent agent.

Some of my critics have said "this Behe fellow" is a known Christian. He has been seen entering and leaving churches. Therefore, his design theory is a religious idea, not a scientific one. I am charged with letting my religious beliefs interfere with my scientific work.

I appreciate the concern, but I think the concept of intelligent design is a completely empirical idea. It is based entirely on the premise that the physical evidence leads to a conclusion of intelligent design. Every day you walk down the street, you decide that someone has arranged some element in a pleasing pattern. You notice if that pattern has been blown by the wind into something random in arrangement. People are by nature good at detecting intelligent design.

One of the ways to appreciate the distinction between intelligent design and random order can be appreciated in a panel of "The Far Side" comic.[8] A troop of explorers walks through the jungle. The lead explorer has been strung up and skewered. One member of this group turns to another and says, "That's why I never walk in front."

Those are words to live by.

Anyone who sees the "Far Side" artist's point will immediately realize that what happened to the expedition leader was designed. His was not an accidental death. As a matter of fact, the humor comes from recognition that the leader's fate was designed. How does one know that this was design? Is it a religious conclusion? Probably not. You know there is design if a number of parts interact to produce a function that none of the parts alone can produce. If you took any part away and the system would not work, design is indicated because there is irreducible complexity.

The conclusion of intelligent design is not based on philosophical, theological, or scriptural concerns. It is a logical deduction, based simply on the empirical evidence.

A fuller discussion on the detection of design and an exploration of questions raised by this are available in mathematician-philosopher William Dembski's *The Design Inference*.[9] Dembski goes into great mathematical and rigorous philosophical detail. While you can treat the matter of design with academic rigor, the conclusion itself is straightforward. This is not a difficult point to grasp if its main point can be illustrated in a "Far Side" comic; we're not talking quantum physics here.

In *Darwin's Black Box*[10] I spell out some of these arguments, which seem to have caught a lot of people by surprise. The book was widely reviewed. The *New York Times*, *Washington Post*, and other major media took a look at this. It's even been reviewed by foreign press. *Aboard* magazine, the in-flight magazine of the Bolivian National Airlines, gave it a four-page review, in Spanish and English. *Christianity Today* named it "Book of the Year," but *Skeptic Magazine* did not. Can't please everybody! There have been a number of reviews by biochemists, molecular biologists, and evolutionary biologists. Not all have been flattering. I think the general reaction is most succinctly exemplified in a book called *The Way of the Cell*, by Franklin Harold, a biochemist at Colorado State University. In his book, he wrote, "We should reject as a matter of principle, the substitution of intelligent design for the dialog of chance and necessity." He cites my book then continues, "But, we must concede that there are presently no detailed Darwinian accounts of the evolution of any biochemical system, only a variety of wishful speculations."[11]

Harold makes two points, which I'll take in reverse order. The second is that Darwinian theory has given no account of these complicated biochemical systems, and the best explanations have no proof. They are "wishful speculations," what are popularly known as "just so stories." In Rudyard Kipling's *Just So Stories*, he tells "how the tiger got its stripes," and "how the rhinoceros got its horn." Evolutionists might add a story concerning "how the bacterium got its flagellum." On one level the situation is amusing; on another it's astounding. The great majority of scientists give allegiance to macroevolutionary theory and use it as a framework to look at many questions. Yet it has been completely sterile in trying to explain the very foundation of life.

The first point that Harold makes is that he sees some principle that forbids us from entertaining the idea that life was designed. We have to look for unguided laws and natural explanations.

What is this principle? What principle tells us we can't entertain an idea of intelligent design when looking at a drawing of the bacterial flagellum (see fig. 3.6)? Why aren't we allowed to consider that? Harold actually doesn't say what the principle is. Nonetheless, I think the principle is worded something like this: Intelligent design appears to have strong *extra*-scientific implications for philosophy and even theology, and that makes many people uncomfortable. Science should avoid theories with such implications. I can understand the objection, but I disagree with it. When I was being trained in science, my classmates and I were always told that science is supposed to follow the evidence wherever it leads. Let other people worry about the philosophical and theological implications. I thought that was good advice back then, and I think it remains good advice as science uncovers more and more pointers toward intelligent design.

Another reaction to the idea of irreducible complexity should be noted. In *Darwin's Black Box* I devoted a chapter to describing the system in our bodies that allows blood to clot. Most people don't give it a moment's thought. While shaving, you nick yourself with a razor and start to bleed a little bit. A few minutes later it stops, and eventually it heals over. It doesn't look particular exciting, but research has shown that the blood clotting cascade is quite complex.

Boston Review published about a dozen essays discussing the implications of *Darwin's Black Box*. In his essay, Russell Doolittle disagreed with my assessment that the blood clotting cascade is irreducibly complex. This obviously was not good for me since Doolittle is a very prominent scientist, a biochemist at the University of California, San Diego, and a member of the National Academy of Sciences. He has studied the blood clotting cascade for the past forty years. He's not the kind of guy you want on the other side. He wrote, "Recently the gene for plaminogen [*sic*], was knocked out of mice and predictably those mice had thrombotic complications because fibrin clots could not be cleared away."[12] Blood clots are made up of a protein called fibrinogen, which forms a kind of net to stop the blood flow. Plasminogen is like chemical scissors, an enzyme that cuts up the clot when the work of the healing over has been accomplished.

Doolittle and supporters point to the case study in which the gene for plasminogen was destroyed in mice. The mice no longer had the substance that clears blood clots once their work is done. Doolittle says those mice had thrombotic complications. They formed numerous clots because fibrin clots could not be cleared. Soon afterward, these researchers knocked out the gene for fibrinogen—what actually forms the clot itself—in another line of mice. "Again, predictably, these mice were ailing, although in this case hemorrhage was a problem" since they couldn't form clots. He continues, "What do you think happened when these two lines of mice were crossed? For all practical purposes, *the mice lacking both genes were normal.* Contrary to claims about irreducible complexity, the entire ensemble of proteins is not needed and music and harmony can arise from a smaller orchestra."[13]

His point was that when you adjust different components of various mice, with resultant problems, but then mate them, their offspring are okay. This result supposedly nullifies the notion of irreducible complexity.

I don't think his argument is a good one and doesn't really affect irreducible complexity in the way he suggests. We don't actually have to go into the details of the argument he poses because it turns out that Russell Doolittle misread the paper that he was citing. The paper that he was talking about was "Loss of Fibrinogen Rescues Mice from the Pleiotropic Effects of Plasminogen Deficiency."[14] Doolittle saw this paper and its title. Then he saw the phrase "rescues mice," and assumed that the mice missing both components were normal. It turns out they were not. In the actual abstract at the very beginning of the paper, the authors write the following, "Mice deficient in plasminogen and fibrinogen are phenotypically indistinguishable from fibrinogen-deficient mice." This means that mice missing both components have all the problems that mice missing only fibrinogen have and cannot form clots. They hemorrhage. Female mice die during pregnancy. They are not promising evolutionary intermediates.

From the paper, these are the symptoms of the different strains of mice. If you take out the component that removes blood clots once their job is finished, then you get blood clots that cannot be dissolved, ulcers, and other problems. When you can't form blood clots in the first place, lacking fibrinogen, then you have the hemorrhage-related suite of problems. When you lack both, you have the same problems as when you just lack fibrinogen. This is a very logical result: Fibrinogen is the stuff that forms the clot, it forms the net, it stops blood from flowing, and plasminogen is the stuff that clears it off once its job is done. But, if you are missing both of them, you can't form clots in the first place, so there is nothing left for plasminogen to take away.

The scientists who were doing this were actually addressing an important question. They wanted to know if plasminogen had any other role in the body besides its role in blood clotting. They decided it didn't because the effects of removing both of these components were the same as the effects of just removing fibrinogen. The point, for our purposes, is that these mice are not the happy campers Doolittle thought they were. The same group of researchers have gone on to knock out a couple of other components of the blood clotting cascade, including prothombin and tissue factor; in each case the blood clotting cascade fails to work and the mice have big problems, which is *exactly* what you would expect if the system were indeed irreducibly complex as I argue.

What can we conclude from the fact that Russell Doolittle made this incorrect claim? Anybody can misread a paper, and scientists are not the clearest writers in the world. No. The point is that the most prominent scientist in the field of blood clotting research, who has worked on it for decades and is a very bright man, does not know how Darwinian processes could have produced the blood clotting cascade. If Russell Doolittle does not know how the blood clotting cascade might have evolved, nobody knows. A lot of people think that they do know, but they're wrong.

Michael Ruse wrote an article titled "Answering the Creationists: Where They Go Wrong and What They're Afraid Of." Michael Ruse is a prominent philosopher of biology. He has testified in several court cases when laws were passed to have creation science taught in classrooms. He's written about a dozen books on Darwinian biology and the philosophy that flows from it. He wrote the following about a year or so after Doolittle's article came out:

> For example, Behe is a real scientist, but this case for the impossibility of a small-step natural origin of biological complexity has been trampled upon contemptuously by the scientists working in the field.

They think his grasp of the pertinent science is weak in the knowledge of the literature curiously, (although conveniently) outdated. For example, far from the evolution of blood clotting being a mystery, the past three decades of work by Russell Doolittle and others has thrown great light on the ways in which clotting came into being. More than this, it can be shown that the clotting mechanism does not have to be a one-step phenomenon with everything already in place and functioning. One step in the cascade involves fibrinogen required for clotting and another, plaminogen [sic], required for clearing clots away.[15]

He goes on to quote exactly the same passage from Russell Doolittle quoted above and even spells *plasminogen* wrong in the same way that Russell Doolittle spelled it wrong—plaminogen. With Doolittle it was a typo, but Michael Ruse, the philosopher, was simply copying Russell Doolittle's argument. Even prominent academics in the field, who think that they do know how these things might have been put together, are wrong.

A more recent example comes from the article by Neil Greenspan, "Not So Intelligent Design," in *The Scientist* magazine. Greenspan is a scientist, a pathologist at Case Western Reserve University. He wrote, "The design advocates also ignore the accumulating examples of the reducibility of biological symptoms, as Russell Doolittle. . . ." He cites the same argument that Michael Ruse cited, and he totally confuses terms when he goes on to say that "mice genetically altered so that they lack either thrombin or fibrinogen. . . ."[16] He should say "*plasminogen* or fibrinogen."

To a lay audience it probably doesn't matter. But here's a man who's supposed to be a scientist, an academic person who could go to the literature and read for himself the original papers that Doolittle relied upon, but he didn't. Since he thought that he knew that Darwinian evolution is obviously true, he simply parroted the arguments in its favor and didn't even consider arguments against it. Another prominent scientist thought he knew something that he obviously did not know.

Greenspan goes on to write, with delicious irony, "These results cast doubt on the claim by proponents of intelligent design that they know which systems exhibit irreducible complexity and which do not."[17] The results he was relying on are actually completely opposite to what he thought they were, so the shoe is now on the other foot. The Darwinists do not know which systems their theory can account for and which their theory cannot account for. They also have been found to be very uncritical of explanations that seem to support their theory.

The extrascientific implications of intelligent design do funny things to the critical capacities of many, including many scientists, philosophers, and other academics. They will look you in the eye and say with great confidence that something is true when it is not. There are many other criticisms of intelligent design and irreducible complexity, philosophical, scientific, other. I and others have responded in book chapters, a couple of articles and journals, and most accessibly on the Internet. A number of articles of mine are available at crsc.org. For those who like to follow this issue closely, this Web site is the place to go for replies to many of the critics.

The progress of science has, in fact, illuminated the question of what type of universe we live in. I hope you see why I agree with Cardinal Ratzinger when he says that we must have the audacity to say that the great projects of the living creation are not the products of chance and error. Today they point to a creating reason and show us a creating intelligence more luminously than ever before.

Five

Why Are We Here?

Accident or Purpose?

JAY W. RICHARDS

Those who are acquainted with the intelligent design movement are probably aware that Phil Johnson might be considered its grandfather. His book *Darwin on Trial* was important to the birth of the movement.[1] One reason why this book is so important is that Phil understood how to frame the issue properly, in a way that can actually win the debate. Rather than getting mired in disputes about the proper interpretation of Genesis 1 or the nature of science, he argued that we should simply consider the evidence for Darwinism empirically. This sets to the side naturalistic or materialistic assumptions that may skew our interpretation of the evidence.

That procedure is a reliable guide for considering the question of intelligent design more broadly, even outside biology. So let's look at the evidence regarding design of the universe empirically, apart from either naturalistic assumptions or interpretations of the first chapter of Genesis. By following this approach, we have an opportunity to divide the united materialistic scientific community, or at least the mandarins in that community. We also can unite the divided Christian community that tends to argue over things biblical rather than wider questions that are easier to answer.

Darwinism deals with the history of life. In particular, it offers a materialistic explanation for a certain type of complexity in biological systems, such as animals and plants. This is adaptive complexity. Things appear to be adapted to particular environments with specific functions. Darwin offered a materialistic mechanism for explaining what might happen in the history of life to explain adaptive complexity. Darwinism, strictly speaking, doesn't address the origin of life itself, though discussion of the history of life bleeds over into consideration of the origin of life.

There are prior questions to all of these debates in biology: How do you get planets or environments that are compatible with biological organisms? How do the necessary conditions for life come to be? To put it differently, what do you need to have a universe that allows for life? How do you get local environments—whether planets or energy sources—where biological creatures like us can exist? These are straightforward empirical questions that anyone can consider. Such questions have to do with everything from the origin of the universe to the origin of life, but I'm going to focus on only a couple of aspects of this massive scope of physical reality. I also want to frame the questions theologically.

The intelligent design movement is not, per se, a Christian movement, though many Christians are involved in it. One can speak about evidence for design without being a Christian. I am a Christian, however, so I understand the issues in Christian theological terms. One concept in the history of Christian theology is that God reveals Himself in two primary ways, or according to two "books"— the Book of Scripture and the Book of Nature. Charles Hodge, the nineteenth-century Princeton theologian, puts it this way: "Theology is properly distinguished as natural and revealed. The former is concerned with the facts of nature so far as they reveal God in our relation to him, and the latter with the facts of scripture."[2]

A book has a purpose; it is meant to be read. If you understand the language in which the book is written, you should understand the message that it is intended to convey. The Christian Scripture writings are literally in a book; but what of the sense in which nature itself is a book that is intended to be read and interpreted? A book always points beyond itself to the intentions and ideas of the author. This way to understand nature fits naturally with Christian thought. It may be a uniquely Christian way of looking at nature. I would suggest that many in the design movement are developing proper ways to read and interpret the Book of Nature. Nature has its own language, and as any language, it has a vocabulary and a grammar. Unless you know that language, it's very difficult to read what is written in it. If you are a Christian who views nature as in this literary metaphor, then you have a perspective from which to understand the design movement, even though design theorists may not normally describe or understand their work this way.

Perhaps one of the effects of the materialistic science of the nineteenth century was to silence the Book of Nature, to confuse its language so that nature couldn't testify to anything beyond itself. If that is a correct way of looking at the history of science, then the design movement of recent years, if successful, can teach us anew how to read the Book of Nature.

I do think things are being revealed in these days that have not been revealed since the foundations of the world. We've only known about the exquisite structure of the DNA molecule and how the cell uses it to build proteins for half a century. Much of what we discovered in late-twentieth-century biology contradicts assumptions of nineteenth-century science. Biologists believed that the cell was a simple homogenous globule of protoplasm—like a simple glob of green gelatin. We've discovered that the cell functions through wonderfully complex machinery. This knowledge was hidden from science until the twentieth century.

Just as we have recently discovered so much about the microscopic world, we have discovered far more about the universe beyond us. Genesis 1 and other passages of Scripture have told us for a very long time the spectacular nature of our universe. The writer of Psalm 19 says,

> The Heavens declare the glory of God. The skies proclaim the work of his hands. Day after day they pour forth speech, night after night they display knowledge. (vv. 1–2)

When the Hebrew psalmist refers to the heavens, he is talking about the sky; in particular, the night sky. This passage implies that the Book of Nature is not simply a book meant to be read. Rather, the Book of Nature actively conveys information: "There is no speech or language where their voice is not heard. Their voice goes out to all the earth; their words to the ends of the world" (Ps. 19:3–4a). This book is available everywhere, communicating not just to one ethnic group or at one particular time in history. It has always been available. Consequently, arguments and insights we gain from this Book of Nature potentially have universal applicability. There may be arguments based on the Book of Nature that should be considered by any open-minded person who is willing to consider whether the natural world points beyond itself. It is exciting to be alive at a time when the Book of Nature is speaking anew through science.

The New Testament refers to this language. Paul, in his letter to the church at Rome says, "For since the creation of the world God's invisible qualities—his eternal power and divine nature—have been clearly seen, being understood from what has been made, so that men are without excuse" (Rom. 1:20). According to Paul, nature tells us more than that God exists; it tells something about God. When one reads on in Paul's argument in Romans, it becomes clear that he is not referring to salvation history. You can't find out by studying the bacterial flagellum or astronomy that God became incarnate in the man Jesus and died for our sins. But the natural world tells enough about God that we are without excuse for our failure to follow His moral law.

Many of the official authorities of the scientific community have claimed that nature does not testify to anything beyond itself. This claim is made in a modest form: Whether there is a God is not a question that natural science is competent to address. The stronger form of this claim is simply that the physical universe is all there is. I am reminded of perhaps the most eloquent statement of this perspective. In the popular Public Broadcasting Service series "Cosmos," based on the book of that name, astronomer Carl Sagan told viewers with calm assurance, "The cosmos is all there is, or ever was or ever will be." This is a doctrinal statement of materialism, and Sagan's eloquent television teaching of it is still one the most popular PBS series ever produced.

Sagan gave a concise statement of the materialistic worldview; unfortunately he taught it as if it were an unassailable truth of natural science. If Sagan is right, of course, the Christian claim is wrong. If the Christian claim is true that the books of Scripture and Nature testify to God's existence, then something is profoundly wrong about Sagan's statement. His philosophy can never adequately explain the natural world.

We included another quotation of Sagan's at the beginning of the book *The Privileged Planet*. The rest of this chapter will consider his statement of an idea called the Copernican Principle, which is popular in the fields of astronomy and cosmology. If materialism in biology manifests itself in Darwinian terms, the Copernican Principle is materialism's manifestation in astronomy and cosmology.

The Copernican Principle is tied to Nicholas Copernicus (1473–1543). In a book published at his death, this founder of modern cosmology challenged the view that the stars, the planets, and the sun traveled in their course across our sky with the earth stationary in the center. He wrote that the earth travels *with* the other planets around the sun. And so Copernicus led the change from the so-called geocentric cosmology, with the earth at the center, to heliocentric cosmology, with the sun at the center.

Copernicus was not teaching that we are insignificant because we are not in the physical center of the universe. In fact, before the time of Copernicus, many people understood Satan's throne to be the center of the universe. The surface of the earth was sort of an intermediate place where humans existed, and where death and decay occurs. This was in contrast to the heavens, with the moon, the sun, the stars, and the planets, which were thought to be eternal and unchanging. So the center of the universe as theorized before Copernicus was not a good place to be. It was more like the sump of the universe.

In the nineteenth and twentieth centuries, however, the history was rewritten to claim that Copernicus's discovery reveals that we are not important in the scheme of things. This is a story many science educators continue to teach, even though it is historical nonsense. Only if being in the physical center of the universe is necessary for our significance, should we believe the earth and its inhabitants are insignificant in the wider picture of the universe. There's no good reason to believe that.

Of course, one could make this point in a more subtle form. After all, we now know that the earth is one of many planets around one star in a galaxy of one hundred billion stars, which is itself just one of a hundred billion galaxies. Until the twentieth century, many scientists believed the universe was eternal. Add to that the idea that the universe and our place in it are without purpose, and you get the idea of the Copernican Principle. It has nothing to do with Copernicus's perspective, and doesn't even follow from his insight.

Again, Carl Sagan expressed the basic idea well. In 1977, the United States National Aeronautics and Space Administration (NASA) launched two satellites that were jointly called Voyager. These traveled to the outer reaches of the solar system to take pictures of the outer planets. The purpose of the Voyager satellites was to take pictures of Jupiter, Saturn, Uranus, and Neptune. In 1990, however, Sagan persuaded NASA to turn one of the Voyager satellites' cameras around, just as it was reaching Pluto, which is about 4 billion miles from the sun. This would allow it to take a distant picture of the earth. When these pictures were developed, one sees a picture of a tiny little dot and, because of the optics in the camera involved, it looks like there is a beam of sunlight cutting across the earth. But it is otherwise a tiny blue dot.[3] In his reflection on this picture, Sagan writes,

> Because of the reflection of sunlight, the earth seems to be sitting in a beam of light as if there were some special significance to this small world, but it's just an accident of geometry and optics. Our

posturing, our imagined self-importance, the delusion that we have some privileged position in the universe are challenged by this point of pale light. Our planet is a lonely speck in the great enveloping cosmic dark. In our obscurity and all this vastness there is no hint that help will come from elsewhere to save us from ourselves.[4]

Sagan's perspective is a depressing evaluation of our existence. Because we are not the center of the universe, and we are small in comparison to the universe, Sagan considers us too insignificant to be saved from ourselves. This is an important issue. Is the earth really an insignificant speck in an impersonal universe? Do we exist for no purpose?

Or is the truth otherwise? If the truth is otherwise, how can we tell?

In the last twenty years, a discipline called astrobiology has emerged in science. My colleague Guillermo Gonzalez is one of the key figures in this scientific community. Astrobiology is an interdisciplinary science that studies what is needed at the astronomical level to have life. A dogma in astrobiology is that life is common in the universe. This isn't an empirical discovery. Rather, it's the result of a large community of scientists accepting the Copernican Principle. The Copernican Principle says that we are insignificant, that there is nothing special about the earth or its circumstances. By implication, whatever happened here must have happened countless times elsewhere. So there's nothing unusual or rare or special about our circumstances. If it happened here, it must have happened elsewhere. If life is here, it must be elsewhere.

In recent years, though, some within the astrobiology community have come to realize that it is much more complicated than that. There are a number of things you need to bring about a habitable planet, one that could even possibly be inhabited by any sort of life. This issue is what many astrobiologists are concerned with now.

There is one almost unanimously agreed upon criterion for any habitable planet: you need a terrestrial planet—that is, a planet like the earth, with liquid water. You need a rocky planet with a hard surface, not a gas planet like Jupiter or Saturn, which have no surface on which organisms can dwell and energy can be stored: one that will support complex carbon and water-based life. Water might not seem that important to life—especially for those who have watched too much science fiction—but it is essential for the existence of chemical life.

Some might wonder whether there might be ammonia life, or alcohol life, or some other base of organism, but remember that NASA spent $800 million to send a probe to Mars. Its purpose was to determine whether Mars ever had liquid water on its surface. We wouldn't be spending that much money if we didn't think water was important for life. I tell you that simply so you realize that it's widely recognized how important water is for life.

Water is called the universal solvent; it dissolves more compounds than virtually any other liquid. It also has strange, heat-storing capacities. As a result, it moderates temperatures both in the body and on the planet. There is a very unusual coincidence here, a fitness between water and carbon: Carbon is almost certainly the only way in the universe to build biological organisms. Only with carbon can you build certain types of complex molecules and structures that bear information and allow you to have biology. The coincidence is that the very temperature range in which water is liquid is the temperature range in which most carbon reactions take place. So there is a perfect chemical fit between the solvent water and carbon.

Liquid water on the surface of a rocky planet is just a precondition for life. Water, carbon, and the sun are things you need, but you cannot simply stir them together and out pops a little green man. For life to exist, one also needs a planet in what is called the circumstellar habitable zone. The planet must be in the zone of orbit around a star at which water stays in the right temperature to remain liquid. Think of a planet that contains liquid water. If this planet is in a wild, oval orbit, through much of its year, it will be too far from its star, and the water will be frozen. At other times, it will be too close, and water will boil or actually vaporize. At best, its water would be a medium for life through only part of its year. For a planet to have liquid water, it must maintain an orbit that is almost perfectly circular and at the right distance from the star—the circumstellar habitable zone. This is sometimes called the "Goldilocks Zone," neither too close nor too far, but where the climate is just right.

The earth is the only planet in our solar system that is within a circumstellar habitable zone as it revolves around our sun. On Venus, the planet next closest to the sun, the surface temperature is about 800 degrees Fahrenheit. It is very hostile to life, so we don't waste any money sending probes there to search for life. Even Mars, which revolves just outside the zone, has temperatures too cold for any kind of complex life.

You also need a planetary system that is in the right place in the galaxy, the galactic habitable zone. There is just the right place in a galaxy for a planetary system to support life. This is a much newer concept than the circumstellar habitable zone, but NASA has already started to take it into account in funding astrobiological research. Some reasons that there is a galactic habitable zone will be explained below.

Other things are needed for a planet to be habitable, conditions that must coincide in order to have even the possibility of life. So, even if Darwinism's naturalistic origin of life were true, all these preconditions would have to be in place for biological organisms.

A terrestrial planet would have to be the right type of terrestrial planet. At least twenty-five factors must be just right for that one variable. Let us look at a brief list of some major requirements. Not all of the following are accepted by all scientists, but I will mention nine that are commonly accepted.

1. *A stabilizing moon.* The earth without a moon would wobble on its axis over fairly short periods of time. The earth is tilted on its axis at about 23.5 degrees, relative to the plane at which it orbits the sun. This is why we have seasons. If the moon were not large and were not so well-placed, the earth would wobble from about 0 degrees to over 60 degrees on its course around the sun. Mars has two moons that are not large enough to stabilize the planet's tilt, so it wobbles. This creates hostile, planetwide sandstorms. If the earth somehow lost its moon, before very long the entire surface of the planet could no longer be inhabited by large, complex life. Until recently, we had no idea that the moon preserves life on earth.

2. *Plate tectonics to recycle the elements and minerals that life needs on this surface.* Without such recycling, life-enriching nutrients would eventually sink into the crust. They wouldn't be available to life on the planet surface.

3. *An earthlike nitrogen and oxygen rich atmosphere.* Without this, you wouldn't be able to have large animal life.

4. *The right kind of planetary neighbors.* Beyond Earth and Mars lies an asteroid belt, and then the very large planets Jupiter and Saturn, near the middle of the solar system. During the 1990s, computer simulations calculated what would happen to a comet in the solar

system without the gravitational pull of Jupiter and Saturn. Calculating all of the known factors, the computer model determined that the inner solar system where we are would be visited more frequently by comets. A dramatic illustration of this occurred in July 1994 when comet Shoemaker-Levy 9 broke up and collided with Jupiter. Any one of these comet fragments would have caused more devastation than that from the atom bomb dropped on Hiroshima. Science found that we have guardian sentinels that protect us from life-sterilizing bombardment by comets. These planets figure prominently in our existence.

5. *The right kind of star.* The solar system requires a single star for stable orbits. Most stars in the galaxy are binary stars or triplets, stars that are in orbit around each other. We need a single star that's not too variable, one very much like our sun.

6. *The right kind of galaxy.* The galaxy must be the right age and size to have heavy elements, yet not too irregular so that stars collide or "perturb" each other.

7. *The right galactic location.* The system must be in that galactic habitable zone noted above.

8. *The right cosmic time.* A habitable planet must exist at the right point in the history of the cosmos, so that the sort of elements are available to build rocky planets. Too early and the planet would be bathed in deadly radiation permeating the universe.

9. *A universe that is fine-tuned for life.* Imagine a sort of universe-creating machine, like a giant safe in which there are master locks and dials that fix the settings for laws of physics, gravity, electromagnetism, and a strong nuclear force. Among other factors, the universe must be expanding.

The fine-tuned universe in itself is a serious problem for naturalism. Let's say you walk into the control center for this universe-creating machine, and all the dials have been set and are fixed on very particular numbers. A view pad on the side shows a picture of the actual universe those settings are maintaining. An attendant explains that this machine determines the constants of the universe. You might ask what would happen if the settings were changed. He invites you to change the dials and hit the preview button to see what might happen. You decide to weaken the force of electromagnetism and its force of gravity just a tad. You carefully touch the preview button. Suddenly galaxies and planets and stars and other celestial bodies fall apart. That's how precisely tuned the gravitational constant has to be with electromagnetism.

Strengthen electromagnetic force too much, and suddenly you can't build terrestrial planets the right size. They are too big for life. Also, stars burn up quickly and erratically. That's the idea of fine-tuned constants of physics.

This is a partial laundry list of conditions needed to build just one habitable planet. This stands in contrast to this claim of Sagan that earth is ordinary and insignificant. It is very unlikely that these conditions come together very many places. In fact, almost everything we learn suggests that the conditions must be even more precise and unlikely than previously thought. We don't know how rare these variables might be over the universe, but the trend seems to be moving toward an assumption that they are extremely rare.

In the 1920s and 1930s, it was widely believed in the United States that Mars was inhabited by intelligent beings. *Cosmopolitan* magazine had a story about what Martians may be like. In 1938, Orson Welles produced a radio adaptation of H. G. Wells's 1898 novel, *War of the Worlds*, imagining what a news broadcast might be like if there was a Martian invasion. His fictional broadcast caused widespread panic, as thousands thought it was a real news report. That could only have happened if the population more or less accepted the existence of Martians. After probing Mars with the Viking Lander in 1976, however, astronomers realized that there was certainly no complex life on the planet. Notice how perceptions have been downgraded, from assuming that intelligent Martians exist to looking for evidence that liquid water might have been on the Martian surface at some point in the past. This is just one example of a trend in the growing realization that habitable planets are exceedingly rare.

We now come to the central question: Doesn't all this complexity and order in the solar system and universe indicate design and intentionality? Isn't it just the sort of thing that an intelligent being like God would do? A hiker finds a properly working watch on a heap in the middle of a forest. The finder would not suppose that the watch did not just appear there, without an intelligent agent involved.

Now I think that intuition is reasonable, but the intelligent design movement is interested in more than simply appealing to intuition, because intuitions are sometimes unreliable. My daughter used to have the strong intuition that clouds are designed to look like cartoon characters. Unfortunately her intuition was wrong unless the Disney Corporation has become more powerful than I realize. All of us have had intuitions that proved to be incorrect. They must be tested to see if independent evidence confirms them. Does our intuition that rarity demonstrates evidence prove design, or could it be simple luck that this planet had all the right conditions?

The option of luck is not utterly irrational. Don Brownlee and Peter Ward, who are colleagues of Gonzalez, wrote an influential book in 2000 called *Rare Earth*. In this book, the two described all of the things needed for a habitable planet.[5] In a documentary, "The Privileged Planet," Brownlee argued that it's very likely that complex life is rare in the universe. He went on to say that it looks like we won the grand cosmic lottery.[6] Someone had to win it, and it was us. Of course, if somebody was going to win it, then whoever that was would look up around and say, wow, it's amazing that things came together so well. Nevertheless, Brownlee and Ward argue, as amazing as it might look, the earth is habitable by simple luck.

Others may see the same evidence of the rarity of conditions needed for life and go straight to say that design is the only possibility. But as an argument, that does not work well. Here's why. Imagine multiplying the probabilities for all these conditions for habitability. What are the chances that in a solar system one planet will be in the circumstellar habitable zone? We don't know, but let's be generous and say that one in ten planets in a planetary system will be in the circumstellar habitable zone. That's 10 percent. What is the chance that these planetary systems circumnavigate a single star of the right type? Let's say that's 10 percent as well. What are the chances that you're going to get a moon around the planet in the circumstellar habitable zone of the right kind of star? Let's say it's 10 percent again. The chances are probably much lower than that, but no one knows what the numbers are, so for the purposes of illustration we should be conservative.

Multiply these probabilities: $.10 \times .10 = .01$. Imagine that, of thirteen factors to get a habitable planet, each has the same 10 percent probability. That would mean that there would be one chance in 10^{13} or a one followed by thirteen zeros. That sounds like a very low probability. Surely you'd have to have design for that.

The problem is that there are about 10^{11} stars in the Milky Way galaxy, and this is something we know with a fair degree of certainty. Not all those stars will be compatible with life. That is one of the variables. But, given how many chances there are in this galaxy, there could be a 1 percent chance of having one habitable planet in the Milky Way. That's still a pretty low probability, even using very conservative numbers. But Brownlee and Ward know that there are about 100 billion *galaxies* in the observable universe. Given one hundred galaxies, theoretically there would be one habitable planet.

Another example of this reasoning would be to walk into a room and watch me flip a coin ten times. Each time the coin lands with "heads" showing. It would be reasonable to conclude that either this is a two-headed coin or I'm really skillful at flipping coins. You're not going to think that ten heads in a row just happened by chance. The low probability means that this pattern is fishy. An explanation is needed.

What if you then learned that I had been trapped in this room for ten years, flipping the coin once a second for the entire ten-year period? What if you had witnessed me flipping the coin during all that time? Your impression would change. If you flip coins long enough, you're eventually going to get ten heads in a row because you've got so many chances to do it. You have more of what philosophers call "probabilistic resources." You have few probabilistic resources if you just flip a coin ten times. If you flip it a billion times, you're far more likely to get ten heads in a row at some point. That's the problem with arguing for design from mere rarity, as wondrous as the outcome seems and as intuitively plausible as the evidence for design seems.

When this problem first occurred to me, it seemed strange that all of the things needed for a habitable planet couldn't bear evidence for design when so many other parts of the natural world scream design. I suspected that we needed something more than mere probability for our argument for design. Then, around 1999 I read an op-ed essay in the *Wall Street Journal* by Gonzalez, who was complaining about the dogma regarding the existence of extraterrestrials. His essay was a mere 850 words, but as I read it I thought, "This guy thinks like a design theorist."

I learned that he was at the University of Washington in Seattle, so I called him. I identified myself as affiliated with the Discovery Institute, involved in work on questions regarding intelligent design theory. He said, "Oh, I've been meaning to call you guys for years. Actually, I think I'm on to something." Lots of scientists are like that. They work away at their computer screens and never look up and realize the implications of their work. Through several conversations, we talked about his idea, which, when developed, marshals the evidence for rarity in favor of design. It answers the question, "If rarity and the conditions for a habitable planet were, in fact, the result of design and not mere chance or luck, how could we tell? Is there some way to know that we should favor design over chance?"

That's what *The Privileged Planet* is about.[7] Let me briefly review this argument. You now know a little about the conditions that have to come together in a habitable planet, and that the chance for the simultaneous occurrence of these conditions is exceedingly rare. Given only the facts so far given, the answer could be that the habitable planet came about by design or by chance. We have that open question because the universe is so large and there are so many chances available. Maybe it could happen once just by luck.

What if we add the information that the conditions required to create these very rare places were the same conditions required for scientific discovery? What if those rare places in which observers can exist in the universe are the best overall places for observation? This is the idea that Gonzalez helped develop. Our thesis is simply that the same narrow circumstances that allow us to exist also provide us with the best overall setting for making scientific discoveries. We argue that the very conditions that make earth hospitable to intelligent life also make it well suited to viewing and analyzing the universe as a whole.

We think there is a general principle in the universe that we call the "correlation." Gonzalez had wanted to title the book *The Correlation Between Habitability and Measurability*. That title probably would not have attracted many readers on Amazon.com. From what we know of biology, it seems that the conditions for habitability correlate or overlap with the conditions for measurability. Measurability is required to discover things about the universe, such as the laws of gravity. Newton needed visible planets in order to make his calculations and develop his understanding of gravity. We need to be able to discover that we are on a planet, going around a star with other planets. To do large-scale astronomy and cosmology, we need to discover that we are in a galaxy, and that many galaxies are far away and seem to be receding from us.

We'd like to be able to discern whether the universe had a beginning or has always existed. What conditions are required in order to discover those things? The conditions required for a habitable planet are, in fact, the same conditions required for scientific discovery. Gonzalez first considered this wonder in 1995 while he was observing a perfect solar eclipse in India.

Let me just give two examples of the correlation, where a condition for habitability is also an important condition for making a scientific discovery: perfect solar eclipses and galactic zones.

Perfect Solar Eclipses

Solar eclipses are interesting for their intuitive power, and we have noted that the idea first came to Gonzalez during a solar eclipse. For a solar eclipse to occur, a bright body is needed to provide light, an eclipsing body to block the light, and an observer platform where the light is blocked. These all must be the right distances apart, and in a straight line in space. All of these components coming together produces a solar eclipse.

The earth, the moon, and the sun provide the necessary objects, and they are in the proper proportion to their distances from each other. For an observer on earth, the size of the sun in the sky and the size of the moon in the sky appear to match almost precisely. The moon, however, is about four-hundred times smaller than the sun, but almost exactly four-hundred times closer than the sun to the surface of the earth. Because of this coincidence, the sun and the moon appear to be the same size in the sky so, to an observer on earth, they match, making possible what we call perfect solar eclipses.

After making his observation, Gonzalez decided to do research to determine where else in the solar system solar eclipses appear and where perfect solar eclipses appear. Gonzalez worked on this for months and published his findings in his article "Wonderful Eclipses" in the journal *Astronomy and Geophysics*. Think about the size of any moon in proportion to the size of the sun as it appears in the sky from the surface of that moon's planet. Where one of the horizontal lines crosses the vertical line in the middle, the angular size ratio is one (see fig. 5.1). A one-to-one ratio means there is a perfect match between the two things. Looking at the earth, you see a little horizontal line that crosses the vertical line. From the

Figure 5.1. Eclipse Sizes

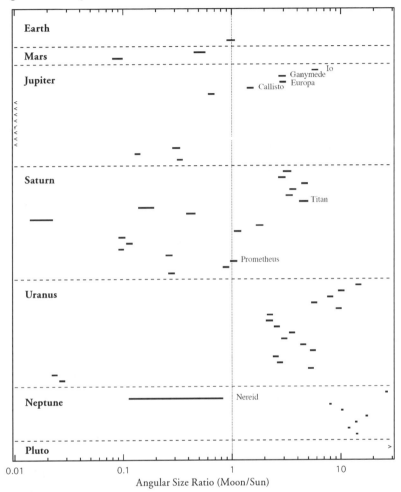

surface of the earth, then, there is a one ratio in the apparent size of the earth's moon and sun.

Venus and Mercury don't have moons. For Mars, there is no match. Jupiter has many, many moons, none of which match. The eclipses are either tiny or they are so-called supereclipses. Saturn has a partial match, in one of its moons, called Prometheus. The problem is that Prometheus is shaped like a potato. It's not spherical, and it whips around Saturn very quickly. So, being very generous with the data, we can find one other place in the solar system that comes close to perfect solar eclipses.

This means that the one place in the solar system where there are observers is the one place in the solar system where there are perfect solar eclipses to observe. That is a strange coincidence. I don't know how to describe it, except that it's "fishy." The implication gives chills.

Almost any introductory astronomy textbook teaches that perfect solar eclipses have been profoundly important in the history of scientific discovery. If it weren't for perfect solar eclipses, we might never have realized what stars are made of. A very important experiment in the nineteenth century allowed astronomers to learn that the sun is a giant ball of gas. They determined what its atmosphere is made of, and that helped them determine what other stars are made of and to be able to do astrophysics of the entire universe. Using data from the sun's composition, they compared the signs and found that stars everywhere are somewhat similar, at least chemically. So perfect solar eclipses helped human astronomers to be able to do astrophysics.

It also was an important test of Albert Einstein's Theory of General Relativity. One implication of Einstein's theory was that gravity bends the trajectory of starlight. Gravity is a relatively weak force, so to test this theory a really narrow beam of light must pass precisely beside a very massive body like the sun. Imagine finding starlight behind the sun, and trying to know where it would be if the sun was not there and then figure the change where it is passes right by the edge of the sun. It is necessary to see the sun and the starlight to do this. That just doesn't work (not to mention the consequences for your eyes). Only one set of conditions allow a test to be successful: a perfect solar eclipse. During the 1919 solar eclipse, Sir Arthur Eddington and a group of astronomers did the test and confirmed general relativity, making Einstein a world celebrity. This experiment has been confirmed in more rigorous and accurate tests since 1919.

It's not just interesting to see perfect solar eclipses; they are important for scientific discovery. Now let's connect this fact with habitability. Perfect solar eclipses are produced because of two very important variables for having a habitable planet. The planet has to be the right distance from its sun, and it needs to have the right kind of moon. Now your star is going to be a certain size by virtue of being in the circumstellar habitable zone. Moreover, the moon is going to have to be the right size and distance from your earth to stabilize the tilt of your planet's axis. As it happens, when you get these two independent conditions, you end up with your sun and moon aligned properly for producing the solar eclipses needed to make important scientific discoveries.

That the requirements for producing scientifically valuable eclipses contribute to habitability led to the hypothesis that the universe is designed for discovery. If it is designed in such a way as to benefit its inhabitants, then this kind of correlation will be seen in other places. The components for a habitable planet will in multiple ways be crucial for scientific discovery, so that if you didn't have these habitability factors, the scientific advance of civilization would be far more difficult.

The Galactic Habitable Zone

Here we will use one more example: our location in our galaxy. Only some galaxies are habitable, and even in the best candidates there is a galactic habitable zone where a planet has to be in order to be habitable. The system cannot be too close to the center of a galaxy or too far out on the edge.

The best opportunity for a habitable zone would be in a spiral galaxy like the Milky Way. It's called a spiral galaxy because it looks like a whirlpool. In an irregular galaxy, the orbits of the stars are too irregular. You also want to be in a large spiral galaxy, because the large galaxies have enough heavy elements for the forming of rocky planets. These heavy elements are what astronomers call metals. This includes basically all the elements past hydrogen and helium on the periodic table. Metals are required in terrestrial planets.

At some places in the galaxy, elements build up through a recycling of star cycles. Closer to the center of the galaxy, it is much denser with stars and star-forming activity, having a lot of heavy elements for building terrestrial planets. Farther from the center of the galaxy, these elements dissipate. This gives a planet building quandary. Stars in the outlying reaches of the galaxy are probably not going to have terrestrial planets because there are just not enough materials available. Heavy elements are found close to the center, where a massive black hole and other factors create conditions hostile to life. The black hole is a body so massive that it bends the trajectory of light and absorbs the stars unfortunate enough to be near it. It belches gamma and X-ray radiation. The center is also packed with stars. Finally, the spiral arm, where star formation is still taking place,

Figure 5.2. The Galactic Habitable Zone

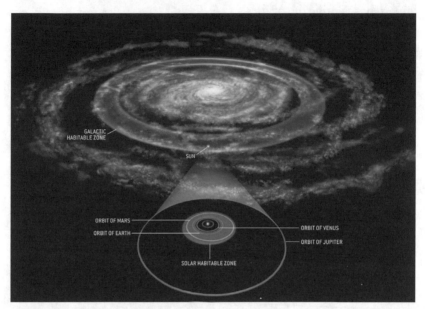

Guillermo Gonzalez, Donald Brownlee, and Peter D. Ward, "Refugees for Life in a Hostile Universe," *Scientific American* (October 2001): 63.

is not habitable. The gravitational pull of too many stars nearby could pull comets into the inner solar system.

Where, then, is earth located? A habitable planet must be between spiral arms, about midway between the galactic center and the outer edge, orbiting around the center of the galaxy at about the same rate as the spiral arms, so that it doesn't cross them too frequently. That's the galactic habitable zone (see fig. 5.2).

The picture of the galactic habitable zone exhibited here is not quite accurate. That circular zone identifies the galactic habitable zone. The real zone, however, is within a dashed line, in those spaces between the spiral arms. That's where you want to be in order to be a habitable planet in this galactic habitable zone.

The point here is not simply that there are habitable places in the galaxy, but that the habitable places are also going to have the best overall conditions for scientific discovery. To make the most scientific discoveries about nearby stars, the planets, and the structure of the galaxy and other galaxies, the best place to be is in the galactic habitable zone. It is the best place from which to view into the distant universe. If we were in a spiral arm, the nearby part of space would be cloudy due to dust and other objects. It would be like a murky day in Seattle. In many places, it would be difficult to see the planets, let alone other stars. The most important scientific discoveries of the twentieth century would never have been made.

As noted, it helps not be in the center of the galaxy if one wants to figure out the structure of our galaxy. Up on a mountain on a clear night, it is possible to see that Milky Way band across the sky that looks like a cloud. In that band we see the galaxy edge-on. We're looking at the part of the galaxy that is dense with stars and therefore brighter. Our location also allows us to see other galaxies.

As was the case with the perfect solar eclipse, the place in a galaxy most conducive to life is the place most conducive to science. Look at correspondence as a design argument. Bill Dembski, a leading design theorist, argues that when you infer design, it's not just that you find something that's really improbable. Rather you infer design when you find something that's improbable that also conforms to a particular kind of pattern. When you find pattern plus improbability, you must rationally infer design. You've detected something that's the product of an intelligent agent. We know that Mount Rushmore, for instance, was designed by intelligent agents. It's the result of sculptors and not merely wind, erosion, and rock formation. An extraterrestrial who landed on earth and didn't know what American presidents looked like would still see that the structure was designed. It's not just that the structure is improbable. The pile of rocks at the bottom of the mountain is also improbable. The pile of rocks is complex; if bulldozers took all those rocks away, one could never get them repositioned in the same place, so it's very complex, which is another way of saying it's improbable.

Figure 5.3. Mount Rushmore

Unlike the pile of rocks, however, the presidential faces conform very tightly to a meaningful, independent pattern, the pattern of the human face. We can recognize that pattern.

Or think of the way we read text. It's not just that a sequence of letters in some written text is improbable. Lots of jumbles of letters are improbable but they don't say anything. Meaningful text conforms to the pattern of a particular language. The combination of the properties of a meaningful pattern and improbability, Dembski argues, allows us to infer design.

Now with our argument, the issue of probability is somewhat different than with other arguments. We need habitable planets to be somewhat rare compared to most of the universe so we can compare habitable environments with uninhabitable ones. This provides the contrast medium by which we can discover a meaningful pattern. That meaningful pattern is the correlation between habitability and measurability.

Yoking the conditions for life with the conditions for discovery is just the sort of thing that an intelligent agent would be interested in doing. If the universe was intended or designed to be discovered, then this combination of habitable factors is *just what one would expect*. It would resolve our sense of surprise to realize that the universe is designed for discovery. However, if the universe is a mere concatenation of chance events, constrained by purposeless regularities that we refer to as "laws," we would not expect discovery.

In learning about perfect eclipses, you immediately see that there is something "fishy" about the idea that the only planet in the solar system where you can see perfect eclipses is just where there are observers to see them. Well, this unlikely scenario that we are observing helps us to recognize a meaningful pattern. It makes sense to put observers at the best place for observing. That's why we put telescopes on the tops of mountains like Mauna Kea in Hawaii. Telescopes go on the tops of the mountains, where the conditions for observing are best.

If our argument is correct, then the universe exhibits the same kind of meaningful pattern. That pattern may not constitute a knock-down-drag-out proof for God's existence; but if nature really is a book that's meant to be read, then this is just what you would expect.

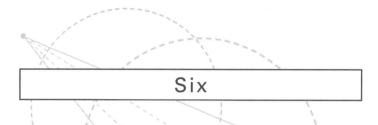

Six

Philosophical Implications of Neo-Darwinism and Intelligent Design

Theism, Personhood, and Bioethics

EDDIE N. COLANTER

The New Religion

In 1859, Charles Darwin published *The Origin of Species*,[1] One hundred years later Darwin's work was heralded at a Centennial Celebration in Chicago as an established fact and the beginning of "the new religion."[2] Sir Julian Huxley, the grandson of Darwin's primary advocate, T. H. Huxley, proclaimed:

> Future historians will perhaps take this Centennial Week as epitomizing an important critical period in the history of this earth of ours—the period when the process of evolution, in the person of inquiring man, began to be truly conscious of itself. . . . This is one of the first public occasions on which it has been frankly faced that all aspects of reality are subject to evolution, from atoms and stars to fish and flowers, from fish and flowers to human societies and values—indeed, that all reality is a single process of evolution. . . . In the evolutionary pattern of thought, there is no longer either need or room for the supernatural. The earth was not created; it evolved. So did all the animals and plants that inhabit it, including our human selves, mind and soul as well as brain and body. So did religion. . . . Finally, the evolutionary vision is enabling us to discern, however incompletely, the lineaments of the new religion that we can be sure will arise to serve the needs of the coming era.[3]

What is the "new religion" that claims that nothing was created or intelligently designed, but that everything that exists, including religion itself, has evolved? The "new religion" is neo-Darwinism (ND). This view of ND could also be called strong ND in contrast to weak ND. It is important to distinguish between these two wings of ND. What I am addressing in this paper is strong ND,[4] with its total commitment to philosophical naturalism. This commitment is candidly announced by biologist Richard Lewontin:

Our willingness to accept scientific claims that are against common sense is the key to an understanding of the real struggle between science and the supernatural. We take the side of science in spite of its failure to fulfill many of its extravagant promises of health and life, in spite of the tolerance of the scientific community of unsubstantiated just-so-stories, because we have a prior commitment to materialism. It is not that the methods and institutions of science somehow compel us to accept a material explanation of the phenomenal world, but on the contrary, that we are forced by our *a priori* adherence to material causes to create an apparatus of investigation and a set of concepts that produce material explanations, no matter how counterintuitive, no matter how mystifying to the uninitiated. Moreover, that Materialism is absolute, for we cannot allow a Divine Foot in the door.[5]

Philosophical naturalism is the view that the only thing that exists is the material or natural world; it is also known as scientific materialism. It is a materialistic view of reality that is consistent with physicalism or ontological materialism. As Lewontin claims, "Materialism is absolute." Immaterial entities such as God or souls do not exist. Weak ND, in contrast, is sometimes held or believed without having the same philosophical implications as strong ND. For example, many believe in weak ND and still believe in God, souls, and other supernatural elements that are not consistent with philosophical naturalism.[6] Unless otherwise stated, I will use ND to refer to strong ND.

Huxley's quote illustrates that there are philosophical implications of a ND scientific position. From Darwin's evolutionary theory, Huxley concludes that, "all reality is a single process of evolution." This position necessarily excludes intelligent design (ID) or any other scientific theory that is not consistent with "the new religion" as the ultimate explanation for "all reality." Huxley's statement is just one example of how ND as a scientific theory has practical consequences for one's philosophical and theological positions concerning reality, theism, and ethics.

The Biology Class

In the early 1990s, I experienced the weight of the "new religion" as an undergraduate student at the University of California, San Diego. In one of my first biology classes, the professor began his course by confidently asking the following question, "How many of you still believe in creation?" I remember the awkward silence that followed in the classroom as I reluctantly raised my hand for a nanosecond. Sadly, I do not think I raised it very high, perhaps just above my waist-high desk. The question did not weaken my warranted belief and commitment to God or the knowledge that life has objective meaning, purpose, and value. It did cause me to reflect, however, on the efficaciousness of ND's gravitational pull on my own hand, as well as the faith of some of the other undergraduate students in the class, whom I know did not adhere to the "new religion" of ND.

The Philosophical Implications of Neo-Darwinism

The experience in my biology class also demonstrates the philosophical implications of ND. Philosophical implications are practical consequences: How people act or behave is in accordance to their beliefs or accepted ideas about theism and reality. In this case, those who accept ND's foundation of philosophical naturalism are more likely to reject the need for theism or any other type of designing intelligence to account for the origin of life. In addition, those that accept ND often reject any notion that the human species has any special moral status among living things. *Homo sapiens*, in this view, are merely the result of mindless material processes, the chance result of matter evolving over time. In this respect, to regard human beings as living organisms that possess some unique moral status is to be guilty of speciesism, the view that some special status or value attaches to one species over another. Thus, ND seems to undermine any notion of objective morality except in regard to morality merely being a naturalistic mechanism in place only to further the survival of the human species. This form of morality is, therefore, relative to the individual or society, having no universal status to make prescriptions of what human beings "ought" to do.

Ideas have consequences, and perhaps the most important ones are our ideas of God and origins. ND is the position that all living organisms came to exist as they are solely as the result of purposeless, random chance, over a necessary amount of time and with sufficient matter, through processes of natural selection and genetic mutation. All life is seen as the result of nondirected evolutionary processes. In contrast, ID[7] is the position that intelligent causation is the best explanation for the complex, information-rich structures of biological systems and that these causes are empirically detectable.[8] The philosophical implications of these two contrasting theories are obvious: If ND is correct and human beings are products of purposeless, random, nondirected, materialist, naturalistic processes, how can there be any objective theism, morality, meaning, purpose, and value? Further, if this is the case, human beings do not have a unique nature and any intrinsic moral status by virtue of being human; the only human rights are those that we arbitrarily give to ourselves.

Neo-Darwinism, as proffered by many prominent scientists, seems to contradict a foundation for theism and objective morality. Moreover, ND cannot consistently object to, or even distinguish between, acts of good and evil. As a result, there would be no objective moral difference between the deeds of Mother Teresa and the terrorists who flew planes into the World Trade Center on September 11, 2001. Philosopher and theologian William Lane Craig illustrates the fact that life can have no objective meaning, purpose, or value in a merely material universe without God:

> Without God the universe is the result of a cosmic accident, a chance explosion. There is no reason for which to exist. As for man, he is a freak of nature—a blind product of matter plus time plus chance. Man is just a lump of slime that evolved into rationality. There is no more purpose in life for the human race than for a species of insect; for both are the result of the blind interaction of chance and necessity.[9]

In contrast to ND, the philosophical implications of ID are consistent with a foundation for a theistic reality where life has objective meaning, purpose, and value. Moreover, perhaps a designer in fact did have the human species in mind. This carries with it a possible hope for humankind that is not entailed in ND. Namely, ID allows a strong plausibility structure for objective morality and the life immortal.

Views of human origins have vast philosophical implications for life; therefore, the importance of these views cannot be underestimated. This is why the question asked by my biology professor was so penetrating. The implication of his assertion that evolution is an obvious empirical dogma reduced ID or any view not consistent with ND to pure subjectivism, outside the realms of science and knowledge. Moreover, he was implying that ND counts as knowledge against theism and theistic truth claims. Intentional or unintentional, this was an intellectual assault on many students' theistic beliefs and views of reality. Philosopher Dallas Willard and others have claimed that "ideas have consequences," whether we like it or not and whether we know it or not. Willard states:

> Bluntly [regarding theism] . . . we must think straight; and crooked thinking, unintentional or not, always favors evil. And when the crooked thinking gets elevated into group orthodoxy, whether religious or secular [scientific], there is always, quite literally, "hell to pay." That is, hell will take its portion, as it has repeatedly done in the horrors of world history.[10]

These words by Willard illustrate the importance of understanding our ideas, their implications, and their consequences. This awareness is important whether or not the ideas are, in fact, true and correspond to reality. To be ignorant of implications can be tragic. Scientific ideas have philosophical implications, directly or indirectly, regarding theism, reality, or ultimate causes; therefore, they are not neutral. That is, these accepted ideas often influence us as individuals and as a society with respect to what we think and believe, how we act, and what we value.

The Contrast Between Neo-Darwinism and Intelligent Design

The contrasting philosophical implications of ND and ID are integral to the growing debate concerning the bioethical issues such as personhood, human cloning, embryonic stem cell research, and reproductive technology. Public policy, law, medicine, business, and education are influenced by which scientific theory society and individual leaders accept. Specifically, accepted beliefs of origins and reality influence how we answer the pertinent questions "Is there a God?" "What is reality?" "What is a human being?" "What does it mean to be human?" "Who is and who is not a member of the human community?" "How should we treat human beings?" "Is there a significant moral difference between humans and other animals?" and "Do we have a duty to all human beings by virtue of their humanness?"

Again, it is important to understand the philosophical implications of ND and ID because a person's formation of beliefs and ideas about theism, reality, meaning, personhood, and morality are based on whether one accepts, in part or in whole, the theories of ND or ID. Practical consequences stem from one's views of reality and theism in general and origins in particular.

In a Southern California public high school newspaper, students replied to the question of origins.[11] When asked, "What do you think?" in regard to the issues surrounding the concepts of origins, creation, evolution, and intelligent design, the students responded:

I believe both evolution and creation are connected; you can't have one without the other.   —Student 1 (freshman)

We believe in the Word of God. We came from Adam and Eve.
    —Students 2 and 3 (seniors)

Everything God makes is wonderful, evolution is crap.
    —Student 4 (sophomore)

I believe that God created all things.   —Student 5 (senior)

I know a couple of people that look like monkeys.
    —Student 6 (sophomore)

There are so many facts that can prove evolution.
    —Student 7 (senior)

If God created man, then how could you ignore the science of dinosaurs?   —Student 8 (senior)

I don't believe in God, so I believe in evolution.
    —Student 9 (freshman)

I think it's a mixture of both. I believe there is some higher power of creation because there is too much of a pattern in nature to be a coincidence.   —Student 10 (senior)

There are several interesting aspects to these high school student responses, but one obvious theme is what I have been referring to as the philosophical implications of ND and ID. A strong relationship invariably exists between one's views of origins, theism, reality, and science. Student 9 does not believe in God, and this is in part why this person believes in evolution. The reverse is also true. How one views theism has philosophical implications for one's views regarding ND and ID.

This paper is limited to philosophical implications of ND and ID and not to the scientific strengths and weaknesses of either position. I do believe that ID as a scientific and empirical theory better explains some of the scientific data regarding the information-rich biological systems and their DNA. Many prominent educators of the scientific community have a scientific commitment to strong ND, so they conclude that no God and no objective morality exist. In addition, they conclude that human beings do not have any special moral status or unique nature. Commitment to this new religion influences their lives and those they touch because of their societal positions as educators and policy makers. I will give further examples of reasoning by prominent educators who advocate ND, and I will specifically address the philosophical implications in regard to theism, personhood, and bioethics.

Important Concepts

Neo-Darwinism Supports a Scientific Materialistic Worldview

As mentioned earlier, ND supports worldviews that are consistent with scientific materialism. A worldview is a comprehensive set of basic or ultimate beliefs used to view the world, interpret the facts, and attempt to answer the deep serious questions. The primary questions are "Is there a God?" "What is reality?" "Who and what are we?" and "Where did we come from?" Scientism as a worldview asserts that the only type of truth or knowledge that exists or that is important is that which can be known or verified through the scientific method. There is no knowledge or truth outside the discipline of science. Scientism is a context for philosophical naturalism.

What Is Science?

Do all scientists agree on what science is? Webster's dictionary defines *science* as

> 1. A branch of knowledge or study dealing with a body of facts or truths systematically arranged and showing the operation of general laws . . . 2. systematic knowledge of the physical or material world. . . .[12]

The definition and discipline parameters of science are not always agreed upon. As stated by philosopher J. P. Moreland in *Christianity and the*

Nature of Science: A Philosophical Investigation, defining science can be a difficult project with no clear definition; it is largely philosophical.[13] Moreland states, "Science cannot be separated from other disciplines by stating necessary and sufficient conditions for science . . . [it] is not an isolated . . . field of study."[14]

Science is often presented as if the scientific method was the foundation of all knowledge and the only given truism. According to Moreland, however, there are presuppositions that must be accepted by those who believe the scientific method is efficacious. These include

1. the existence of the external world;
2. the orderly nature of the external world and its knowability;
3. the uniformity of nature and induction;
4. laws of logic, epistemology, and truth, and the correspondence theory of truth;
5. the reliability of the senses and the mind;
6. the adequacy of language to describe the world;
7. mathematics and the existence of numbers; and
8. the concepts of formal ontology.[15]

Many of these presuppositions are either not recognized or are unfairly dismissed. In addition, when science addresses singularity events, for example the big bang theory or the origin of life, the discipline of history must be part of the scientific process as well. That is, with nonrepeatable historical events, scientists must rely to some extent on the historical method.

Methodological and Philosophical Naturalism

To better understand the philosophical implications of ND, it is vital to differentiate between methodological naturalism and philosophical naturalism.[16] Methodological naturalism is the presupposition that science must confine all scientific methodologies and empirical explanations within the scope of random and undirected natural processes.[17] Thus, according to ID theorist William A. Dembski, "So long as [methodological naturalism] sets the ground rules for how the game of science is to be played, [ID] has no chance for success."[18] If this is the case, then according to philosopher Francis J. Beckwith, "a prior commitment to methodological naturalism makes evolution to be the only reasonable explanation accounting for the origin of the universe and, thus, organic life."[19] In other words, ID as a position that some empirical phenomena and data of the natural world might be best explained as the result of nonrandom, directed, and or intelligent causation is rejected *a priori* regardless of any evidence, reason, or empirical data that would indicate otherwise.

Philosophical naturalism is a more foundational claim than methodological naturalism. Philosophical naturalism is the view that everything that exists or has being is solely material and therefore reducible to material properties. This view is also referred to as ontological materialism. Whereas methodological naturalism is a presupposition used as a tool of science, philosophical naturalism is a worldview. Philosophical naturalism restricts all of reality and everything that exists to explanations that are ultimately reducible to material properties. Consequently, immaterial beings—such as God, angels, and human souls—do not necessarily exist as, or are not necessarily composed of, immaterial substances or properties. In respect to the relationship between philosophical naturalism and methodological naturalism, Dembski argues that it was the power of philosophical naturalism that influenced the culture to adopt methodological naturalism.[20]

Evolutionary Theory and Intelligent Design Theory

Evolutionary theory was primarily introduced in Darwin's *The Origin of Species* in 1859. The basic tenets of evolutionary theory are that all organisms are related through a common ancestry and arose through the process of mutation and natural selection, and that organisms further arose and persisted because of the random chance processes of nature.

Evolution works by four primary steps. First, random chance mutations cause changes, or variation, in a population of organisms. Second, these different organisms compete to survive and reproduce. Third, the organisms that are best able to survive and reproduce leave the most offspring. This is called natural selection. Fourth, given enough time, if some organisms survive and reproduce more than others, a new species will evolve. Neo-Darwinism is a modern Darwinian theory that explains the origin of species in respect to genetic mutations and natural selection. Notably, microevolution pertains to mutations and variations *within* species, and is not debated by evolutionists or creationists.

There is confusion and controversy concerning what intelligent design refers to. ID is a scientific theory that has its roots in information theory and observations about intelligent action. ID tenets are not equivalent to those of scientific creationism.[21] ID theorists argue that information and specified complexity are found in biological systems; for example, DNA and a bacteria flagellum. The existence of systems with specified complexity is best accounted for as a product of design by an intelligent agent. ID makes no explicit statements about the identity of the intelligent designer. It is simply the view that intelligent action was involved at some point in the origins of various aspects of biological life, and that design can be detected empirically. ID is the view that certain physical features of living organisms and the universe are not the result of random and undirected natural processes. This view is based on empirical evidence, scientific research, and reason.

Moreover, ID is more than just a naïve notion about living things with the mere appearance of design, as the atheist zoologist Richard Dawkins has explained it: "Biology is the study of complicated things that give the appearance of having been designed for a purpose."[22] Darwinists hold that natural selection did the "designing." However, ID theorist Stephen C. Meyer notes, "in all cases where we know the causal origin of 'high information content,' experience has shown that intelligent design played a causal role."[23] ID implies that life exists as a result of the purposeful action of an intelligent designer. This is in stark contrast to ND, which postulates that life is the product of, and can be explained by, natural processes alone. According to ND, all life is merely the result of time plus chance plus matter via purposeless, blind forces of nature.

The Entry of Neo-Darwinism into the Religious Realm

Despite claims of some that ND is only science and does not speak to issues of religion or philosophy, neo-Darwinist arguments are often used to discount beliefs that are not consistent with those of a materialist worldview. The following are examples of philosophical implications of ND that affect theistic beliefs:

1. Science is used to support or advocate atheistic worldviews. Dawkins, a zoologist, concludes that Darwinian science contributed strong evidence for atheism: "[A]lthough atheism might have been logically tenable before Darwin, Darwin made it possible to

be an intellectually fulfilled atheist."[24] Dawkins is using ND as evidence in support of atheism.

2. Biologist William B. Provine asserts that Darwin clearly understood the philosophical implications of his own naturalistic theory; namely that

    1) no gods worth having exist;
    2) no life after death exists;
    3) no ultimate foundation for ethics exists;
    4) no ultimate meaning in life exists; and
    5) human free will is nonexistent.[25]

    If ND is true, then there is no God, no life after death, no ultimate foundation for ethics, no ultimate meaning in life, and no human free will, according to Provine's assessment of Darwin's theory. The first two, "no gods worth having exist" and "no life after death exists," were also articulated in the views of Epicurus (341–270 B.C.), well over two thousand years ago.

3. Regarding ND's philosophical implication for human origins, paleontologist Stephen Jay Gould stated, "We are here because one odd group of fishes had a peculiar fin anatomy that could transform into legs for terrestrial creatures. . . . We may yearn for a 'higher' answer—but none exists. This explanation, though superficially troubling, if not terrifying, is ultimately liberating and exhilarating."[26] According to Gould, the human species was not planned by an intelligent designer who had us in mind. It logically follows that human beings have no unique essence, nature, intrinsic meaning, value, or purpose.

4. Likewise, paleontologist George Gaylord Simpson asserted, "Man is the result of a purposeless and natural process that did not have him in mind."[27]

5. If ND is used as an ultimate explanation for the existence of all life, there is no need to suggest any type of theism to account for human existence. All of life is merely the result of ND and needs no other explanation. In this respect, sociobiologist Edward Wilson writes, "[L]ife . . . has arisen by evolution. . . . [T]he human brain and all its activities have arisen from the same. . . . [N]o more complicated explanation is needed to account for human

existence, either scientifically or spiritually."[28] The consequences of this view of the human brain are that any idea of human consciousness is reducible to material properties and not to an immaterial self or soul.

6. In line with these advocates of ND, D. J. Futuyma, an evolutionary biologist, states:

> By coupling undirected, purposeless variation to the blind, uncaring process of natural selection, Darwin made theological or spiritual explanations of the life processes superfluous. Together with Marx's materialistic theory of history and society and Freud's attribution of human behavior to influences over which we have little control, Darwin's theory of evolution was a crucial plank in the platform of mechanism and materialism—of much of science, in short—that has since been the stage of most Western thought.[29]

This reasoning behind ND and its practical consequences are well established in Western thought today. The above examples illustrate this point. Philosophical naturalism is the dominant foundation for this practice of science and the interpretation of scientific data to the exclusion of other viable scientific alternatives such as ID. Proponents advance ND as an ultimate explanation of reality and thus are heralding the new religion. Here, advocates of ND have exited science and entered the domain of philosophy or theology, maybe without realizing they have done so. Intentional or not, they are setting parameters around other disciplines that influence and or are influenced by science.[30]

Personhood and Bioethics

What is personhood? Who and what are we? Do we have souls? Do we have a nature? Are we merely physical culmination of time plus matter plus chance via purposeless naturalistic processes? Or are we the result of an intelligent designer? Who is and who is not a member of the human community? What kind of beings are persons? When does a being become a person? What criteria ought to be used to determine who is and is not a person?

To answer such questions, it is crucial to understand the concept of personhood. Personhood is a status that some beings have by virtue of what they are by nature. It is important that moral status is given to all persons, the condition that each human being has in order to be considered for direct moral concern by other persons.

The Relationship of Personhood to the Value of Human Life

One's worldview has a major influence on how a concept of personhood is formed. If one holds to ND, then human beings are viewed as the result of the blind forces of nature and do not have an essence. Human life is without inherent meaning, purpose, or value. ND is not consistent with a coherent notion of personhood. This point is demonstrated by philosopher and materialist Paul Churchland:

> For . . . the important point about the standard evolutionary story is that the human species and all of its features are the wholly physical outcome of a purely physical process. Like all but the simplest of organisms, we have a nervous system. And for the same reason: a nervous system is just an active matrix of cells, and a cell is just an active matrix of molecules. We are notable only in that our nervous system is more complex and powerful than those of our fellow creatures. Our inner nature differs from that of simpler creatures in degree, but not in kind.[31]

The philosophical implications of ND, that human beings have a nature that is different in degree but not in kind from other animals, has tremendous ramifications for how we view humanity. This view affects our moral actions toward other humans and animals. According to Churchland and those who agree with him, there is no substantial difference between a human being and a monkey. In fact, Churchland has said that if a computer or some form of artificial intelligence could do everything that a human being could do, to call it anything less than human would be racism (or perhaps "thingism," valuing some things improperly over other things).[32]

If one holds that human beings are the result of impersonal naturalistic forces, it is difficult to conceive how personal beings could result from such impersonal beginnings. A coherent concept of personhood seems reasonable only if a personal intelligence is the source of human existence. One philosophical implication of ID is that intelligent agency is the cause of human existence. This is consistent with the possibilities of theism, personhood, and objective morality that is beyond the limit of philosophical naturalism.

Personhood is closely linked to the notion that human beings have an essence that defines them and guides their change and development. Every human being is a composite of an immaterial soul and a material body.[33] Together, the soul and body are one substance. This is a hylomorphic view in which the soul is the form of the body. In such a case, the human being or the person is essentially that composite. Neither the form nor the matter is a whole individual substance, only the composite of both. This view is in sharp contrast to ND and beliefs such as materialism or physicalism, which hold, if they are consistent, that human beings are merely the sum total of their parts, without any essence or immaterial soul. If ND is true, then there is no immaterial soul and no human essence.[34] If ID is correct, then an intelligent designer could design human beings with or without souls. We do not know what an intelligent designer would or would not design unless we knew more about this intelligent designer.

The philosophical implications of ID are consistent with the position that human beings have inherent personhood qualities or capacities that are directed by an essential nature. These include consciousness, rational thought, the ability to make moral choices, and the capacity to love. At the moment of conception, all human beings have the capacity or potential to manifest these qualities. Scientifically we know that the human embryo is of the species *Homo sapiens*. Coherent with ID is the position that the human embryo is not a potential human being but a human being with potential.

What Defines Personhood?

Personhood carries the idea that all human beings have a personal identity and a unity of self that is sustained through age, growth, and development.[35] For example, every adult was once an embryo that developed from a fetus to a baby to a child to an adolescent to an adult. These physical, developmental, and functional changes never changed the person's essence or nature. There is a sustained personal identity and a unity of self throughout all these stages of life.[36] There also is a teleology to human development that would not be consistent with ND.

It seems incoherent to define personhood as anything other than a status and essence that all human beings possess by virtue of being human. Every human being is necessarily a person, and no other criterion seems satisfactory. For example, if consciousness is a criterion for personhood, you must consider if human beings are still persons when asleep or in a coma if you are to be consistent. Of course they are. If viability of the fetus is the criterion, consider how technological advancements make viability earlier and earlier in gestation. Can we honestly say that twenty-four-week fetuses were not persons in the past, but they are now because technology makes viability possible earlier? This seems arbitrary. As Hadley Arkes states, "If the definition of 'human' life were to depend, then, on the point of 'viability,' we would again fall into the technological fallacy: in this case, the definition of human being would be made to rest on the current state of the art in incubator science."[37]

Other inadequate criteria for personhood include evidence for brain activity, desires, or independence. When these types of characteristics become criteria for what makes human beings valuable with personhood, human beings become instrumental. That is, human qualities are valuable and not the human beings themselves.[38] What is more valuable, these qualities, or the human being that have the qualities? If ND is correct, then the philosophical implications are that there are no objective criteria for value in human beings or personhood. Consistent with ND, an individual could be human and yet not a person.[39]

How we ought to treat human beings enters the area of ethics or morality. Medical ethics refers to how we ought to treat human beings concerning medical matters. Medical ethics is also known as applied ethics or bioethics. Bioethics deals with abortion, embryonic stem cell research, euthanasia, cloning, reproductive technology, eugenics, and other life issues.

When addressing an issue such as abortion, the question to ask is "What is being killed?" If ND is correct, the philosophical implications would not lead to an objective answer to the value of the fetus or the moral status of an abortion. In this respect, bioethics and ethics in general become illusory, as stated by the evolutionist E. O. Wilson:

> The time has come to take seriously the fact that we humans are modified monkeys, not the favored Creation of a Benevolent God on the Sixth Day. . . . We must think again especially about our

so-called "ethical principles." . . . As evolutionists, we see that no (ethical) justification of the traditional kind is possible. Morality, or more strictly our belief in morality, is merely an adaptation put in place to further our reproductive ends. Hence, the basis of ethics does not lie in God's will. . . . In an important sense, ethics as we understand it is an illusion fobbed on us by our genes to get us to cooperate. It is without external grounding. . . . Ethics is illusory inasmuch as it persuades us that it has an objective reference. This is the crux of the biological position. Once it is grasped, everything falls into place.[40]

ND is only concerned with the biological position. Morality is only seen in a materialistic context and so has no objective reference.

This position of ethics found in ND can be traced to an earlier time according to Benjamin Wiker. In his book *Moral Darwinism: How We Became Hedonists,* Wiker contends that Epicurus was the designer of what we know as modern science.[41] Wiker believes that modern materialism can be traced back to Epicurean materialism and that this materialism is consistent with what we know as moral Darwinism.[42] Epicureanism, founded by Epicurus, was an atheistic philosophy.[43] This philosophy viewed ethics as hedonistic. Pleasure was one's intrinsic natural goal and pain the only evil.[44] Epicurus attempted to eliminate what he considered to be the two major sources of human suffering, namely, the fear of gods and death.[45] Wiker points out other connections between Epicureanism and moral Darwinism.[46] He concludes that it is Epicurean reasoning that explains the acceptance of abortion in today's culture.[47] With a materialist worldview, the moral Darwinist has no concern about any consequences or justice from a divine source:[48]

If a human being has no soul, and there is no God (or God is metaphysically locked out of the universe), then there is no reason to fear that procuring an abortion or engaging in infanticide will produce some dreadful effect. Once a fetus, as a biological growth dependent on the woman, has been terminated, the woman is simply relieved of a burden or pain which she is experiencing, and the fetus, as a material entity, is no more. There is no hell to fear, no spirit of the dead child to haunt the woman or doctor, no God to exact punishment. There is only relief, or in Epicurus's words, freedom from disturbance.[49]

If the soul, personhood, and the possibility of divine judgment are removed from the equation of ethical responsibility, then people are "free," *de facto*, to arbitrarily construct their own morality.

The moral bankruptcy of ND in regard to personhood and bioethics is further articulated by Richard Weikart. In his research concerning the influence of Darwinism on Hitler's bioethical and moral atrocities, he finds:

> Many argued that by providing a naturalistic account of the origin of ethics and morality, Darwinism delivered a death-blow to the prevailing Judeo-Christian ethics, as well as Kantian ethics and any fixed moral code. If morality was built on social instincts that changed over evolutionary time, then morality must be relative to the conditions of life at any given time. . . . Darwinists who made the evolutionary process the new criteria for morality radically altered the way that people thought about morality . . . [thus] improving vitality and mental prowess—especially of future generations—became the highest moral virtue. . . . This new stress on evolutionary progress and health as the norm for behavior spawned the eugenics movement . . . which was overtly founded on Darwinian principles.[50]

To what degree did Darwinism bring about the Holocaust? In answering this question, Weikart says:

> Darwinism by itself did not produce the Holocaust, but without Darwinism, especially in its social Darwinist and eugenics permutations, neither Hitler nor his Nazi followers would have had the necessary scientific underpinnings to convince themselves and their collaborators that one of the world's greatest atrocities was really morally praiseworthy. Darwinism—or at least some naturalistic interpretations of Darwinism—succeeded in turning morality on its head.[51]

The philosophical implications of ND seem to have no limit in regard to negative consequences for future generations. A notion of personhood consistent with ID should be ascribed to every human being from conception through adulthood, regardless of level of function or dependency, based on his or her human nature alone. Characteristics of human person-hood include (but are not limited to)

1. having moral status, a soul, personal identity, and unity of self throughout time and change;
2. having the capacity for rational thought, understanding, language, personal relationships, and moral responsibility; and
3. having the potential to love God and neighbor.

The philosophical implications of ND are not compatible with this notion of personhood and the resulting view of bioethics. The source of most bioethical concerns and human rights issues stem from our concept of personhood. Issues of abortion, embryonic stem cell research, eugenics, euthanasia, and cloning are primarily related to who is, and who is not, a member of the human community. If we acknowledge that every human being has the status of personhood, many of our bioethical dilemmas and human rights issues could be more readily resolved, and many human lives would be preserved and valued. The philosophical implications of ND not only have no reference for objective morality, but also have nothing ethically to say about whether past or future holocausts are right or wrong.

Conclusion

Neo-Darwinism and intelligent design theory have vastly different implications regarding theism, personhood, and bioethics. If one believes in the tenets of strong ND, they are likely to embrace some form of atheism and integrate it as a worldview to interpret reality and humanity. In contrast, one who holds to ID will likely be more critical of philosophical naturalism and more inclined to embrace some notion of theism and integrate it as a worldview when interpreting reality and humanity.

It may also be the case, and often is, that an individual will claim to hold conflicting views of ND, theism, and objective morality in tension. This occurs because a person has not integrated their beliefs or views of the nature of religion and science, or they consider theological beliefs to be outside the realm of knowledge. They do not consider religious claims or statements to be propositional. That is, religious claims, by their very nature, are subjective and cannot be true or false. Religion and its claims about reality then cannot contradict or be contradicted by anything because it is part of the subjective realm, and not knowledge-based.

Either way, if one holds as true or mostly true that ND is the only explanation of origins and biological systems, then it often follows that that individual is likely to be a materialist or atheist and embrace some evolutionary ethic in respect to theism, personhood, and bioethics. If one accepts the evidence for ID as the best explanation of origins and the information-rich biological systems, then it is also likely for that person to embrace some view of theism (at least as plausible), and to be open to a concept of personhood that is consistent with theism, objective morality, and the belief that human beings have a special place in the cosmos.

In addition, I would contend that the philosophical implications of ND are not consistent with the concepts of truth, justice, education, a meaning in life, or free will. Under these conditions, the viability of science itself as a knowledge-based discipline is compromised. If philosophical naturalism is correct, then human beings are reduced to pieces of impersonal matter. Moreover, all human cultures and societal achievements and hopes ultimately end in the grave of a cold, dark universe. Every living being, whether human or monkey, will become extinct, given the laws of thermodynamics, and there will be no lasting record of its history. Evils will go unpunished and goods will go unrewarded. There is no truth, good or bad ideas, worthy or unworthy arguments, or love, but only determined chemical processes and the firing of neurons in brains. Science itself ends up a meaningless endeavor with no one left to share in its alleged benefits.

The science of ND as prophet of the new religion foretells ultimate doom and meaninglessness of the universe and all life. We find this reasoning from Kenneth R. Miller in a biology textbook that was widely used in the 1990s in regard to believing in philosophical materialism as a result of accepting Darwinian evolution:

> Darwin knew that accepting his theory required believing in *philosophical materialism*, the conviction that matter is the stuff of all existence and that all mental and spiritual phenomena are its byproducts. Darwinian evolution was not only purposeless but also heartless—a process in which the rigors of nature ruthlessly eliminate the unfit. Suddenly, humanity was reduced to just one more species

in a world that cared nothing for us. The great human mind was no more than a mass of evolving neurons. Worst of all, there was no divine plan to guide us.[52]

This is why the philosophical implications of ND concerning the question of God's existence are of the utmost importance. Armand M. Nicholi Jr., who juxtaposes the lives and work of Sigmund Freud and C. S. Lewis regarding "The Question of God?" states:

> Freud and Lewis agreed that the most important question concerned God's existence: Is there an Intelligence beyond the universe? Both spent a significant portion of their lives addressing this question, realizing its profound implications for understanding our identity, our purpose, and our destiny.[53]

A good example of how a person's acceptance or rejection of the scientific evidence for ID can change their position on theism can be found in the story of English atheistic philosopher Antony Flew. A few years ago, Flew embraced theism, primarily due to the scientific evidence supporting ID. He speaks of this worldview transition in a 2004 interview with the philosopher Gary Habermas:

> HABERMAS: You very kindly noted that our debates and discussions had influenced your move in the direction of theism. You mentioned that this initial influence contributed in part to your comment that naturalistic efforts have never succeeded in producing "a plausible conjecture as to how any of these complex molecules might have evolved from simple entities." Then in your recently rewritten introduction to the forthcoming edition of your classic volume *God and Philosophy*, you say that the original version of that book is now obsolete. You mention a number of trends in theistic argumentation that you find convincing, like big bang cosmology, fine tuning, and Intelligent Design arguments. Which arguments for God's existence did you find most persuasive?

> FLEW: I think the most impressive arguments for God's existence are those that are supported by recent scientific discoveries . . . the argument to Intelligent Design is enormously stronger that it was when I first met it.[54]

Later in the interview:

HABERMAS: So of the major theistic arguments, such as the cosmological, teleological, moral, and ontological, the only really impressive ones that you take to be decisive are the scientific forms of teleology?

FLEW: Absolutely. It seems to me that Richard Dawkins constantly overlooks the fact that Darwin himself, in the fourteenth chapter of *The Origin of Species*, pointed out that his whole argument began with a being which already possessed reproductive powers. This is the creature the evolution of which a truly comprehensive theory of evolution must give some account. It now seems to me that the findings of more than fifty years of DNA research have provided materials for a new and enormously powerful argument to design.[55]

Flew's honest examination is a good example of how a scientific theory and new scientific discovery have philosophical implications on one's view of theism. Before he accepted the evidence for ID, Flew was a staunch advocate for atheism. His pilgrimage from atheism to theism was primarily the result of a scholarly assessment of the more recent scientific evidence for ID, coupled with ND's inability to explain the scientific evidence in regard to origins.

My intent concerning the philosophical implications of ND and ID is not to personally criticize those who advocate ND or similar positions. Instead it is to encourage discussion and debate because of what is at stake. This entails serious research and examination of the scientific merit of any theory that has such sweeping influence and consequences regarding many issues that affect all of life.

Intelligent design is not anti-evolution. Rather, it is a viable scientific theory that better explains the fine-tuning of the universe and the origin of life, as well as the specified complexity found in the smallest of living organisms. History has demonstrated that science must change to accommodate the latest discoveries and data when reason dictates. True scientific discovery accounts for evidence even when it seems inconsistent with personal, institutional, or cultural presuppositions, as well as beliefs concerning reality, theism, and personhood.

My suggestion is for everyone to consider the evidence and the practical implications of neo-Darwinism and intelligent design, listen to each other with awareness of one's own worldview, and let truth and reason be the final arbiters.

Seven

Darwinism and the Law

H. WAYNE HOUSE

The other chapters in this book have been concerned with scientific and philosophical arguments regarding the matter of naturalistic evolution and intelligent design theory and with whether intelligent design may legitimately enter into an ever-broadening public square. This chapter relates to the latter issue and specifically how this theory may pass muster in the legal arena, considering that the judiciary is now severely biased against the presentation of any view of origins in the public arena.

The intent of debate is to let light shine on facts and truth, but often this is not allowed for fear of the supposed mixture of law and religion, church and state. So, whether something is true does not necessarily mean that it will have a fair hearing in contemporary society. One oftentimes deals with power more than with truth, so that those who control the ability to hear information in government and the press control access to facts and truth.

This is especially so in the area of law. A judge who has little understanding of philosophy, religion, or science makes decisions that impact the availability of information, particularly in the government learning institutions: public schools, museums, and similar public forums.

I will set forth the history of the legal debate over evolution in the American experience and then look at various attempts to open up educational centers to an alternative, nonnaturalistic theory of origins. After looking at the arguments in the courts, we can look for ways in which intelligent design can receive a fair hearing.

The Scopes Trial

Before the Trial

The legal wrangling over the teaching of origins in the public schools goes back to the second decade of the twentieth century, to an obscure

This chapter is an adaptation of "Darwinism and the Law: Can Non-Naturalistic Scientific Theories Survive Constitutional Challenge?" *Regent University Law Review* 13, no. 2 (Spring 2001).

city and a strange set of events. The Scopes trial in Dayton, Tennessee, in 1925 captures the imagination of all who read the reports, or who have seen the play or movie *Inherit the Wind.* The story told in *Inherit the Wind* makes a very entertaining movie, but is very inaccurate in its depiction of the facts.

Several events led to what is often called the Scopes "Monkey trial." The Butler Act was enacted by the Tennessee legislature in 1925.[1] This law by J. W. Butler made it "unlawful for any teacher in any of the . . . public schools of the State which are supported . . . by the public funds of the State, to teach any theory that denies the story of the Divine Creation of man as taught in the Bible, and to teach instead that man has descended from a lower order of animals."[2]

This law brought a strong reaction from the ACLU, a newly formed organization ostensibly created to protect constitutional liberties. After the Butler Act was signed into law, the ACLU began a newspaper ad campaign asking for a volunteer to test the act. They wrote in the *Daily Times* in Chattanooga, May 4, 1925, "We are looking for a Tennessee teacher who is willing to accept our services and testing this law, that is the Butler Law, in the courts."[3]

The actual violation of the Butler Act that occasioned the trial was staged. The reason for this instigation related to the difficult economic times. Business leaders of Dayton, a small town near Chattanooga, took advantage of the ACLU ad to stimulate the economy. The bottom line was "what can we do to draw a crowd?" At a drugstore in Dayton, various business leaders met to discuss a plan to bolster the economy. The ACLU offer seemed like something that might work. With the opening of the trial, the town acquired a car-

Figure 7.1 Joe Mendi

Movie star chimpanzee Joe Mendi, who was brought to Dayton during the Scopes trial. Photograph courtesy of Bryan College.

nival atmosphere. There were vendors, reporters from all over the world, and a chimpanzee that was regularly paraded by the owner of the drugstore. The trial room was packed with inquisitive attendees each day.

What is ironic about the trial is that an offense was never really committed. John Scopes admits, "I didn't violate the law. I never taught that evolution lesson." Speaking to William K. Hutchinson of the International News Service, Scopes said:

> There's something I must tell you. It's worried me. I didn't violate the law . . . I never taught that evolution lesson. I skipped it. I was doing something else the day I should have taught it, and I missed the whole lesson about Darwin and never did teach it. Those kids they put on the stand couldn't remember what I taught them three months ago. They were coached by the lawyers. Honest, I've been scared all through the trial that the kids might remember I missed the lesson. I was afraid they'd get on the stand and say I hadn't taught it and then the whole trial would go blooey. If that happened they would run me out of town on a rail.[4]

When Hutchinson replied that would make a great story, Scopes said, "My god no! Not a word of it until the Supreme Court passes my appeal. My lawyers would kill me."[5]

This is all duplicity, of course, but it is not surprising.[6] Such falsehood is not unheard of to further a cause or to acquire wealth, the one as strong a motive for deception as the other.

George Hunter's *Civic Biology* was alleged to have been used by Scopes in teaching on evolution in violation of the law. This book presents not only unproved allegations regarding evolution but also a racist view of human development. According to Hunter,

> At the present time there exist upon the earth five races or varieties of man, each very different from the other in instincts, social customs, and, to an extent, in structure. These are the Ethiopian or negro type, originating in Africa; the Malay or brown race, from the islands of the Pacific; the American Indian; the Mongolian or yellow race, including the natives of China, Japan, and the Eskimos; and finally, the highest type of all, the Caucasians, represented by the civilized white inhabitants of Europe and America.[7]

181

If that sounds racist, it should not surprise us. The complete title for Darwin's original book had a racist component: *On the Origin of Species by Means of Natural Selection, or The Preservation of Favoured Races in the Struggle for Life*.[8] The very beginning of the public push for evolutionary dogma was not very acceptable from a social or moral standpoint.

During the Trial

Each day the courtroom was so packed that people had to arrive early each morning to get a seat. Outside people loitered to get news of the proceedings, and vendors sold popcorn and hot dogs. Monkeys did tricks, and reporters from all over the world reported the news.

The attorney representing Scopes for the ACLU was Clarence Darrow. For the prosecution was William Jennings Bryan, a noted orator, former cabinet member for Woodrow Wilson, and three-time Democrat Party nominee for President of the United States. Though *Inherit the Wind* insinuates that they hated each other, in reality Darrow and Bryan generally got along amicably throughout the trial.

One of the most unusual things about this trial was the examination of Bryan by Darrow. Today this would be an unheard of scenario, but the transcripts of the trial reveal a most fascinating witness by Bryan, who gives as his reason for succumbing to this:

> The reason I am answering is not for the benefit of the superior court. It is to keep these gentlemen from saying I was afraid to meet them and let them question me, and I want the Christian world to know that any atheist, agnostic, unbeliever, can question me anytime as to my belief in God, and I will answer him.[9]

This may have been a statement of valor but it was not a great legal strategy, and it has been greatly mischaracterized. Before submitting to this examination, Bryan received a promise that he would also have the opportunity to examine Darrow, but that never happened.

Unlike the popular perception, Bryan's intelligence and wit are revealed in his testimony. It should be noted that he was not strictly a "fundamentalist" in his views of science and the Bible, though he held to a high view of Scripture. Darrow posed several different types of questions, but his underlying intent was to bring into doubt the literal interpretation of the Bible:

Figure 7.2. Darrow Addresses the Court

Photograph courtesy of Bryan College.

Q. But when you read that Jonah swallowed the whale—or that the whale swallowed Jonah—excuse me please—how do you literally interpret that?

A. When I read that a big fish swallowed Jonah—it does not say whale.

Q. Doesn't it? Are you sure?

A. That is my recollection of it. A big fish, and I believe it, and I believe in a God who can make a whale and can make a man and make both what He pleases. . . .

Q. Now, you say, the big fish swallowed Jonah, and he there remained how long—three days—and then he spewed him upon the land. You believe that the big fish was made to swallow Jonah?

A. I am not prepared to say that; the Bible merely says it was done.[10]

At other times Darrow became arrogant and belittling, while Bryan demonstrated considerable calm and wit:

DARROW. You insult every man of science and learning in the world because he does not believe in your fool religion.

THE COURT. I will not stand for that.

Figure 7.3. Bryan Addresses the Court

Photograph courtesy of Bryan College.

DARROW.   For what he is doing?

THE COURT. I am talking to both of you. . . .

Q.   (*Directed at Bryan:*) Wait until you get to me. Do you know anything about how many people there were in Egypt 3,500 years
ago, or how many people there were in China 5,000 years ago?

A.   No.

Q.   Have you ever tried to find out?

A.   No, sir. You are the first man I ever heard of who has been in
interested in it. (*Laughter*)

Q.   Mr. Bryan, am I the first man you ever heard of who has been
interested in the age of human societies and primitive man?

A.   You are the first man I ever heard speak of the number of people
at those different periods.

Q.   Where have you lived all your life?

A. Not near you. (*Laughter and applause*)

Q. Nor near anybody of learning?

A. Oh, don't assume you know it all.[11]

Bryan's answers at times demonstrated that he was not a six-day cre-ationist, though he was familiar with the historical and biblical data:

Q. Have you any idea how old the earth is?

A. No.

Q. The Book you have introduced in evidence tells you, doesn't it?

A. I don't think it does, Mr. Darrow.

Q. Let's see whether it does; is this the one?

A. That is the one, I think.

Q. It says b.c. 4004?

A. That is Bishop Usher's calculation.

Q. That is printed in the Bible you introduced?

A. Yes, sir. . . .

Q. Would you say that the earth was only 4,000 years old?

A. Oh, no; I think it is much older than that.

Q. How much?

A. I couldn't say. . . .

Q. Do you think the earth was made in six days?

A. Not six days of twenty-four hours.

Q. Doesn't it say so?

A. No, sir. . . .

Q. . . . Does the statement, "The morning and the evening were the first day," and "The morning and the evening were the second day," mean anything to you?

A. I do not think it necessarily means a twenty-four-hour day.

Q. You do not?

A. No.

Q. What do you consider it to be?

A. I have not attempted to explain it. If you will take the second chapter—let me have the book. (*Examining Bible.*) The fourth verse of the second chapter says: "These are the generations of the heavens and of the earth, when they were created in the day that the Lord God made the earth and the heavens," the word "day" there in the very next chapter is used to describe a period. I do not see that there is any necessity for construing the words, "the evening and the morning," as meaning necessarily a twenty-four-hour day, "in the day when the Lord made the heaven and the earth."

Q. Then, when the Bible said, for instance, "and God called the firmament heaven. And the evening and the morning were the second day," that does not necessarily mean twenty-four hours?

A. I do not think it necessarily does.

Q. Do you think it does or does not?

A. I know a great many think so.

Q. What do you think?

A. I do not think it does.

Q. You think those were not literal days?

A. I do not think they were twenty-four-hour days.

Q. What do you think about it?

A. That is my opinion—I do not know that my opinion is better on that subject than those who think it does.

Q. You do not think that?

A. No. But I think it would be just as easy for the kind of God we believe in to make the earth in six days as in six years or in 6,000,000 years or in 600,000,000 years. I do not think it important whether we believe one or the other.

Q. Do you think those were literal days?

A. My impression is they were periods, but I would not attempt to argue as against anybody who wanted to believe in literal days. . . .

Q. The creation might have been going on for a very long time?

A. It might have continued for millions of years.[12]

186

Bryan's retort to questioning is interesting because Darrow tries to get Bryan to subscribe to a very recent earth, 4004 B.C., but Bryan was a cautious thinker in this regard. Bryan apparently did not believe in a creative day of twenty-four-hours but believed that the earth was probably millions of years old. Now I am not trying to make an argument here for any age of the earth but merely seek to point out that one could not pigeonhole this man.

The Disposition of the Case

Several irregularities occurred in the course of the trial. First, scientists presented testimony of recognized fallacious evidence. For example, note the following:

> Dr. Fay-Cooper Cole, anthropologist at the University of Chicago, used the Piltdown man and Heidelberg man as examples of the proofs of evolution.[13]

> Dr. Kirtley F. Mather, listed the Cro-Magnon and Neanderthal as examples of the missing links,[14] boldly commented that "There are in truth no missing links in the record which connects man with the other members of the order of primates,"[15] and argued for the discredited theory of ontogeny recapitulates phylogeny.[16]

Second, rather than Darrow allowing himself to be questioned by Bryan, the case took an interesting twist as he short-circuited the trial. Darrow wanted to lose the case and even admitted to the court that the charges against Scopes were true. Consider the tact of Darrow. He said to the judge, "I think to save time we will ask the court to bring in the jury, and we expect the jury to find the defendant guilty."

That is an interesting attack. You hire someone as a defense attorney, and he goes to the judge, "Your honor, I would like you to instruct the jury to find my client guilty." There is a reason he did that. This move prepared for an appeal. He said in the beginning that they were only doing this as a test case because they wanted to overturn the law. They couldn't overturn the law if he was found innocent, a definite possibility. The ACLU had to get into an appeal process, and he wanted it to go up to the U.S. Supreme Court.

This also allowed Darrow to escape being questioned by Bryan, an event that could have been very embarrassing for him since Bryan was

Figure 7.4. Scopes Being Sentenced

Photograph courtesy of Bryan College.

very skilled and knowledgeable. In addition, this did not allow for the final summation of William Jennings Bryan, who was viewed as one of the most famous orators of his day. No doubt he would have had produced an outstanding oration for the jury and the public.

The Scopes Trial Versus *Inherit the Wind*

Most people who are familiar with the Scopes trial know it through the movie *Inherit the Wind*, starring superstar Spencer Tracy, playing Clarence Darrow. There are superficial resemblances between them, something acknowledged by the authors of the book that became the movie:

> *Inherit the Wind* is not history. . . . Only a handful of phrases have been taken from the actual transcript of the famous Scopes Trial. Some of the characters of the play are related to the colorful figures in that battle of giants; but they have life and language of their own— and, therefore, names of their own. . . . So *Inherit the Wind* does not pretend to be journalism. It is theatre. It is not 1925.[17]

Following are a number of discrepancies between the facts and the fiction:

1. The trial originated not in Dayton but in the New York offices of the American Civil Liberties Union, for it was this organization that ran an announcement in Tennessee newspapers, offering to pay the expenses of any teacher willing to test the new Tennessee anti-evolution law.

2. When a group of Dayton leaders decided to take advantage of this offer, their main reason was not so much defense of religion as it was economics, for they saw the trial as a great means of publicity that would attract business and industry to Dayton.

3. Others responsible for the trial were the media, who worked hard to persuade Bryan and Darrow to participate in the trial.

4. John T. Scopes was not a martyr for academic freedom. Primarily a coach of three sports, he also taught mathematics, physics, chemistry, and general science. He agreed to help test the law even though he could not remember ever teaching evolution, having only briefly substituted in biology. He was never jailed, nor did he ever take the witness stand in the trial. The people of Dayton liked him, and he cooperated with them in making a test case of the trial.

5. William Jennings Bryan was not out to get Scopes. Bryan thought the Tennessee law a poor one because it involved fining an educator, and he offered to pay Scopes's fine if he needed the money.

6. Bryan was familiar with Darwin's works, and he was not against teaching evolution—if it were presented as a theory, and if other major options, such as creationism, were taught.

7. The trial record discloses that Bryan handled himself well and when put on the stand unexpectedly by Darrow, defined terms carefully, stuck to the facts, made distinctions between literal and figurative language when interpreting the Bible, and questioned the reliability of scientific evidence when it contradicted the Bible. Some scientific experts at the trial referred to such "evidence" of evolution as the Piltdown man (now dismissed as a hoax).

8. Bryan and his wife were on good terms, and she did not admire Clarence Darrow. Scopes dated some girls in Dayton but did not have a steady girlfriend.

9. The defense's scientific experts did not testify at the trial because their testimony was irrelevant to the central question of whether a

law had been broken, because Darrow refused to let Bryan cross-examine the experts, and because Darrow did not call on them to testify. But twelve scientists and theologians were allowed to make statements as part of the record presented by the defense.

10. The topic of sex and sin did not come up in the trial. Neither did Bryan believe that the world was created in 4004 B.C. at 9 AM.

11. Instead of Bryan being mothered by his wife, he took care of her, for she was an invalid.

12. The people of Dayton in general and fundamentalist Christians in particular were not the ignorant, frenzied, uncouth persons the play pictures them as being.

13. Scopes was found guilty partly by the request of Darrow, his defense lawyer, in the hope that the case could be appealed to a higher court.

14. Bryan did not have a fit while delivering his last speech and die in the courtroom.[18]

The Aftermath

The Scopes trial started a myriad of court cases in the second half of the twentieth century over the teaching of creation in the government school system of the United States. Whereas Europe had already succumbed to evolutionary teaching, most of the people of the United States during this period believed in divine creation.

After the conviction of John Scopes, the case went up on appeal to the Tennessee Supreme Court, which overturned the lower court. The reversal was not based on the facts of the case but on a technicality, that the judge should not have imposed the amount of the fine. The jury should have determined this. That the state supreme court chose not to concern itself with a violation of the federal constitution's First Amendment reflected the fact that the U.S. Supreme Court had not yet incorporated the establishment clause of the First Amendment against the states. Consequently, there was no basis in Tennessee law to consider the legislative prohibition of evolution, on religious grounds, to violate the law.

After this decision, little more was said about the Scopes decision, though not of the attempt by citizens to forbid evolution in the schools of Tennessee.[19]

Attempts to Balance Evolution and Creation

Balanced Treatment Acts

In response to the negative rulings against attempts to circumscribe the teaching of evolution in the public schools, which will be discussed below, several states, beginning in the early 1980s, introduced legislation to have balanced teaching on origins in the public schools. Generally these have been named a "balanced treatment act."[20] The reason for this relates to the efforts of different people within the creationist movement to have both evolution and creation presented in the public school classrooms.

Balanced treatment bills took different forms but had a common thread indicating a single source for the form in which the legislation was drafted.[21] This uniformity was the result of the prodigious efforts of Wendell R. Bird, attorney for the Institute for Creation Research in California. Bird was well suited to this task since he majored in science, history, and political science at Vanderbilt University.[22] He had been an editor with the *Yale Law Journal,* in which he published an important note on the matter of balanced treatment.[23]

The balanced treatment approach had its test case in Arkansas, the disposition of which was not favorable to creationism. *McLean v. Arkansas* was only a federal district court case and had no precedential value, but its persuasive authority far exceeded its legal authority.[24] Within the opinion several elements of the Arkansas Balanced Treatment Act are enumerated:

(1) Sudden creation of the universe, energy, and life from nothing; (2) The insufficiency of mutation and natural selection in bringing about the development of all living kinds from a single organism; (3) Changes only within fixed limits of originally created kinds of plants and animals; (4) Separate ancestry of humans and apes; (5) Explanation of the earth's geology by catastrophism, including the occurrence of a worldwide flood; and (6) A relatively recent inception of the earth and living kinds.[25]

A variety of similarities can be observed when one compares this Arkansas bill with others:

State	Sudden Creation from Nothing	No Evolution from Single Organism	Changes Within Fixed Limits	Separate Ancestry for Humans and Apes	Catastrophism or Worldwide Flood	Recent Earth
Georgia	Yes	Ambiguous	Only inferred	Ambiguous	No	No
Missouri	Yes	Yes	Yes	Yes	Yes	Yes
Oklahoma	Yes	Yes	Yes	Yes	Yes	Yes
South Dakota	Yes	Yes	Yes	Yes	Yes	Yes
Texas	Yes	Yes	Yes	Yes	Yes	Yes
Washington	Yes	Yes	Yes	Yes	Yes	Yes

Success of the Balanced Treatment Movement

Several states, as may be seen in the chart, enacted legislation, but none have survived the defeat of the idea of balanced presentation of evolution and creation that came out of *McLean*.[26] The U.S. Supreme Court case of *Edwards v. Aguillard* struck down the Louisiana Balanced Treatment law.[27]

The Evolution-Creation Controversy in the Courts

The issue of whether alternate paradigms of origins may be offered within the public schools has been a cultural and educational controversy since the Scopes trial in 1925.[28] Repeated efforts were made to introduce legislation blocking the introduction of the teaching of evolution in public classrooms in the first half of the twentieth century.[29] During much of the latter half of the twentieth century, the efforts were to prohibit the teaching of scientific evidence for a creationist paradigm of origins.[30] Creationism has primarily been contested through the court system. I will limit discussion to only a few of the court cases that have challenged the creation model of origins.[31]

Epperson v. Arkansas

From 1927 until 1967 the legal landscape regarding the teaching of evolution was fairly quiet, but after the one hundredth anniversary of Darwin's *The Origin of Species* in 1959, there was a major proevolution push in the schools of the United States. In response, there also were attempts to restrict the teaching of evolution.

Approximately forty years after Scopes was tried, the legislature of Arkansas passed a statute that prohibited any teacher in a state-supported school or university "to teach the theory or doctrine that mankind ascended or descended from a lower order of animals" or "to adopt or use in any such institution a textbook that teaches [this theory]." The statute reads:

> It shall be unlawful for any teacher or other instructor in any University, College, Normal, Public School, or other institution of the State, which is supported in whole or in part from public funds derived by State and local taxation to teach the theory or doctrine that mankind ascended or descended from a lower order of animals and also it shall be unlawful for any teacher, textbook commission, or other authority exercising the power to select textbooks for above mentioned educational institutions to adopt or use in any such institution a textbook that teaches the doctrine or theory that mankind descended or ascended from a lower order of animals. [32]

The act was violated by a young teacher named Susan Epperson, who was hired to teach tenth grade biology in the Little Rock school system. She initiated an action in the Chancery Court of Arkansas, asking that the Arkansas statute be declared void and to enjoin the state from dismissing her for using a textbook in violation of the state law.[33]

The Chancery Court concurred with Epperson and found the state statute in violation of the First[34] and Fourteenth Amendments,[35] but on appeal the Arkansas Supreme Court reversed the lower court.[36] Since the state legislature was deemed to have constitutional authority to make such a law, in reasoning similar to the Tennessee Supreme Court finding in Scopes, the supreme court of Arkansas said that "statutes pertaining to teaching of theory of evolution is constitutional exercise of state's powers to specify curriculum in public schools."[37]

On appeal, the U.S. Supreme Court in *Epperson v. Arkansas* (1968) reversed the Arkansas Supreme Court on grounds of infringement of First and Fourteenth Amendment grounds.[38] The court chose not to address the matter of Free Exercise of Religion,[39] but rather ruled that the law violated the establishment clause of the Constitution:

> [T]he law must be stricken because of its conflict with the constitutional prohibition of state laws respecting an establishment of religion or prohibiting the free exercise thereof. The overriding fact is that Arkansas' law selects from the body of knowledge a particular segment which it proscribes for the sole reason that it is deemed to conflict with a particular religious doctrine; that is, with a particular interpretation of the Book of Genesis by a particular religious group.[40]

In making its decision that the state's law violated the establishment clause, it offered no proof other than averring that the law was similar to the Tennessee statute under which Scopes was tried.[41] The Court did not define "religion" nor indicate how the state could satisfy the requirement that the law be secular.[42] As in subsequent opinions by the U.S. Supreme Court regarding laws on creation, the Court questions the sincerity of the legislature in passing the law, suggesting that the legislators sought to slip the biblical account of creation into law:

> Its antecedent, Tennessee's "monkey law," candidly stated its purpose: to make it unlawful "to teach any theory that denies the story of Divine creation of man as taught in the Bible, and to teach instead that man has descended from a lower order of animals." Perhaps the sensational publicity attendant upon the Scopes trial induced Arkansas to adopt less explicit language. It eliminated Tennessee's reference to the "story of the Divine Creation of man" as taught in the Bible, but there is no doubt that the motivation for the law was the same: to suppress the teaching of a theory which, it was thought, "denied" the divine creation of man.[43]

Part of the difficulty in understanding the *Epperson* decision is that the Supreme Court fails to explain how the statute lacked a secular purpose. This is especially troubling since legislative intent or purpose is difficult to define, and in fact it does not do so in this case.[44] Such questionable efforts by the Court are rebuffed by constitutional scholar John Hart Ely, who has said, "The Court should stop pretending it does not remember principles for deciding on what occasions and in what ways the motivation of legislators or other government officials is [sic] relevant to constitutional issues."[45]

This failure to accept legislative intent is uncharacteristic of the Court,[46] but has become increasingly frequent when dealing with religious participation in the political process.[47] Nonetheless the secular purpose test is severely flawed, as Hall explains:

> Motivation analysis could be used to invalidate a wide variety of laws under the establishment clause. Although religion is largely ignored by political scientists, studies indicate that religion frequently plays a major role in the political process. Religious persons frequently vote as a block on referenda. Epperson suggests that these referenda therefore might violate the establishment clause. Furthermore, religious groups have played a key role in conservative and liberal legislation, such as prohibition, civil rights, and welfare legislation. The Court's analysis in McGowan and Edwards suggests that the activity of these religious groups may have invalidated the resulting legislation.[48]

The Court's desire for neutrality in religious matters says that the state "may not be hostile to any religion or to the advocacy of nonreligion; and it may not aid, foster, or promote one religion or religious theory against another. . . . The First Amendment mandates governmental neutrality between religion and religion, and between religion and nonreligion."[49] If Arkansas had simply eliminated the teaching on the origin of man altogether, this presumably would have been satisfactory:

> Arkansas' law cannot be defended as an act of religious neutrality. Arkansas did not seek to excise from the curricula of its schools and universities all discussion of the origin of man. The law's efforts was confined to an attempt to blot out a particular theory because of its supposed conflict with the Biblical account, literally read.[50]

Moreover, the Court said that the Fourteenth Amendment was also violated, but it considered analysis of this amendment unneeded in light of First Amendment religion violations.[51] Justice Fortas, delivering the judgment of the Court, reflecting on *Meyer v. Nebraska*,[52] said, "Today's problem is capable of resolution in the narrower terms of the First Amendment's prohibition of laws respecting an establishment of religion or prohibiting the free exercise thereof."[53]

The Tennessee Law of 1973

One of the major laws post-Scopes, sometimes called the antimonkey or antievolution laws, was passed by the Tennessee legislature in 1973. The legislature attempted to avoid the appearance of prohibition that had damaged the Butler Act. The 1973 law simply said that no textbook used in the state present evolution as scientific fact. It must be referred to as a theory. Additionally, if evolution was presented in a textbook, alternate theories, including the Genesis account, also had to be presented.[54]

No sooner had the law been passed than it was challenged.[55] Two years later, the U.S. Sixth Circuit Court declared the Tennessee law "patently unconstitutional," based on the view that the provisions of the first amendment establishment clause could be applied against the states.[56] The court used the three-prong test established in *Lemon v. Kurtzman*, in which the U.S. Supreme Court articulated how an establishment of the First Amendment might be determined:[57]

> First, the statute must have a secular legislative purpose; second, its principal or primary effect must be one that neither advances nor inhibits religion, *Board of Education v. Allen, 392 U.S. 236, 243 (1968)*; finally, the statute must not foster "an excessive government entanglement with religion."[58]

The circuit court ruled that, though the law did not forbid the teaching of evolution, it did prefer the biblical version of creation over any scientific theory: "We believe that in several respects the statute under consideration is unconstitutional on its face, that no state court interpretation of it can save it, and that in this case, the District Court clearly erred in abstaining from rendering a determination of the unconstitutionality of the statute on its face."[59]

The rationale of the court was that the law required, if evolution is taught, that the biblical account of origins also be taught, and that all theories but the biblical account had to have a disclaimer. This clearly preferred the biblical version of creation, in the court's opinion, to scientific views based on scientific reasoning. Such an approach, the court believed, would establish religion in violation of the first prong of the Lemon test.

Additionally, such action on the part of the state would violate the third test against entanglement with religion.[60]

Whenever you hear on the news about a violation of church and state, it is usually based on a court's interpretation of the Lemon test. Some have said that the Lemon test is aptly named and believe that the tests are artificial creations of the Supreme Court, often incapable of being properly applied. Therefore the test should be abandoned. The Court has been very slow to do so.

Daniel v. Waters

Several other cases could be discussed, but *Daniel v. Waters*[61] (1975) is important because it contributed to several federal court decisions, including *McLean v. Arkansas Board of Education* et al.,[62] and *Edwards v. Aguillard*.[63] In *Daniel* the Sixth Circuit used the three Lemon tests mentioned above, to determine that the state had violated the Establishment Clause of the First Amendment.[64] The court held that the Tennessee law preferred the biblical version of creation over a scientific perspective, violating the establishment clause of the First Amendment. Joyce Francis relates, "Just as Scopes had launched the creation-evolution controversy, Daniel launched the balanced treatment aspect of the controversy."[65]

McLean v. Arkansas Board of Education

McLean v. Arkansas Board of Education (1982) is a federal court decision that has significance far beyond the importance it should have, since it is a court of original jurisdiction and so has no binding authority over other states.[66] However, it has often been quoted by other courts on cases dealing with teaching evolution and creation in the government schools.

Arkansas passed a law mandating the balanced treatment of evolution and creation. The federal district judge ruled that the law[67] violated the establishment clause of the U.S. Constitution as it applied to the Fourteenth Amendment.[68]

Judge William Overton said that the act was an attempt by religious fundamentalists to impose their beliefs of an inerrant Scripture on the schools, and that he would judge the case using the standards set forth in *Lemon*.[69] He said, "First, the statute must have a secular legislative purpose; second, its principal or primary effect must be one that neither advances nor inhibits religion . . . ; finally, the statute must not foster 'an excessive

197

government entanglement with religion.'"[70] The judge held that the statute violated the First Amendment prohibition against establishment of religion because

> the statute was simply and purely an effort to introduce the Biblical version of creation into public school curriculum and thus its specific purpose was to advance religion, the fact that creation science was inspired by the Book of Genesis and that statutory definition of creation science was consistent with a literal interpretation of Genesis left no doubt that primary effect of the statute was advancement of particular religious beliefs. Thus, continuing involvement of state officials in questions and issues of religious concepts in creation science created excessive and prohibited entanglement with religion.[71]

One observes in *McLean* a radically different disposition on the part of the judge. Judge Overton demonstrated extreme prejudice against the defendants, and went to substantial effort to demonstrate that "creation-science" was not science.[72]

There were several irregularities during the trial.[73] Though the trial was not a circus like *Scopes*, it was highly publicized, and facts about the law and the trial were sometimes misrepresented.[74] The State of Arkansas was at a considerable disadvantage since the ACLU had twenty-two lawyers working full-time, while the state of Arkansas had but six.[75]

McLean is the first decision in which a federal court had ruled that simply the mention of creation in school was a religious teaching, per se, and that naturalism was a necessary element of science.[76] The judge said that mention of a sudden creation of the universe out of nothing was "inescapable religiosity"[77] and required a deity as is believed in Western religions.[78] Judge Overton then set forth what he considered to be necessary elements of science:

1. It is guided by natural law;
2. It has to be explanatory by reference to natural law;
3. It is testable against the empirical world;
4. Its conclusions are tentative, i.e., are not necessarily the final word; and
5. It is falsifiable (Ruse and other science witnesses).[79]

Judge Overton's analysis falls far short of demonstrating his thesis under his five elements. First the definition of religion as given by the U.S. Supreme Court demands ultimate commitment rather than simply acknowledging the existence of a deity.[80] Second, if one excludes religion as a source for science, then many of the great scientific discoveries of the past would be viewed as nonscientific.[81] Third, the definition of science that Judge Overton posits does not agree with the definition found in the literature of the philosophy of science:

> The *McLean* definition does not resemble, or come close to resembling, any definition of science existing in the philosophy of science literature, and has not been endorsed subsequently by any philosopher of science, except by certain courtroom witnesses from the *McLean* trial. The witness on whose testimony the judge's opinion was based, Ruse, later revised his points and offered a six-point list of major characteristics.[82]

Moreover, Larry Laudan, a philosopher of science, says regarding the definition of science in *McLean*:

> Once the dust has settled, however, the trial in general and Judge William R. Overton's ruling in particular may come back to haunt us; for, although the verdict itself is probably to be commended, it was reached for all the wrong reasons and by a chain of argument which is hopelessly suspect. Indeed, the ruling rests on a host of misrepresentations of what science is and how it works.
>
> The heart of Judge Overton's Opinion is a formulation of "the essential characteristics of science." These characteristics serve as touchstones for contrasting evolutionary theory with Creationism; they lead Judge Overton ultimately to the claim, specious in its own right, that since Creationism is not "science," it must be religion. . . .
>
> The victory in the Arkansas case was hollow, for it was achieved only at the expense of perpetuating and canonizing a false stereotype of what science is and how it works. If it goes unchallenged by the scientific community, it will raise grave doubts about that community's intellectual integrity. No one familiar with the issues can really believe that anything important was settled through anachronistic

efforts to revive a variety of discredited criteria for distinguishing between the scientific and the nonscientific.[83]

Then Laudan specifically addresses the characteristics used by Overton and mentioned above.

"[McLean] offered five 'essential characteristics of science.' I have shown that there are respectable examples of science which violate each of Overton's desiderata, and moreover that there are many activities we do not regard as science which satisfy many of them."[84]

Another scientist, Philip Quinn, also rejects these criteria:

> Unfortunately, it is all too clear that it is unsound. The problem is that [the McLean definition] is demonstrably false. None of the characteristics it alleges to be necessary conditions for an individual statement to have scientific status is, in fact, a necessary condition of scientific status of an individual statement.[85]

Judge Overton's definition of science and its concomitant rejection of creation is built on a faulty legal and philosophical foundation.

Edwards v. Aguillard

The major case dealing with the "model legislation" is *Edwards v. Aguillard* (1987).[86] The state of Louisiana passed a law[87] similar to that enacted by Arkansas.[88] A group of educators, religious leaders, and parents challenged the constitutional standing of the statute. The federal district court held that the act violated the state constitution. After going through the state courts of Louisiana,[89] the U.S. District Court[90] and the Fifth Circuit Court of Appeals,[91] it worked itself to the U.S. Supreme Court.

The Supreme Court, in 1987, ruled that the Louisiana act was unconstitutional because it had the primary purpose of advancing religion.[92] It used the well-known Lemon three prongs to determine this,[93] though it found no reason to judge the statute under the second and third test since it believed the act failed to meet the first test, that of secular purpose.[94] It states that if the "law was enacted for the purpose of endorsing religion, 'no consideration of the second or third criteria [of Lemon] is necessary.' . . . In this case, appellants have identified no clear secular purpose for the Louisiana Act."[95]

Also, the Court held that the statute undercut academic freedom and served no secular purpose when it prohibited the teaching of evolution unless creation science was taught.[96]

> If the Louisiana Legislature's purpose was solely to maximize the comprehensiveness and effectiveness of science instruction, it would have encouraged the teaching of all scientific theories about the origins of humankind. But under the Act's requirements, teachers who were once free to teach any and all facets of this subject are now unable to do so. Moreover, the Act fails even to ensure that creation science will be taught, but instead requires the teaching of this theory only when the theory of evolution is taught. Thus we agree with the Court of Appeals' conclusion that the Act does not serve to protect academic freedom, but has the distinctly different purpose of discrediting "evolution by counterbalancing its teaching at every turn with the teaching of creationism. . . ."[97]

The U.S. Supreme Court did not totally close the door to teaching creation but indicated that it could have a secular purpose if the law mandated divergent scientific theories be taught:

> We do not imply that a legislature could never require that scientific critiques of prevailing scientific theories be taught. Indeed, the Court acknowledged in Stone that its decision forbidding the posting of the Ten Commandments did not mean that no use could ever be made of the Ten Commandments, or that the Ten Commandments played an exclusively religious role in the history of Western Civilization. . . . In a similar way, teaching a variety of scientific theories about the origins of humankind to schoolchildren might be validly done with the clear secular intent of enhancing the effectiveness of science instruction. But because the primary purpose of the Creationism Act is to endorse a particular religious doctrine, the Act furthers religion in violation of the Establishment Clause.[98]

The dissenting opinion by Justice Scalia, joined by Chief Justice William Rehnquist, reprimanded the majority for rejecting the statements of the members of the legislature regarding the purpose for the act,[99] as well as the definition of creation science given by the legislature.[100]

Though the Supreme Court in *Edwards* did invalidate the Louisiana law, it is less restrictive than *McLean*, as seen in a newsletter from the Creation Science Legal Defense Fund:

> The U.S. Supreme Court today held that Louisiana's "Act for Balanced Treatment of Creation-Science and Evolution" is unconstitutional because it had an unconstitutional *legislative purpose.* "The Act violates the Establishment Clause of the First Amendment because it seeks to employ the symbolic and financial support of government to achieve a religious purpose." (P. 17.)

> However, the Court ruling was narrow and did *not* say that teaching creation-science is *necessarily* unconstitutional *if* adopted for a secular purpose. In fact, the Court said the exact opposite:

> "[T]eaching a variety of scientific theories about the origins of humankind to schoolchildren might be validly done with the clear secular intent of enhancing the effectiveness of science instruction." (P. 14.)[101]

The letter also has an evaluation by Bird, who argued the case before the Supreme Court,

> . . . we are disappointed that the Supreme Court majority struck down the Louisiana law for an allegedly nonsecular purpose, but delighted that it did *not* say that balanced treatment for creation-science and evolution necessarily advances religion with an impermissible purpose.[102]

Should we be optimistic about the possibility of finally getting a favorable hearing in the courts? Much of this depends on how this issue is handled in the future by judges, legislators, and interest groups.[103]

Federal Circuit Court Cases

Since the decision in *Edwards*[104] a number of other cases have arisen in the federal appellate system, all of which reveal that courts tend to be prejudiced at present against the teaching of creationism in the school system and do not accept the fact that evolution promotes a religious view. We will only briefly look at these lower court decisions before turning to an analysis of what approach might be successful.

Mozert v. Hawkins County Board of Education

Ten years after the *Daniel* decision, a district court of Tennessee was presented with *Mozert v. Hawkins County Board of Education* (1987),[105] a case in which students and parents found offensive a textbook that taught the theory of evolution, and other objectionable material.[106] Initially the children were allowed to read an older text not containing the objectionable material, but afterward the school board decided that all students had to use the approved textbook. The students, in their suit, alleged that they were being required to read schoolbooks that inculcated values in violation of their religious beliefs. This was a violation of their free exercise of religion.[107]

The district court held that the school board "has effectively required that the student plaintiffs either read the offensive texts or give up their free public education."[108] However, the Sixth Circuit Court reversed the lower court, holding that the requirement did not burden their rights of free exercise. The court noted that omitting all objectionable topics would be the only way to avoid the conflict and this would violate establishment articulated in the *Epperson* decision, in which "the Supreme Court has clearly held that it violates the Establishment Clause to tailor a public school's curriculum to satisfy the principles or prohibitions of any religion."[109] The Court continued that, even if the plaintiffs might find some of the material in the schoolbooks to be offensive, no student was "required to affirm his or her belief or disbelief in any idea or practice mentioned in the various stories and passages contained in the Holt series."[110] In order to trigger a violation of free exercise, "a litigant must show that challenged state action has a coercive effect that operates against a litigant's practice of his or her religion."[111]

Webster v. New Lenox School District

In *Webster v. New Lenox School District*[112] (1990), the issue was that a school district prohibited a public school teacher from teaching theories other than evolution in his classroom[113] to which he responded that this prohibition violated his First[114] and Fourteenth[115] Amendment rights. The school district argued that Webster's actions were an establishment of religion.[116]

The Seventh Circuit Court agreed with the school district that a teacher may be proscribed from teaching creation so as not to violate the establishment of religion,[117] and that such prohibition was not a violation of his free speech rights since allowing him the right to teach creation would be a form of religious advocacy.[118] The Seventh Circuit, in rejecting Webster's claim, said that the First Amendment is not "a teacher license for uncontrolled expression at variance with established curricular content."[119]

The court's analysis is troubling since it never explains how Mr. Webster's actions established religion, and how his intent to "explore alternate viewpoints was any form of indoctrination. In addition, the court does not offer any criteria for distinguishing religious from secular teaching."[120]

Bishop v. Aronov

Bishop v. Aronov (1991) is different from the former cases in that a university professor brought action against a university board of trustees.[121] He was enjoined from introducing religious beliefs during his class time, and he was not allowed to conduct optional classes to discuss religious perspectives on different academic topics.[122] Since this was a college level course, one would think the court would not have been so concerned since the students would not be impressionable.[123] Nor were the classes mandatory.[124]

The federal district court gave Bishop a summary judgment, having determined that the "University had created a forum for students and their professors to engage in a free interchange of ideas,"[125] relying on *Widmar v. Vincent.*[126] The court also held that Professor Bishop had a primary secular purpose that did not violate the establishment clause.[127]

The Seventh Circuit Court of Appeals reversed the district court, denying that the university's actions infringed on the professor's free speech or established religion.[128] It said that the university is not a public forum in which the professor had a right to express views contrary to those directed by the university.[129]

The appeals court makes a number of faulty arguments.[130] It does not develop a meaningful understanding of academic freedom with the framework of the university.[131] Additionally, its perspective on a public forum[132] does not distinguish between the varying criteria for a primary and secondary school from that of a university.[133] Also, the court used a rational basis standard of review rather than a strict scrutiny standard since viewpoint discrimination was at issue.[134]

Freiler v. Tangipahoa Parish Board of Education

In *Freiler v. Tangipahoa Parish Board of Education* (1999, 2000),[135] a board of education approved a disclaimer in the endorsement of evolution.[136] The disclaimer read that the phrase was "not intended to influence or dissuade the Biblical version of Creation."[137] After being challenged[138] the U.S. District Court held that it could not find any secular purpose for the disclaimer[139] and found this resolution an unconstitutional violation of the establishment clause.[140]

On appeal, the Fifth Circuit upheld the decision of the lower court, using a number of legal tests, including *Lemon* and the endorsement tests.[141] What is most interesting about this case is that this is the first court that uses the term *intelligent design*, and equates it with the teaching of creation science.[142]

The Teaching of Intelligent Design in Public Schools

Intelligent design is a scientific theory that was formulated in the 1980s and 1990s by a group of scholars dissatisfied by neo-Darwinian accounts of life. Many, if not most, of these scholars were not biblical creationists under the *McLean* definition of *creationism*. Intelligent design thus holds that some aspects of the universe are best explained by an intelligent cause rather than an undirected cause such as natural selection. The theory aims to detect specified and complex information in nature, which is taken as a reliable indicator of design.

In contrast to creationism, design theory does not try to specify the age of the earth, nor does it try to address religious questions about the identity of the designer or determine whether the designer is natural or supernatural. Given that the intelligent design movement includes both theists and nontheists of various religious viewpoints, it seems clear that the theory is not focused around a particular interpretation of Scripture. Rather, philosopher Antony Flew, atheist turned theist, stated, "the findings of more than fifty years of DNA research have provided materials for a new and enormously powerful argument to design."[143] The intelligent design movement is united around such a core conviction that design in nature is real, and that it is empirically detectable through scientific methods.

Is Intelligent Design Science?

Much of the difficulty of the origins debate relates to the definition of *science* and *religion*. The Oxford Dictionary defines science as "A branch of study which is concerned either with a connected body of demonstrated truths or with observed facts systematically classified and more or less colligated by being brought under general laws, and which includes trustworthy methods for the discovery of new truth within its own domain."[144] The emphasis in this definition is on demonstration and observation for the purpose of further study.

This definition, however, may be inadequate, since some view science as also referring to a system or a worldview that is based upon what are considered to be facts. Under this definition, science would be a philosophy. Related to this perspective of "science as philosophy" is the nature of "commonsense assumptions" that are made by scientists. For example, science operates from an assumption that an external world exists. That assumption might be debated philosophically, since this is understood through sense organs and it is not certain how accurate the senses are. Science depends as well on an assumption that the external world works in an orderly fashion and that the external world is knowable. The existence of truth and laws of logic must be assumed by scientists, along with the reliability of our cognitive and sensory faculties to serve as truth-gatherers. There must be a source of justified beliefs in our intellectual environment. Science as a discipline assumes the adequacy of language to describe the world. The importance of some working values is assumed (e.g., "test theories fairly and report test results honestly"). Those who practice science assume the uniformity of nature and induction and the existence of numbers.[145]

When Is Science Not Really Scientific?

Science, then, is not devoid of presuppositions or free of circular reasoning. If a "watchmaker" is carefully excluded at the beginning, we need not be surprised if no "watchmaker" appears at the end. Speaking of the thinking of Michael Polanyi, in his book *Personal Knowledge*, Donald Calbreath says,

> The scientist enters into a study with certain preconceived notions and interprets the results of the study with the same preconceived

notions. True objectivity simply does not exist in the scientific world. A creationist and an evolutionist can agree on the data, the physically observable phenomena (whether it be the distribution of radioisotopes in a given geological structure or the bone formations of a living animal or fossil). They will then proceed to interpret that data according to their own presuppositions ("God created this" or "It all happened by accident"). Both employ the same data, but reach strikingly different conclusions.[146]

Science as a method of seeking to discover truth should be distinguished from scientism, a commitment to a supposed scientific method at the expense of truth. J. P. Moreland observes,

> Scientism is the view that science is the very paradigm of truth and rationality. If something does not square with currently well-established scientific beliefs, if it is not within the domain of entities appropriate for scientific investigation, or if it is not amenable to scientific methodology, then it is not true or rational. Everything outside of science is a matter of mere belief and subjective opinion, of which rational assessment is impossible. Science, exclusively and ideally, is our model of intellectual excellence.[147]

Moreland distinguishes between strong and weak scientism:

> Note first that strong scientism [there are no truths apart from scientific truths; all truths must be tested according to scientific methodology] is self-refuting. A proposition (or sentence) is self-refuting if it refers to and falsifies itself. For example, "There are no English sentences" and "There are no truths" are self-refuting. Strong scientism is not itself a proposition *of* science, but a second-order proposition *of* philosophy *about* science to the effect that only scientific propositions are true or rational to believe. And strong scientism is itself offered as a true, rationally justified position to believe.
>
> There are two more problems that count equally against strong and weak scientism. First, scientism (in both forms) does not adequately allow for the task of stating and defending the necessary presuppositions for science itself to be practiced (assuming scientific realism). Thus scientism shows itself to be a foe and not a friend of science.

Science cannot be practiced in thin air. In fact, science itself presupposes a number of substantive philosophical theses that must be assumed if science is even going to get off the runway. Each of these assumptions has been challenged, and the task of stating and defending these assumptions is one of the tasks of philosophy. The conclusions of science cannot be more certain than the presuppositions it rests on and uses to reach those conclusions.

There is a second problem that counts equally against strong and weak scientism: the existence of true and rationally justified beliefs outside of science. The simple fact is that true, rationally justified beliefs exist in a host of fields outside of science. Strong scientism does not allow for this fact, and it is therefore to be rejected as an inadequate account of our intellectual enterprise.[148]

Has the *McLean* Decision Disqualified Intelligent Design as Science?

Judge Overton set forth standards for determining what qualifies as science. We have already seen that these do not square with the current definition of science.[149] While intelligent design lacks components of young earth creationism, many critics assert that it refers to the supernatural and thus might fail Overton's criteria that science must be explained by natural laws.[150]

First, it is not clear that this is a proper criterion for science. This simplistic guide excludes much of what is understood by most scientists as true science. Take, for example, the distinction between existence and explanation:

> For centuries scientists have recognized a difference between establishing the existence of a phenomenon and explaining that phenomenon in a lawlike way. Our ultimate goal, no doubt, is to do both. But to suggest, as the *McLean* Opinion does repeatedly, that an existence claim . . . is unscientific until we have found the laws on which the alleged phenomenon depends is simply outrageous. Galileo and Newton took themselves to have established the existence of gravitational phenomena, long before anyone was able to give a causal or explanatory account of gravitation. Darwin took himself to have established the existence of natural selection almost a half-century

before geneticists were able to lay out the laws of heredity on which natural selection depended. If we took the *McLean* Opinion criterion seriously, we should have to say that Newton and Darwin were unscientific; and, to take an example from our own time, it would follow that plate tectonics is unscientific because we have not yet identified the laws of physics and chemistry which account for the dynamics of crustal motion.[151]

The denial of *creatio ex nihilo* or a creator as nonscientific, as in *McLean*[152] and followed by at least one federal court,[153] solves no problems for modern science. The big bang assumes that everything came into existence from nothing,[154] and scientists regularly speak of creation, implying creator, in contrast to the eternality of matter with no creator.[155] The universe gives strong indication of an intelligent designer and denial of such makes a distracter appear less than straightforward.[156]

Second, regardless of whether this criterion is legitimate, it is not clear that it even applies to intelligent design. As Dean Kenyon and Percival Davis explain in the *Of Pandas and People* textbook, intelligent design does not even purport to invoke the supernatural:

[T]he place of intelligent design in science has been troubling for more than a century. That is because on the whole, scientists from within Western culture failed to distinguish between intelligence, which can be recognized by uniform sensory experience, and the supernatural, which cannot. Today we recognize that appeals to intelligent design may be considered in science, as illustrated by current NASA search for extraterrestrial intelligence (SETI). Archaeology has pioneered the development of methods for distinguishing the effects of natural and intelligent causes. We should recognize, however, that if we go further, and conclude that the intelligence responsible for biological origins is outside the universe (supernatural) or within it, we do so without the help of science.[157]

Moreover, design theorist William Dembski explains that intelligent design needs not invoke *creatio ex nihilo*: "Intelligent design does not claim that living things came together suddenly in their present form through the efforts of a supernatural creator. Intelligent design is not and never will be a doctrine of creation."[158]

Thus it is not clear that intelligent design would fail Judge Overton's definition of science.

Is Intelligent Design Religious?

The *McLean* opinion argued that creation, by definition, must be viewed as a religious concept,[159] but the Supreme Court has ruled that a religious view consistent with a secular view does not violate the establishment clause.[160] Judge Overton wrote regarding creation out of nothing:

> To the contrary, "creation out of nothing" is a concept unique to Western religions. In traditional Western religious thought, the conception of a creator of the world is a conception of God. Indeed, creation of the world "out of nothing" is the ultimate religious statement because God is the only actor. . . .
>
> The idea of sudden creation from nothing, or creation ex nihilo, is an inherently religious concept. (Vawter, Gilkey, Geisler, Ayala, Blount, Hicks.)
>
> The argument advanced by defendants' witness, Dr. Norman Geisler, that teaching the existence of God is not religious unless the teaching seeks a commitment is contrary to common understanding and contradicts settled case law. . . .[161]

Judge Overton's simplistic understanding of science and religion are clearly revealed here. First, *creatio ex nihilo* did not originate in Western thinking, but was Hebraic in origin—the Christian West borrowing the idea from the Near Eastern view of the Hebrews.[162] Second, as noted, the big bang theory of the origin of the universe presupposes creation out of nothing, but is not an inherently religious theory.[163] Third, the settled law, wrongly stated by Judge Overton, is that religion requires commitment and devotion, not dispassionate analysis of the existence of a higher being.[164] Justice Antonin Scalia recognized this when he affirmed that the idea of a prime mover or designer in ancient Greek thought was not religious in nature.[165] Fourth, *McLean* seems to imply that if something is not scientific, it must be religious, but such thinking has puzzling results for explaining philosophical views that are not scientific but are also not religious.[166] Thus, regardless of whether intelligent design implicates creation *ex nihilo* (which it does not), it is not clear that it therefore would be religion.

Can Intelligent Design Survive Constitutional Challenge?

Given the history of the debate regarding the teaching of biological origins within the classroom in the twentieth century and the eventual enthronement of evolution, the question is whether it is possible for any alternative to evolution constitutionally to be taught in the public schools of the United States.

History records a very hectic past, with attempts by creationists to forbid the teaching of evolution, the inclusion of evolution in textbooks, and the denial of biblical creation. Creationist laws have argued for disclaimers against a denial of biblical creation and against evolution based on its religious nature. Those on either side have demanded the freedom to teach or be taught evolution or to teach or be taught creation as free speech or religion. There was a movement to enact laws requiring that a balanced presentation of evolution and creation be given in public schools if either is taught. Those favoring creation have had limited success through all these attempts and most often outright failure.

With such a history, is the well poisoned, so that no creation theory can receive a fair hearing in the courts or society? Unlike evolution, which is consistent with ancient religions and contemporary secular humanistic religion,[167] but without religious association in the minds of the courts,[168] media, and society at large, the teaching of any nonevolutionary view is immediately identified with the biblical account of creation and even religious fundamentalism.[169]

One commentator has argued that, even if creation could be demonstrated to be scientific, its religious nature would preclude it from being taught. Jay Wexler concedes that intelligent design could be considered science, yet would violate the establishment clause as also being a religious doctrine.[170]

Wexler's argument fails because "design theory does not fit the dictionary definition of religion, or the specific test for religion adopted by the Ninth Circuit in its recent cases concerning the establishment of religion."[171] The circuit court adopted the recommendation of constitutional scholar Laurence Tribe that "anything 'arguably non-religious' should not be considered religious in applying the Establishment Clause.'"[172] In another case, the Ninth Circuit relies on a three-part test to define religion, nearer to the original sense of the establishment of the institution of religion intended by the framers of the First Amendment:[173]

> First, a religion addresses fundamental and ultimate questions having to do with deep and imponderable matters. Second, a religion is comprehensive in nature; it consists of a belief-system as opposed to an isolated teaching. Third, a religion often can be recognized by the presence of certain formal and external signs.[174]

Under these two rulings as articulated by the Ninth Circuit, design theory could survive challenge. Intelligent design does not violate the three-part test. Rather than being an attempt to penetrate "ultimate questions," design theory seeks only to answer a question posed by Darwinian theory and contemporary biologists, namely, "[h]ow did biologists acquire their appearance of design?"[175] In contrast to traditional creationism, the ID proposal relates only to a designer, without identifying the designer or specifying whether the designer is natural or supernatural. Intelligent design is consistent with theism, but that in itself does not render the theory unconstitutional, as Justice Lewis Powell says in his concurring opinion in *Edwards v. Aguillard*: "A decision respecting the subject matter to be taught in public schools does not violate the Establishment Clause simply because the material to be taught 'happens to coincide or harmonize with the tenets of some or all religions.'"[176]

Second, intelligent design does not qualify under the legal definition of religion articulated by the Ninth Circuit concerning a comprehensive belief system "as opposed to an isolated teaching":

> Design theory does not offer a theory of morality or metaphysics, or an opinion on the prospects of an afterlife. It requires neither a belief in divine revelation nor a code of conduct; nor does it purport to uncover the underlying meaning of the universe or to confer inviolable knowledge on its adherents. It is simply a theory about the source of the appearance of design in living organisms. It is a clear example of an "isolated teaching," one that has no necessary connections to any spiritual dogma or church institution. Design theory has no religious pretensions. It simply tries to apply a well-established scientific method to the analysis of biological phenomena.[177]

Third, design theory does not trigger the third part of the suggested test by the Ninth Circuit regarding "formal and external signs." There are no sacraments, no sacred texts, observance of holidays, nor ordination.

In December 2005, the *Kitzmiller v. Dover* case finally provided a legal decision regarding the teaching of intelligent design in a public school. The case began when the school board in Dover, Pennsylvania, required biology teachers to read a short oral disclaimer that mentioned intelligent design as an alternative to evolution.[178] Leading proponents of intelligent design actually opposed the Dover school district's policy because they did not feel that intelligent design should be mandated in schools. But the Dover school district followed the advice of the Thomas More Legal Center, resulting in this lawsuit.

The ACLU and Americans United for the Separation of Church and State filed a lawsuit on behalf of various parents in the district to have the oral disclaimer struck down as unconstitutional. Judge John E. Jones ruled harshly against the school board. Not only did he find that the Dover Area School Board had religious motives, but he issued an extensive holding about whether intelligent design is science. While both sides agree that the school district probably had unconstitutional religious motives, it is interesting to note that scholars on both sides have also agreed that Judge Jones overstepped his bounds by ruling on the question of whether ID is science. [179]

Intelligent design proponents have suggested that Judge Jones misunderstood intelligent design by ruling that it necessarily invokes a supernatural creator, ignoring the fact that pro-ID expert witnesses testified otherwise.[180] Moreover, it appears that Judge Jones got basic facts about intelligent design wrong, as he ruled that design theorists have published no peer-reviewed scientific articles supporting the theory, and that its proponents do not do research into the theory.[181] In a stunning revelation, a report showed that Judge Jones copied 90.9 percent of his ruling's section on whether ID is science essentially verbatim from a brief submitted by the ACLU about a month before the ruling.

The *Kitzmiller* case is not binding upon any other parties and will not be appealed to any higher courts. Thus, the blatant errors, and the judicial copying, and the clear judicial overreach will all diminish the impact this ruling has upon the judiciary.

Conclusion

Intelligent design theory does not bring the same concerns as traditional creationism.[182] In fact, its empirical method of argument, its lack of allusion to the fundamentalist wing of Christianity and Christian theology has brought scorn from creationist groups.[183] If future courts recognize the many flaws in the *Kitzmiller* ruling, it may fare better in the courts and in the classrooms. Such a scenario, balancing design and chance rationales for the origins of the universe and life, should be proposed in school boards,[184] taught in public school classrooms,[185] and presented in legislation.[186] For legislators or teachers who are truly *not* seeking to get the "Bible back into school" but simply want fair representation of all competing scientific theories to be presented to students, intelligent design offers a real possibility to achieve that goal.

A Reply to Francis Collins's Darwinian Arguments for Common Ancestry of Apes and Humans

CASEY LUSKIN AND LOGAN PAUL GAGE

Note from the general editor: This appendix is in response to the arguments for Darwinism and human-chimpanzee common ancestry as put forth by the scientist and Christian evolutionist Francis S. Collins in his widely discussed book, *The Language of God: A Scientist Presents Evidence for Belief* (New York: Free Press, 2006).

Introduction

Francis Collins, respected scientist and director of the National Human Genome Research Institute, recently became a prominent figure in the evolution debate. As a self-described proponent of "theistic evolution"[1] and a Christian, Collins's cachet is his ability to communicate his sympathetic viewpoint on religion.[2] Given the antireligious arguments of leading Darwinists such as Richard Dawkins, Collins's voice is a valuable addition to the evolution debate. Unfortunately, his widely discussed 2006 book, *The Language of God: A Scientist Presents Evidence for Belief,*[3] advances several questionable arguments for a Darwinian account of human-ape common ancestry.

Many assume that if common ancestry is true, then the only viable scientific position is Darwinian evolution—in which all organisms are descended from a common ancestor via random mutations and blind selection. Such an assumption is incorrect: Intelligent design *is not necessarily incompatible with common ancestry*.[4] Even if all organisms on earth share a common ancestor, it does not follow that the primary mechanisms causing the differences between the species must be blind, unguided processes such as natural selection. Nonetheless, Darwin's tree of life (see fig. A.1) is an "icon of evolution" and therefore deserves careful examination.[5]

The authors thank Tim Standish for his helpful comments, which aided the crafting of this response.

Darwin's tree of life—the notion that all living organisms share a universal common ancestor—has faced difficulties in the past few decades. Some leading biologists believe that universal common descent cannot explain the beginning of the tree of life. As W. Ford Doolittle explains, "Molecular phylogenists will have failed to find the 'true tree,' not because their methods are inadequate or because they have chosen the wrong genes, but because the history of life cannot properly be represented as

Figure A.1. Lineage

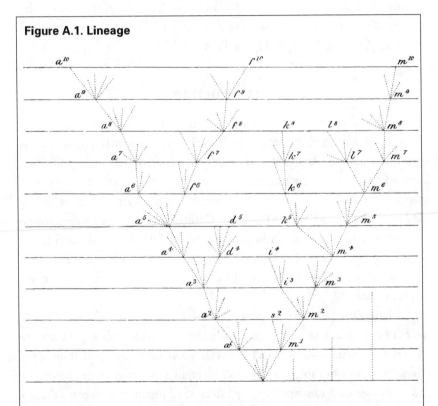

Darwin envisioned the history of life forming a grand tree where all living organisms were descended from a universal common ancestor. In this diagram, the only illustration in Darwin's *The Origin of Species*, Darwin presents his idea that life forms a great "tree of life." Biologists since Darwin have sought to reconstruct this tree of life, but have found that biological traits are often distributed among living organisms in a pattern that does not fit a tree. Many biologists have lamented that life is best represented by a bush, or a tangled thicket, rather than by a nested hierarchy forming a nice, neat tree. The solution to Darwin's tree of life may remain elusive until scientists are willing to consider intelligent design.

a tree."[6] Doolittle, a Darwinist, elsewhere writes that "there would never have been a single cell that could be called the last universal common ancestor."[7] Doolittle attributes his observations to gene-swapping among microorganisms at the base of the tree. But as discussed in chapter 3, Carl Woese finds that such problems exist beyond the base of the tree: "Phylogenetic incongruities [conflicts] can be seen everywhere in the universal tree, from its root to the major branchings within and among the various taxa to the makeup of the primary groupings themselves."[8] A recent study looking at animal relationships concluded, "Despite the amount of data and breadth of taxa analyzed, relationships among most metazoan phyla remained unresolved."[9] Indeed, the Cambrian explosion, during which nearly all of the major living animal phyla (or basic body plans) appeared over 500 million years ago in a geological instant, raises a serious challenge to Darwinian explanations of common descent.[10]

Collins argues for common ancestry at the level of humans and apes rather than focusing on the lower branches of the tree of life. But does common ancestry hold up even at these higher branches? To be sure, if humans and apes share a common ancestor, that would not refute intelligent design. But Collins claims that the evidence for common human-ape ancestry via purely Darwinian means is particularly strong. It is this claim that will be scrutinized here.

To his credit, Collins avoids the usual simplistic argument of claiming that mere genetic similarity is solid evidence for common ancestry. Collins sees through this, noting that genetic similarity "alone does not, of course, prove a common ancestor" because a designer could have "used successful design principles over and over again."[11] Collins is right.

To show how this argument fails by analogy, if one discovers two similar Buicks in a junkyard, one would not conclude one car descended from the other. Rather, one would conclude that intelligent engineers modified plans from the first Buick to make the second. In the same way, genetic similarity between apes (particularly, chimpanzees) and humans—in itself—is compatible with either common descent or common design. For this reason, Collins offers four supplementary arguments for human-ape common ancestry and a Darwinian explanation of human origins:

1. human chromosomal fusion;
2. "junk" DNA in humans and apes;

3. non-coding DNA sequences that have more differences than protein-coding sequences of DNA; and

4. mutations that allegedly caused the evolution of human cognition and language.

Human Chromosomal Fusion

One of the most frequent arguments in favor of human-ape common ancestry is that only common ancestry explains the fact that human chromosome 2 closely resembles chimpanzee chromosomes 2a and 2b.[12] Humans have twenty-three pairs of chromosomes, or forty-six total. Apes such as the chimpanzee have twenty-four pairs of chromosomes, or forty-eight total. Darwinists contend that humans have one less pair of chromosomes than apes because somewhere in the human line, two ape chromosomes became fused into one chromosome. Human chromosome 2 has a structure similar to what one would expect if two chromosomes resembling chimpanzee chromosomes 2a and 2b were fused to one another, end to end. Collins and many other Darwinists claim that this evidence demonstrates common ancestry.

Anyone who compares chimps and humans recognizes a high level of similarity in body structure (also called morphology). Indeed, pre-Darwinian scientists such as Carolus Linnaeus (1707–1778) recognized similarities between species and classified organisms accordingly without assuming common ancestry. Since similar body structures are usually built using similar genes, it is not surprising to learn that our genes are very similar to those of chimps.

We accept that there is good evidence that human chromosome 2 is composed of two fused chromosomes. It seems clear that a chromosomal fusion event took place at some time in our human lineage. This evidence, however, merely confirms something we already knew: humans and chimps have a similar genetic structure. As Collins reminds us, genetic similarity does not prove common ancestry, for genetic similarity may be the result of functional requirements, in this case possibly implicating common design.[13]

Evidence for chromosomal fusion in humans simply indicates that, at some point within our human lineage, two chromosomes became fused. This tells us nothing about whether we share a common ancestor with apes.

Neither Collins nor any other Darwinist of whom we are aware speculates that this fusion event caused our ancestors to *become* human. The fusion evidence merely tells us that our ancestors—whether essentially human or otherwise—once had forty-eight chromosomes. It does not tell us whether our ancestors were related to modern apes.

Predictions of Comparative Morphology?

The Darwinist might respond, "But this evidence shows that our ancestors once had forty-eight chromosomes, just like chimpanzees and other apes. We would expect to see a fused chromosome in humans because that explains the data with the least number of genetic changes in species over evolutionary time. Moreover, our fused chromosome 2 contains segments resembling ape chromosomes 2a and 2b. Evolution would have predicted this evidence, so this confirms that prediction and demonstrates common descent." While they may be correct that a prediction of Darwinian theory has been fulfilled, our chromosomal fusion could have been expected based upon observations and arguments that have nothing to do with Darwinism.

The Darwinist response merely restates the fact that humans and apes (like the chimpanzee) share a similar genetic structure. But long before the evidence for human chromosomal fusion was discovered, we knew about the high genetic similarity between humans and chimps. Moreover, long before we knew about the high level of genetic similarity, we knew that humans and chimps shared a similar morphology. Since our DNA largely determines organismal form, this high level of human-chimp genetic similarity could have been predicted without any knowledge of evolution, based upon observations of human and chimp morphological similarity alone. After all, similar designs usually imply a similar blueprint. Thus, this fusion evidence is not *independent* evidence for common ancestry. Yet as will be seen, the chromosomal fusion evidence simply strengthens the evidence for genetic similarity between chimps and humans. Since similarity could have been expected apart from Darwinism and common ancestry, similarities between organisms may just as easily be the result of functional requirements implemented via common design.

In *The Language of God*, Collins shows the highly similar karyotypes (i.e., sets of chromosomes) of chimps and humans.[14] Should this similarity be surprising? As noted, morphological studies observe that humans and chimps are very similar in their body plan. Again, this similar morphology implies a similar genetic blueprint. Even if we had no concept of common ancestry, we would still *expect* that both species would share similar genetic blueprints, including their chromosomal scheme.

Now consider a hypothetical scenario where human chromosome 2 becomes unfused. In this case, humans would now have forty-eight chromosomes like chimpanzees. This hypothetical karyotype would closely resemble the chimp karyotype. Evidence for chromosomal fusion strengthens our already-strong knowledge that humans and chimps have a similar genetic makeup. But that's all the fusion evidence actually demonstrates.

A Thought Experiment: "The Doublefusers"

As a final illustration of why the chromosomal fusion evidence does not logically provide special evidence for human-ape common ancestry, consider this hypothetical scenario. Assume that in 2015, two members of a small, isolated tribe of humans, who have never had contact with modern civilization, experience a second chromosomal fusion event. Within a few generations, this trait spreads throughout the small tribe until all members have twenty-two pairs of chromosomes (they remain fertile and normal in all other respects). We'll call the tribe the *"Doublefuser"* people. In 2100, war, famine, and sickness kill off the entire human race except for this remote tribe, and the human species experiences a genetic bottleneck. Many centuries later, the descendants of the *Doublefuser* tribe repopulate the earth and rediscover genetics and Darwinian evolution.

The technologically advanced *Doublefusers* examine their karyotype and proclaim, *"Wow, we humans have two pairs of fused chromosomes. Were we to unfuse these two pairs, our karyotype looks just like a chimp karyotype. These two fusion events show that we share common ancestry with apes."*

But of course, from our present vantage point, we understand the second pair of fused chromosomes in *Doublefusers* has nothing to do with chimp genetics and is far removed from any hypothetical common ancestor between humans and chimps: The second fusion event took place in 2015, and there's no logical reason why the second fusion event should cause them to infer common ancestry with apes. Yet modern Darwinists view our one pair of fused chromosomes precisely as the *Doublefusers* view their two pairs of fused chromosomes. We know that the second fused chromosome in the *Doublefusers* logically provides no special evidence for chimp-human ancestry. Why should we assume the case must be any different with our one fused chromosome?

Common Design or Common Descent Explain Fusion Evidence

As the illustration demonstrates, the fusion evidence does not tell us whether human chromosomal fusion took place in a line that leads back to a common ancestor with chimps or in an independent line that was designed separately. What it demonstrates is that at one time our lineage had forty-eight chromosomes, similar to current ape genetic structure. As illustrated below, chromosomal fusion can exist in the human lineage without a human-ape common ancestor.

The evidence for human chromosomal fusion does *not* provide independent evidence that humans share a common ancestor with chimps. As seen in figure A.2, the evidence is equally compatible with common ancestry (A) and separate ancestry (B).

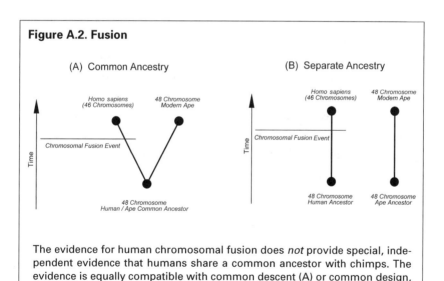

Figure A.2. Fusion

(A) Common Ancestry

Homo sapiens (46 Chromosomes)
48 Chromosome Modern Ape
Chromosomal Fusion Event
48 Chromosome Human / Ape Common Ancestor
Time

(B) Separate Ancestry

Homo sapiens (46 Chromosomes)
48 Chromosome Modern Ape
Chromosomal Fusion Event
48 Chromosome Human Ancestor
48 Chromosome Ape Ancestor
Time

The evidence for human chromosomal fusion does *not* provide special, independent evidence that humans share a common ancestor with chimps. The evidence is equally compatible with common descent (A) or common design, even if there is no common ancestry between the two species (B).

The chromosomal fusion evidence strengthens our knowledge that humans and chimps have similar genetics. But we could have anticipated these genetic similarities without evolution. And Collins himself admits that shared functional similarities between two organisms does little to assist in discriminating between common ancestry and common design with separate ancestry. Thus, the evidence for chromosomal fusion in humans provides no special evidence for common ancestry between humans and apes.

"Junk" DNA in Humans and Apes

Intelligent design can explain functional similarities, but what about non-functional similarities? Like others before him, Collins argues that common ancestry should be inferred from segments of DNA that *appear* to be useless, since such segments are often found to be in the same places in human and chimp chromosomes.

At best, Collins's "junk" DNA arguments explain dysfunction in the genetic text—biological gibberish. What he fails to explain is what generated the biological information in the first place. For this explanation, we must turn to intelligent design.

Intelligent design is primarily a historical science. It studies present-day causes and applies them to the historical record to *infer* the best explanation for natural phenomena. Intelligent design uses uniformitarian reasoning, based upon the principle that "the present is the key to the past."[15] It starts with observations of intelligent agents to establish a cause-and-effect relationship between intelligence and the generation of certain types of information. William Dembski writes that "the defining feature of intelligent causes is their ability to create novel information and, in particular, specified complexity."[16] Stephen Meyer explains that we are justified in inferring design in biology when we find specified complexity:

> [W]e have repeated experience of rational and conscious agents—in particular ourselves—generating or causing increases in complex specified information, both in the form of sequence-specific lines of code and in the form of hierarchically arranged systems of parts. . . . Our experience-based knowledge of information-flow confirms that systems with large amounts of specified complexity (especially codes

and languages) invariably originate from an intelligent source from a mind or personal agent.[17]

Intelligent design accounts for the origin of new genetic information, because in our experience the type of specified and complex information found in human DNA *always* comes from intelligence. In contrast, Collins does not convincingly explain how new functional DNA first originated.

As molecular biologists learn more about DNA, they are continually testing—and refuting—the Darwinian hypothesis that DNA is mainly useless genetic "junk." In the past, Darwinists loudly proclaimed that much of our DNA contained repetitive elements that are meaningless.[18] Darwinists have claimed this major portion of DNA is selfish or parasitic DNA that invades and becomes inserted into our genomes:[19] only eight years ago, Richard Dawkins specifically targeted repetitive DNA as undesigned "junk," writing that "creationists might spend some earnest time speculating on why the Creator should bother to litter genomes with . . . junk tandem repeat DNA."[20]

Collins similarly assumes that these stretches of DNA with a repeating sequence, called "ancient repetitive elements" (AREs), are nonfunctional "genetic flotsam and jetsam."[21] Sounding much like Dawkins, Collins claims that "truncated" or "decapitated" repetitive elements "presen[t] an overwhelming challenge to those who hold to the idea that all species were created ex nihilo."[22] Collins writes, "Unless one is willing to take the position that God has placed these decapitated AREs in these precise positions to confuse and mislead us, the conclusion of a common ancestor for humans and mice is virtually inescapable."[23]

While Collins casts his challenge in theological terms, a scientific assessment is possible. Collins is wrong to make an argument from ignorance and assume that AREs (or "truncated AREs") have no function, merely because no function is currently known. In 2002, evolutionary biologist Richard Sternberg surveyed the literature and found extensive evidence for function in AREs. Sternberg's article concluded that "the selfish DNA narrative and allied frameworks must join the other 'icons' of neo-Darwinian evolutionary theory that, despite their variance with empirical evidence, nevertheless persist in the literature."[24] Reprinted from Sternberg's paper, known genomic/epigenetic roles of REs include:

- satellite repeats forming higher-order nuclear structures;
- satellite repeats forming centromeres;
- satellite repeats and other REs involved in chromatin condensation;
- telomeric tandem repeats and LINE elements;
- subtelomeric nuclear positioning/chromatin boundary elements;
- non-TE interspersed chromatin boundary elements;
- short, interspersed nuclear elements or SINEs as nucleation centers for methylation;
- SINEs as chromatin boundary/insulator elements;
- SINEs involved in cell proliferation;
- SINEs involved in cellular stress responses;
- SINEs involved in translation (may be connected to stress response);
- SINEs involved in binding cohesion to chromosomes; and
- LINEs involved in DNA repair.

Other genetic research continues to uncover functions for allegedly functionless types of repetitive DNA, including SINE,[25] LINE,[26] and ALU elements.[27] Sternberg, along with leading geneticist James A. Shapiro, concludes elsewhere that "one day, we will think of what used to be called 'junk DNA' as a critical component of truly 'expert' cellular control regimes."[28]

Collins asserts that truncated AREs are "junk." But geneticists are constantly disproving the assumption that non-coding DNA is "junk." For example, a 2003 *Scientific American* article, "The Unseen Genome: Gems Among the Junk," explains that types of non-coding DNA were "long ago written off as irrelevant because they yield no proteins."[29] Though written from an evolutionary perspective, the article further says these introns "were immediately assumed to be evolutionary junk"[30] but admits that assumption was hasty. What's more, the author writes that this failure to recognize introns as functional is possibly "one of the biggest mistakes in the history of molecular biology."[31] Similarly, a paper from the *Annals of the New York Academy of Sciences* argues that "neo-Darwinian 'narratives' have been the primary obstacle to elucidating the effects of these enigmatic components of chromosomes," so "a new conceptual framework is needed."[32]

Indeed, the whole notion of "junk" DNA is quickly unraveling, as the *Washington Post* reported: "A project involving hundreds of scientists in 11 countries and detailed in 29 papers" discovered that "the vast majority of the 3 billion 'letters' of the human genetic code are busily toiling at an array of previously invisible tasks."[33] Collins should be wary of repeating the mistaken assumption that types of non-coding DNA have no function, especially when multiple types of functions have been found for AREs.

In another "junk" DNA argument, Collins writes that human pseudogene caspase-12 is functionless and asks, "why would God have gone to the trouble of inserting such a nonfunctional gene in this precise location?"[34] But Collins acknowledges that the caspase-12 gene produces a full-fledged protein in chimps, so this is not a case where humans share a nonfunctional stretch of DNA with another species. There is no evidence that humans inherited the gene's nonfunctional state from a common ancestor with chimps, lending little support to common descent. In fact, 28 percent of people in sub-Saharan Africa have a functioning copy of the caspase-12 gene, as do lower percentages in some other human populations.[35] Collins ignores the obvious explanation that caspase-12 was originally designed to be functional in humans but was rendered nonfunctional by a mutation in most human populations in the very recent past. Like the evidence for chromosomal fusion, this pseudogene tells a story of an event that occurred uniquely within the human lineage and does not necessarily say anything about whether humans share an ancestor with apes.

Functions for other pseudogenes have already been discovered.[36] As with the AREs, why, then, should we assume that even the allegedly broken copy of caspase-12 is functionless "junk"? One study suggested that even in humans with the "premature" stop codon, which is said to turn caspase-12 into a pseudogene, it still produces a "CARD-only protein,"[37] which can be a type of functional protein in humans.[38] The study suggests that the similarity between human caspase-12 and other CARD-only proteins could provide evidence that human caspase-12 interacts in some biological pathways, and it recommends that scientists study the human caspase-12 to determine what it does:

> Since human pseudo-caspase-12 is structurally comparable to ICE-BERG and COP/Pseudo-ICE [CARD-only proteins], it would be interesting to study its involvement in similar pathways.[39]

While the study suggests searching out a function for human caspase-12, Collins makes an argument from ignorance. He would advise that we assume the pseudogene does nothing and stop searching for a function. As in the case of introns, this could be a false Darwinian assumption that hinders research.

It would be more prudent for Collins to acknowledge that functions are already known for many AREs and pseudogenes and to adopt a wait-and-see approach for those types of DNA (like truncated AREs or some other pseudogenes) whose functions we do not yet understand. The history of genetics teaches us not to assume that poorly understood types of DNA are merely functionless junk. And if they aren't functionless junk, this may be another instance where, in Collins's own words, a designer could have "used successful design principles over and over again."[40]

Non-Coding DNA Sequences Have More Differences Than Protein-Coding Sequences of DNA

Despite the rapidly accumulating evidence that non-coding DNA has function, Collins and other Darwinists continue to assume that much non-coding DNA really is "junk."[41] Collins says that "Darwin's theory predicts that mutations that do not affect function (namely, those located in 'junk DNA') will accumulate" more rapidly than those in "the coding regions of the genes."[42] He cites a greater level of differences among species' non-coding DNA than among their protein-coding DNA as evidence that the non-coding DNA is "junk." He assumes that the large differences between non-coding DNA stem from the more-rapid accumulation of random mutations in those allegedly "junk"-filled regions.

Collins's view ignores the hypothesis that non-coding DNA *is* performing a key function, such as controlling gene expression, such that the differences in non-coding DNA have a large influence on organismal development. If this is the case, then the Darwinian "junk" DNA viewpoint has again slowed the progress of science.

In a recent *Time* magazine article, some skeptics of "junk" DNA make precisely this point.[43] They contend that Collins's observation simply demonstrates that many of the genetic differences responsible for physical differences between organisms lie in their non-coding DNA. Because the human genome project revealed that humans have so few genes, the article explains, some scientists have reasoned that the differences between species must be controlled not by genes but by stretches of DNA that *do not code for proteins*. To explain this point, the *Time* article quotes evolutionist Owen Lovejoy:

> This shockingly small number made it clear to scientists that genes alone don't dictate the differences between species; the changes, they now know, also depend on molecular switches that tell genes when and where to turn on and off. "Take the genes involved in creating the hand, the penis and the vertebrae," says Lovejoy. "These share some of the same structural genes. The pelvis is another example. Humans have a radically different pelvis from that of apes. It's like having the blueprints for two different brick houses. The bricks are the same, but the results are very different."[44]

Indeed, a recent article in *Nature* titled, "It's the junk that makes us human," argues this same point:

> Anyone who has ever put together self-assembly furniture knows that having the right parts is important, but what you do with them can make or break the project. The same seems to be true of the vast amounts of DNA in an organism's genome that used to be labelled as junk. Studies now indicate that this DNA may be responsible for the signals that were crucial for human evolution, directing the various components of our genome to work differently from the way they do in other organisms.
>
> The findings seem to bolster a 30-year-old hypothesis that gene regulation—not the creation of new genes—has moulded the traits that make us unique.
>
> The latest work looks for regions of the genome that have changed rapidly in human evolution, based on the theory that they are most likely to have shaped our differences from other animals. But instead of hunting for rapidly evolving DNA in genes, researchers are starting to look at non-coding DNA—stretches of DNA that don't encode proteins.[45]

Thus, the higher level of differences between non-coding DNA is not evidence that it is merely "junk" that is accumulating random mutations at a higher rate than protein-coding DNA. Rather, the large differences show that non-coding DNA has functionality that controls gene expression, which is important for determining the physical characteristics of an organism. This model accounts for the surprisingly low number of genes (i.e., segments of coding DNA) in organisms because it shows that building an organism requires more than merely the gene-coding segments of DNA. This hypothesis easily accounts for the raw data that Collins presents.

In *The Language of God*, Collins provides a chart with the caption, "Likelihood of Finding a Similar DNA Sequence in the Genome of Other Organisms, Starting with a Human DNA Sequence."[46] He then provides statistics that compare the similarities between human DNA sequences and DNA sequences of other species. Two types of DNA sequences are compared: those that code for proteins, and those that do not code for proteins (called "non-coding" sequences). In his chart, protein-coding DNA sequences between humans and other species are more similar than are the non-coding DNA of humans and other species.

Collins reports that some protein-coding DNA sequences between humans and chimps are 100 percent identical. But non-coding DNA sequences between humans and chimps are apparently only 98 percent similar. Following the same pattern, Collins reports that human protein-coding DNA is 99 percent similar to that of dogs or mice. But human non-coding DNA is only 52 percent and 40 percent similar to the non-coding DNA of dogs and mice, respectively. The differences are most pronounced with invertebrates. Human protein-coding DNA is 60 percent similar to fruit flies. But here, non-protein coding DNA is reportedly about 0 percent similar to that of fruit flies. Collins assumes these non-coding sequences are junk, because his chart labels them, "Random DNA Segment[s] Between Genes."

Collins uses this data to assert that the reason species have a greater degree of difference between their non-coding DNA than their coding DNA is because non-coding DNA is junk that accumulates mutations at a higher rate. But if we do not make the questionable evolutionary assumption that non-coding DNA is junk, then this data simply suggests that physical differences between different species are not largely controlled by protein-coding DNA but are rather controlled by the non-coding DNA. Yet Collins considers these vital non-coding differences to be the result of "random DNA segment[s] between genes."[47] Large differences exist in non-coding DNA among widely different species because the non-coding DNA may be largely responsible for differences between species.

Now that differences in non-coding DNA are known to control gene expression (which influences an organism's growth and development), we cannot assume, with Collins, that the differences among "junk" DNA in different species are the result of random mutations. Rather, such differences may be better explained as designed differences tailored precisely to encode the developmental traits among species. In fact, the conclusion that non-coding DNA controls gene expression and helps determine physical characteristics is precisely what intelligent design would predict. ID would not expect that large sections of DNA be mere junk. Collins's argument reveals why the Darwinian "junk" DNA assumption might hinder scientific research.

Mutations That Allegedly Caused the Evolution of Human Cognition and Language

Two arguments made by Collins are repeated in the aforementioned *Time* magazine article on chimp and human similarities.[48] Both appear to invoke extravagant and highly unlikely macromutations to account for the origin of major aspects of human intellect.

A Jaw-Dropping Theory

First, Collins looks at the MYH16 gene, which supposedly mutated into a pseudogene in humans.[49] Since MYH16 affects the production of myosin in jaw muscles, a protein that effectively increases muscle strength, it is said that the alleged loss of this gene caused jaw muscles to be weaker. Some have hypothesized this loss in jaw-muscle strength allowed the human braincase to grow larger, causing an increase in human intelligence.

This is a nice story, but does it make sense? Around the same time this research was first reported, leading paleoanthropologist Bernard Wood explained why simply identifying the effects of a mutation does not imply that we have an accurate evolutionary story:

> The mutation would have reduced the Darwinian fitness of those
> individuals. . . . It only would've become fixed if it coincided with

mutations that reduced tooth size, jaw size and increased brain size. What are the chances of that?[50]

But if we accept the story that human braincases enlarged due to this unlikely mutation, the implication is that this explains human intellectual evolution. But the well-known paleoanthropologist Ian Tattersal observes that simply enlarging the brain does very little to explain the evolution of human cognition:

> [T]he arrival of the modern cognitive capacity did not simply involve adding just a bit more neural material, that last little bit of extra brain size that pushed us over the brink. Still less did it involve adding new brain structures, for basic brain design remains remarkably uniform among all the higher primates.[51]

A Miracle Macromutation Theory of the Evolution of Human Cognition

So how did our higher brain capacities evolve, genetically speaking? Again Collins thinks he has an answer. As his second argument, he discusses what is essentially a highly improbable miracle mutation in which two changes in our FOXP2 gene created some of our major linguistic abilities.[52] The *Time* article makes an even bolder claim, asserting that the two mutations could have caused "the emergence of all aspects of human speech, from a baby's first words to a Robin Williams monologue."[53] Such an optimistic line of reasoning strains credulity. The origin of human speech would have required many changes that make up a suite of interdependent complex traits. Two leading evolutionists writing in a prominent text on primate origins explain that human language could not evolve in an abrupt manner, genetically speaking:

> How could we move from communication systems in nonhuman primates to human language in a manner consistent with evolutionary principles? Arguments that humans are fundamentally different from nonhuman animals either set the stage for creationist explanations or simply avoid the attempt to develop a persuasive evolutionary argument. Bickerton's proposal of a single-gene mutation is, I think, too simplistic. Too many factors are involved in language learning—

production, perception, comprehension, syntax, usage, symbols, cognition—for language to be the result of a single mutation event.[54]

Humans are quite different because they possess language, which underlies every major intellectual achievement of humanity. This discontinuity theory is implausible because evolution cannot proceed by inspired jumps, only by accretion of beneficial variants of what went before.[55]

These authors are correct to reject the "single mutation event" hypothesis—and they would be justified in doing the same for two mutation events because human language is vastly more complex than the form of communication found even in our allegedly closest relative, the chimpanzee. Rather than supporting Collins's "single event hypothesis," these authors would argue that human intellectual capacities are different only in degree from those of other primates, and thus could have evolved in a slow, step-by-step fashion. But this view has its own problems. Ian Tattersal describes the intellectual gulf between humans and other species, saying, "Human language is governed by its structure, which admits endless possibilities; ape vocalization is governed by its content, which is inherently limited by its mode of expression."[56] This miracle macromutation theory of the origin of language is attractive to evolutionists because all humans appear to be hardwired for language.[57] One Darwinist, Elizabeth Bates, suggests that this leaves two unviable options for evolutionists:

> If the basic structural principles of language cannot be learned (bottom up) or derived (top down), there are only two possible explanations for their existence: either Universal Grammar was endowed to us directly by the Creator, or else our species has undergone a mutation of unprecedented magnitude, a cognitive equivalent of the Big Bang.[58]
>
> What protoform can we possibly envision that could have given birth to constraints on the extraction of noun phrases from an embedded clause? What could it conceivably mean for an organism to possess half a symbol or three quarters of a rule? . . . monadic symbols, on a yes-or-no basis—a process that cries out for a Creationist explanation.[59]

Some Darwinists, such as Steven Pinker, think language can evolve piecemeal from forms of protolanguage. But other Darwinists like Tattersal disagree because "language is a unique aptitude that doesn't seem to have emerged from protolanguage."[60] Those who follow Tattersal's view accept the integrated complexity of language and may prefer the miracle macro-mutation hypothesis. But as we've already seen, that explanation doesn't jibe with slow, gradual, step-by-step Darwinian modes of change.

Because of this conundrum, Tattersal is forced to argue that human language and cognition evolved by an accidental, indirect route, where key steps in our evolution did not even provide the types of cognitive advantages humans currently enjoy. Such a process of indirect and purely accidental route of evolution is called "exaptation," and Tattersal thus argues that we have "an exapted brain, equipped since who knows when with a neglected potential for symbolic thoughts." According to Tattersal, language evolved after a change that was "minor in genetic terms, and probably had nothing whatever to do with adaptation in the classical sense."[61] In other words, lower primate brains just happened to have all the tools ready for complex human thought and language, even though they weren't being used for such, and a small random mutation in our hominid ancestors that wasn't even adaptive caused human language. This option, too, seems incredible.

Perhaps language presents the type of complex feature contingent on many variables that Noam Chomsky as well as "some of his fiercest opponents" believe is "incompatible with the modern Darwinian theory of evolution, in which complex biological systems arise by the gradual accumulation over generation of random genetic mutations that enhance reproductive success."[62] Would Collins consider this option?

Conclusion

Francis Collins's position as both a Christian and a Darwinian scientist enables him to make valuable contributions to the debate over evolution. However, his Darwinian arguments in favor of human-ape common ancestry are simply unconvincing:

- Collins argues that chromosomal fusion in humans is strong evidence for the hypothesis of human-ape common ancestry. Yet this fusion event took place entirely within the human line after our alleged split with the chimpanzee line and by itself does not tell us whether the human line extends back to share a common ancestor with apes. At best, this evidence demonstrates that humans and chimps share similar genetics—something we already knew without evolutionary biology. Such similarities are just as easily explained by common design.

- Collins assumes that some non-coding DNA is functionless "junk." That such an eminent geneticist as Collins would make so dubious an assumption, given its well-documented history of failure, makes clear how entrenched the "junk" DNA mind-set is within the Darwinian scientific community.

- Collins argues that the larger degree of difference in non-coding DNA compared to protein-coding DNA among various species indicates that non-coding DNA is functionless junk that has accumulated many random mutations. By extension, Collins suggests this is evidence of common ancestry and a Darwinian past. Yet his assumption of nonfunctionality is increasingly betrayed by data showing that non-coding DNA controls gene expression, which is precisely what helps cause differences in the physical characteristics of different species.

- Collins suggests that the evolution of human cognition and language could be explained by a few small mutations. In reality, the origin of human intellect would have required a complex series of coordinate changes that challenge a Darwinian explanation.

Notes

Foreword

1. Richard Dawkins, *River Out of Eden: A Darwinian View of Life* (New York: Basic Books, 1995), 98.

Preface

1. "A Scientific Dissent from Darwinism," Center for Science & Culture. See at dissentfromdarwin.org.
2. Francis Glasson says that "Darwin expected that his book would arouse violent criticism from the scientific world, and it certainly came from that quarter. According to his own account, most of the leading scientists of the day believed in the ummutability [*sic*] of species." Francis Glasson, "Darwin and the Church," *New Scientist* 99 (September 1, 1983): 638. In his introduction, Darwin confirms this perspective. Charles Darwin, *The Origin of Species: By Means of Natural Selection, or the Preservation of Favoured Races in the Struggle for Life* (n.p., 1859). Owen Chadwick, Regius professor of modern history at Cambridge, wrote, "At first much of the opposition to Darwin's theory came from scientists on grounds of evidence, not from theologians on grounds of scripture." Glasson, "Darwin and the Church," 639. For example, Darwin's geology teacher and friend, Adam Sedgwick, did not accept Darwin's views of evolution: "We venture to affirm that no man who has any name in science, properly so-called has spoken well of the book, or regarded it with any feelings but those of deep aversion. We say this advisedly, after exchanging thoughts with some of the best-informed men in Britain." R. E. D. Clark, *Darwin: Before and After* (Grand Rapids: Grand Rapids International Publications, 1958), 49, quoted in B. Davidheiser, *Evolution and the Christian Faith* (Nutley, NJ: Presbyterian & Reformed, 1969), 166. In Microsoft Encarta Online Encyclopedia 2000 at encarta.msn.com (December 21, 2000): "Darwin, Charles Robert," Garland E. Allen and Randy Bird say,

> The reaction to the *Origin* was immediate. Some biologists argued that Darwin could not prove his hypothesis. Others criticized Darwin's concept of variation, arguing that he could explain neither the origin of variations nor how they were passed to succeeding generations. This particular scientific objection was not answered until the birth of modern genetics in the early

20th century. . . . In fact, many scientists continued to express doubts for the following 50 to 80 years.

3. For example, the National Academy of Sciences states in the same document that "intelligent design, and other claims of supernatural intervention in the origin of life are not science because they are not testable by the methods of science" and "Scientists have considered the hypotheses proposed by [intelligent design] and rejected them because of a lack of evidence." National Academy of Sciences, *Science and Creationism: A View from the National Academy of Sciences*, 2d ed. (Washington, DC: National Academy, 1999), ix, 25.

4. The prominent Darwinist philosopher of science Michael Ruse writes, "[O]ne often sees it said that 'evolution is not a fact, but a theory.' Is this the essence of my claim? Not really! Indeed, I suggest that this wise-sounding statement is confused to the point of falsity: it almost certainly is if, without regard for cause, one means no more by 'evolution' than the claim that all organisms developed naturally from primitive beginnings. Evolution is a fact, fact, FACT!" Michael Ruse, *Darwinism Defended: A Guide to the Evolution Controversies*, 3d ed. (Reading, MA: Addison-Wesley, 1983), 58.

Chapter 1: Bringing Balance to a Fiery Debate

1. Stephen Jay Gould, *Ever Since Darwin* (New York: Norton, 1977), 147.

2. Stephen Jay Gould, "Evolution's Erratic Pace," in *Natural History* 86.5 (May 1977): 12–16.

3. Many Darwinists are not atheists. Darwinist thinking is inherently based on materialist assumptions and leads to atheism if the logic is followed consistently. Nonetheless, there are many sincere Christians, such as the prominent geneticist Francis Collins, who manage to find a satisfying way to be both Christian theist and Darwinist. This compromise involves some careful intellectual juggling, because the two ways of thinking are mutually contradictory once one realizes that the Darwinist system is based mainly on materialist philosophical assumptions rather than experimental confirmation. However, the contradiction stems more from the way Darwinists reason than from their factual claims, and it may be overlooked if one simply assumes that the creative power of the Darwinian mutation/selection mechanism must have been demonstrated rather than established by philosophical reasoning.

4. Julian Huxley, "The Humanist Frame," in *Essays of a Humanist* (1964; repr., Harmondsworth, U.K.: Penguin, 1969), 82–83.

5. For examples, see the following papers in science journals: P. Abelson, "Chemical Events on the Primitive Earth," *Proceedings of the National Academy of Sciences USA* 55 (1966): 1365–72; B. M. Rode, "Peptides and the Origin of Life," *Peptides* 20 (1999): 773–76; and Dante Canile, "Vanadian in peridotites, mantle redox and tectonic environments: Archean to present," *Earth and Planetary Science Letters* 195 (2002): 75-90.

6. See Jonathan Wells, "Peppered Moths," in *Icons of Evolution: Science or Myth? Why Much of What We Teach About Evolution Is Wrong* (Washington, DC: Regnery, 2000), chap. 7. Discussion of the fact that moths don't normally rest upon trees may be found in the following articles: Kauri Mikkola, "On the Selective Forces Acting in the Industrial Melanism of Biston and Oligia Moths (Lepidoptera: Geometridae and Noctuidae)," *Biological Journal of the Linnean Society* 21.4 (1984): 409–21; C. A. Clarke, G. S. Mani, and G. Wynne, "Evolution in Reverse: Clean Air and the Peppered Moth," *Biological Journal of the Linnean Society* 26 (1985): 189–99; Rory J. Howlett and Michael E. N. Majerus, "The Understanding of Industrial Melanism in the Peppered Moth (Biston Betularia) (Lepidoptera: Geometridae)," *Biological Journal of the Linnean Society* 30.1 (1987): 31–44; and Theodore D. Sargent, Craig D. Millar, and David M. Lambert, "The 'Classical' Explanation of Industrial Melanism: Assessing the Evidence," *Evolutionary Biology* 30 (1998): 299–322.
7. For example, Jay Wexler writes that "in 1963–64, the BSCS published three textbooks (dealing with cellular biology, ecology, and molecular analysis) that were thoroughly permeated by evolutionary theory. By 1970, nearly half of American high schools had adopted the BSCS books." Jay D. Wexler, "Of Pandas, People, and the First Amendment: The Constitutionality of Teaching Intelligent Design in the Public Schools," *Stanford Law Review* 49 (1997): 439, 447.
8. Douglas J. Futuyma, *Evolutionary Biology*, 3d ed. (Sunderland, MA: Sinaeur Associates, 1998), 5.
9. Stephen Jay Gould of Harvard University advocated rapid change in species in his theory called punctuated equilibrium. Sometimes less scientifically it is called the "hopeful monster" view.
10. This exchange was reported by William Dembski as forwarded to him by Michael Ruse. The "Remarkable exchange between Michael Ruse and Daniel Dennett" can be found at "Uncommon Descent," the intelligent design blog of William Dembski, Denyse O'Leary, and Friends (February 21, 2006), uncommondescent.com/index.php/archives/844.
11. For example, see Andrew M. Simons, "The Continuity of Microevolution and Macroevolution," *Journal of Evolutionary Biology* 15 (2002): 688–701; and Robert Carroll, *Patterns and Processes of Vertebrate Evolution* (Cambridge, U.K.: Cambridge University Press, 1997), 8–10.
12. A long listing of resources about the Ohio debate can be found at the Center for Science and Culture, Discovery Institute, "Ohio Science Standards Resource Page: Information on the Critical Analysis of Evolution Science Curriculum" (February 14, 2006) at discovery.org/scripts/viewDB/index.php?command=view&id=3180.
13. This policy was repealed in February 2006 pending review by the Ohio State Board of Education, but similar policies have been passed in five addi-

tional states that are currently emplaced into statewide science standards: Kansas, Minnesota, New Mexico, Pennsylvania, and South Carolina.

14. Patricia Princehouse, quoted by Stephanie Simon, "Ohio Drops Demand That Evolution Be Challenged," *Los Angeles Times*, February 15, 2006.

15. Barbara Forrest and Paul R. Gross, *Creationism's Trojan Horse: The Wedge of Intelligent Design* (New York: Oxford University Press, 2004).

16. See Discovery Institute, "The 'Wedge Document': 'So What?'" (February 3, 2006), discovery.org/scripts/viewDB/filesDB-download.php?id=349.

17. Phillip E. Johnson, *The Wedge of Truth: Splitting the Foundations of Naturalism* (Downers Grove, IL: InterVarsity Press, 2000), 17.

18. Michael Ruse and E. O. Wilson, "The Evolution of Ethics," in *Religion and the Natural Sciences: The Range of Engagement*, ed. James E. Huchingson (Fort Worth, TX: Harcourt Brace, 1993), 308–12.

19. Steven Pinker, "Why They Kill Their Newborns," *New York Times*, November 2, 1997, sec. Magazine Desk.

20. American Association for the Advancement of Science, "AAAS Board Resolution on Intelligent Design Theory" (October 18, 2002), aaas.org/news/releases/2002/1106id2.

21. *Kitmiller v. Dover*, 400 F. Supp. 2d 707 (M.D.Pa. 2005). For a good response to this court decision from the pro-ID perspective, see David DeWolf, John West, Casey Luskin, and Jonathan Witt, *Traipsing into Evolution: Intelligent Design and the Kitzmiller v. Dover Decision* (Seattle, WA: Discovery Institute, 2006).

Chapter 2: Intelligent Design and the Nature of Science

1. Neal Gillespie, *Charles Darwin and the Problem of Creation* (Chicago: University of Chicago Press, 1979), 19.

2. Robert C. Cowen, "Science Is What Can Be Argued, Not What Is Believed," *The Baltimore Sun*, July 8, 1987. The quote used the term *creationists*, not *ID advocates*.

3. Michael Behe makes it clear that the designer need not be supernatural "The Modern Intelligent Design Hypothesis," *Philosophia Christi*, 2nd ser., 3, no. 1 (2001): 165.

4. Gillespie, *Charles Darwin*, 19.

5. For the text of Judge Overton's ruling with a thorough critique, see J. P. Moreland, *Christianity and the Nature of Science* (Grand Rapids: Baker, 1989), 23–35.

6. It should be noted that ID need not violate even methodological naturalism. ID does not try to decide whether the designer is natural or supernatural. Thus, ID does not necessarily make claims that must go beyond the natural world.

Chapter 3: Finding Intelligent Design in Nature

1. The type of information that reliably indicates intelligent design is called complex and specified information. William A. Dembski, *No Free Lunch: Why Specified Complexity Cannot Be Purchased Without Intelligence* (Lanham, MD: Rowman & Littlefield, 2002), xiv.

2. There are many examples of possible intelligent agents, including animals, humans, extraterrestrials, or even supernatural beings, any of which can have intelligence. The scientific theory of intelligent design, however, is not focused upon studying the *intelligence* responsible for design in nature life as much as it is interested in studying nature to find signs of intelligent agency. Intelligent design is not focused on investigating the identity or nature of the intelligence responsible for life. William Dembski thus defines intelligent design as follows: "Intelligent design is the science that studies signs of intelligence. Note that a sign is not the thing signified. . . . As a scientific research program, intelligent design investigates the effects of intelligence and not intelligence as such." William A. Dembski, *The Design Revolution: Answering the Toughest Questions About Intelligent Design* (Downers Grove, IL: InterVarsity Press, 2004), 33.

3. A common objection to intelligent design is that archaeologists can infer intelligent design in archaeology because we have observation-based experience with human intelligence creating such artifacts, but biologists have no direct experience with intelligent agents making designed objects and, thus, are not justified in invoking design in biology.

   This objection has a fundamental logical flaw that fails to grasp the basis for inferring design. Many of us may not fully grasp the purpose of Stonehenge, but we immediately recognize that it is the result of intelligent design and not natural processes. This is because Stonehenge contains a complex arrangement of stones that match a pattern. We may know very little about the purposes, beliefs, or identity of the designer of Stonehenge, but we know it was designed.

   An underlying assumption of intelligent design is that intelligence is a property that we can generally understand through our observations of intelligent agents in the natural world. An intelligent agent could have at least some predictable modes of designing (see fig. 3.1, step [a]) because it has the property of intelligence, regardless of whether or not the agent was human. Indeed, the Search for Extra-Terrestrial Intelligence assumes that we can detect intelligent design of radio signals sent by nonhuman extraterrestrial intelligent civilizations. Intelligent design assumes that there are certain properties of intelligence that will be constant regardless of whether or not that intelligent agent was human, natural, or even supernatural. Thus when we find objects in biology that have informational properties that we know stem from intelligent design—encoded information, language-based information processing capability, and irreducibly complex molecular machines—we have a valid rationale for inferring that those biological structures were designed even if we cannot precisely determine the identify of the designing intelligence.

4. William A. Dembski, *The Design Inference* (Cambridge, U.K.: Cambridge University Press, 1998), 62.
5. Stephen C. Meyer, "The Cambrian Information Explosion," in *Debating Design*, ed. William A. Dembski and Michael Ruse (Cambridge, U.K.: Cambridge University Press, 2004), 388.
6. Stephen C. Meyer, "The Origin of Biological Information and the Higher Taxonomic Categories," *Proceedings of the Biological Society of Washington* 117.2 (2004): 213–29.
7. Irreducible complexity is a special case of specified complexity. See Dembski, *No Free Lunch*, 115.
8. Michael Behe, *Darwin's Black Box: The Biochemical Challenge to Evolution* (New York: Free Press, 1996), 39.
9. If the machine continues to function when a part is removed, this process can be repeated until an irreducible core is determined.
10. By advanced life, I mean multicellular organisms. However, many physical parameters must be finely tuned to permit the existence of any form of life.
11. Fred Hoyle, *The Intelligent Universe* (New York: Holt, Rinehart & Winston, 1983), 189.
12. Paul Davies, "The Unreasonable Effectiveness of Science," in *Evidence of Purpose*, ed. John Marks Templeton (New York: Continuum, 1996), 49.
13. William Lane Craig, "Design and the Anthropic Fine-tuning of the Universe," in Neil A. Manson, *God and Design: The Teleological Argument and Modern Science* (New York: Routledge, 2003), 157.
14. Paul Davies, *The Accidental Universe* (Cambridge, U.K.: Cambridge University Press, 1982), 118.
15. David Gross, quoted in Brumfiel, "Outrageous Fortune," 10–12.
16. Arthur Eddington, (no title), *Nature* 450 (1931): 127.
17. Michael Polanyi, "Life's Irreducible Structure," *Science* 160.3834 (June 21, 1968): 1308–12.
18. Leslie E. Orgel, *The Origins of Life: Molecules and Natural Selection* (Toronto, Ontario: John Wiley & Sons Canada, 1973), 189.
19. J. T. Trevors and D. L. Abel, "Chance and Necessity Do Not Explain the Origin of Life," *Cell Biology International* 28 (2004): 729–39.
20. D. L. Abel and J. T. Trevors, "Self-organization vs. Self-ordering Events in Life-origin Models," *Physics of Life Reviews* 3 (2006): 211–28.
21. Ibid.
22. Polanyi, "Life's Irreducible Structure," 1308–12.
23. Meyer, "Origin of Biological Information," 213–29.
24. Bill Gates, *The Road Ahead* (New York: Penguin, 1995), 188.
25. Richard Dawkins, *River Out of Eden: A Darwinian View of Life* (New York: Basic Books, 1995), 17.

26. See Donald Voet, Judith G. Voet, and Charlotte W. Pratt, *Fundamentals of Biochemistry: Life at the Molecular Level*, 2d ed. (Hoboken, NJ: John Wiley & Sons, 2006), 974.

27. Trevors and Abel, "Chance and Necessity," 729–39.

28. Ibid.

29. Øyvind Albert Voie, "Biological Function and the Genetic Code Are Interdependent," *Chaos, Solitons and Fractals* 28.4 (2006): 1000–1004.

30. Richard Dawkins, "The Information Challenge," *The Skeptic* 18.4 (December 1998), at simonyi.ox.ac.uk/dawkins/WorldOfDawkins-archive/Dawkins/Work/Articles/1998 12 04infochallange.

31. Ibid.

32. Jonathan Wells, "Using Intelligent Design Theory to Guide Scientific Research," *Progress in Complexity, Information, and Design* 3.1 (November 2004).

33. Helen Pearson, "Genetic Information Codes and Enigmas," *Nature* 444 (November 16, 2006): 259.

34. Ibid.

35. Jonathan Marks, *What It Means to Be 98% Chimpanzee: Apes, People, and Their Genes* (Berkeley, CA: University of California Press, 2002), 34.

36. Richard V. Sternberg, "On the Roles of Repetitive DNA Elements in the Context of a Unified Genomic–Epigenetic System," *Annals of the New York Academy of Sciences* 981 (2002): 154–88.

37. Richard V. Sternberg and James A. Shapiro, "How Repeated Retroelements Format Genome Function," *Cytogenetic and Genome Research* 110 (2005): 108–16.

38. Shinji Hirotsune, Noriyuki Yoshida, Amy Chen, Lisa Garrett, Fumihiro Sugiyama, Satoru Takahashi, Ken-ichi Yagami, Anthony Wynshaw-Boris, and Atsushi Yoshiki, "An Expressed Pseudogene Regulates the Messenger-RNA Stability of Its Homologous Coding Gene," *Nature* 423 (May 1, 2003): 91–96.

39. Sternberg, "On the Roles of Repetitive DNA Elements," 154–88.

40. Tammy A. Morrish, Nicolas Gilbert, Jeremy S. Myers, Bethaney J. Vincent, Thomas D. Stamato, Guillermo E. Taccioli, Mark A. Batzer, and John V. Moran, "DNA Repair Mediated by Endonuclease-Independent LINE-1 Retrotransposition," *Nature Genetics* 31.2 (June 2002): 159–65.

41. Galit Lev-Maor, Rotem Sorek, Noam Shomron, and Gil Ast, "The Birth of an Alternatively Spliced Exon: 3' Splice-Site Selection in Alu Exons," *Science* 300.5623 (May 23, 2003): 1288–91; and Wojciech Makalowski, "Not Junk After All," *Science* 300.5623 (May 23, 2003): 1246–47.

42. W. Wayt Gibbs, "The Unseen Genome: Gems Among the Junk," *Scientific American* 289.5 (November 2003). Emphasis added.

43. Ibid.

44. Ibid.

45. Sternberg, "On the Roles of Repetitive DNA Elements," 154–88.

46. Bruce Alberts, "The Cell as a Collection of Protein Machines: Preparing the Next Generation of Molecular Biologists," *Cell* 92 (February 6, 1998): 291, emphasis in original.

47. David J. DeRosier, "The Turn of the Screw: The Bacterial Flagellar Motor," *Cell* 93 (1998): 17–20.

48. Transcript of Testimony of Scott Minnich, *Kitzmiller et al. v. Dover Area School Board*, No. 4:04–CV-2688 (M.D.Pa., November 3, 2005), 103–12. Other experimental studies have identified over thirty proteins necessary to form flagella. See table 1 in Robert M. Macnab, "Flagella," in *Escheria Coli and Salmonella Typhimurium: Cellular and Molecular Biology*, ed. Frederick C. Neidhart, John L. Ingraham, K. Brooks Low, Boris Magasanik, Moselio Schaechter, and H. Edwin Umbarger (Washington DC: American Society for Microbiology, 1987), 1:73–74.

49. Kenneth R. Miller, "The Flagellum Unspun: The Collapse of 'Irreducible Complexity,'" in *Debating Design*, ed. William A. Dembski and Michael Ruse (Cambridge, U.K.: Cambridge University Press, 2004).

50. Hiroaki Kitano, "Systems Biology: A Brief Overview," *Science* 295 (March 1, 2002): 1662–64.

51. Ibid.

52. Paul Nelson and Jonathan Wells, "Homology in Biology," in *Darwinism, Design, and Public Education*, ed. John Angus Campbell and Stephen C. Meyer (East Lansing, MI: Michigan State University Press, 2003), 316.

53. R. Quiring, U. Walldorf, U. Kloter, and W. J. Gehring, "Homology of the Eyeless Gene of Drosophila to the Small Eye in Mice and Aniridia in Humans," *Science* 265.5173 (1994): 785–89.

54. "No theorist in evolutionary biology will ever derive chicken and insects from a winged common ancestor, and yet, clearly related sequences are specifically expressed in wing buds and imaginal disks." Wolf-Ekkehard Lönnig, "Dynamic Genomes, Morphological Stasis, and the Origin of Irreducible Complexity," in *Dynamical Genetics*, ed. Valerio Parisi, Valeria De Fonzo, and Filippo Aluffi-Pentini (Kerala, India: Research Signpost, 2004), 101–19; quoting M. J. Cohn and C. Tickle, *Trends Genet* 12 (1996): 253–57.

55. Nelson and Wells, "Homology in Biology," 316.

56. Morphology is the physical shape or other physical properties of an organism.

57. Emile Zuckerlkandl, "Evolutionary Divergence and Convergence in Proteins," in *Evolving Genes and Proteins*, ed. Vernon Bryson and Henry J. Vogel (New York: Academic Press, 1965), 101.

58. C. Patterson, D. M. Williams, and C. J. Humphries, "Congruence Between Molecular and Morphological Phylogenies," *Annual Review of Ecology and Systematics* 24 (1993): 179.

59. Matthew A. Wills, "The Tree of Life and the Rock of Ages: Are We

Getting Better at Estimating Phylogeny?" *BioEssays* 24 (2002): 203–7, reporting on the findings of Michael J. Benton, "Finding the Tree of Life: Matching Phylogenetic Trees to the Fossil Record Through the 20th Century," *Proceedings of the Royal Society of London B* 268 (2001): 2123–30.

60. E. Bapteste, E. Susko, J. Leigh, D. MacLeod, R. L. Charlebois, and W. F. Doolittle, "Do Orthologous Gene Phylogenies Really Support Tree-thinking?" *BMC Evolutionary Biology* 5 (2005): 33.

61. Lynn Margulis, "The Phylogenetic Tree Topples," *American Scientist* 94.3 (May–June 2006). See at redorbit.com/news/health/504208/the_phylogenetic_tree_topples/index.

62. Ibid.

63. Hervé Philippe and Maximilian J. Telford, "Large-scale Sequencing and the New Animal Phylogeny," *Trends in Ecology and Evolution* 21.11 (November 2006): 614–20.

64. Antonis Rokas, Dirk Krüger, and Sean B. Carroll, "Animal Evolution and the Molecular Signature of Radiations Compressed in Time," *Science* 310 (December 23, 2005): 1933–38.

65. Antonis Rokas and Sean B. Carroll, "Bushes in the Tree of Life," *PLOS Biology* 4.11 (November 2006): 1899–1904 (internal citations and figures omitted).

66. Ibid.

67. Ibid.

68. Ibid.

69. Carl Woese, "The Universal Ancestor," *Proceedings of the National Academy of Sciences USA* 95 (June 1998): 6854–59.

70. Stephen C. Meyer, Marcus Ross, Paul Nelson, and Paul Chien, "The Cambrian Explosion: Biology's Big Bang," in Campbell and Meyer, eds., *Darwinism, Design, and Public Education*, 386.

71. Ibid.

72. Charles Darwin, *The Origin of Species* (1859; repr., London, U.K.: Penguin, 1985), 292.

73. Ibid.

74. Stephen Jay Gould, "Is a New and General Theory of Evolution Emerging?" *Paleobiology* 6.1 (1980): 119–30.

75. Darwin, *The Origin of Species*, 292.

76. Stephen Jay Gould, "Evolution's Erratic Pace," *Natural History* 86.5 (May 1977): 12–16.

77. M. J. Benton, M. A. Wills, and R. Hitchin, "Quality of the Fossil Record Through Time," *Nature* 403 (February 3, 2000): 534–36.

78. Niles Eldredge and Ian Tattersall, *The Myths of Human Evolution* (New York: Columbia University Press, 1982), 59.

79. David S. Woodruff, "Evolution: The Paleobiological View," *Science* 208 (May 16, 1980): 716–17.

80. Michael J. Benton and G. William Storrs, "Testing the Quality of the Fossil Record: Paleontological Knowledge Is Improving," *Geology* 22 (February 1994): 111–14.
81. Susumu Ohno, "The Notion of the Cambrian Pananimalia Genome," *Proceedings of the National Academy of Sciences USA* 93 (August 1996): 8475–78.
82. R. S. K. Barnes, P. Calow, P. J. W. Olive, and D. W. Golding, *The Invertebrates: A New Synthesis*, 2d ed. (Oxford, U.K.: Blackwell Scientific, 1993), 10.
83. Philippe Janvier, "Catching the First Fish," *Nature* 402 (November 4, 1999): 21–22.
84. See Meyer, Ross, Nelson, and Chien, "The Cambrian Explosion," 326.
85. Arthur Strahler, *Science and Earth History: The Evolution/Creation Controversy* (New York: Prometheus, 1987), 408.
86. Richard M. Bateman, Peter R. Crane, William A. DiMichele, Paul R. Kenrick, Nick P. Rowe, Thomas Speck, and William E. Stein, "Early Evolution of Land Plants: Phylogeny, Physiology, and Ecology of the Primary Terrestrial Radiation," *Annual Review of Ecology and Systematics* 29 (1998): 263–92.
87. Niles Eldredge, *The Monkey Business: A Scientist Looks at Creationism* (New York: Washington Square, 1982), 65.
88. A. Cooper and R. Fortey, "Evolutionary Explosions and the Phylogenetic Fuse," *Trends in Ecology and Evolution* 13.4 (1998): 151–56.
89. J. Hawks, K. Hunley, L. Sang-Hee, and M. Wolpoff, "Population Bottlenecks and Pleistocene Evolution," *Journal of Molecular Biology and Evolution* 17.1 (2000): 2–22.
90. Ibid.
91. "New Study Suggests Big Bang Theory of Human Evolution" (January 10, 2000), University of Michigan Anthropology Department press release, at umich.edu/~newsinfo/Releases/2000/Jan00/r011000b.
92. For example, see Pat Shipman, *Taking Wing: Archaeopteryx and the Evolution of Bird Flight* (New York: Touchstone, 1998).
93. Carl C. Swisher III, Yuan-qing Wang, Xiao-lin Wang, Xing Xu, and Yuan Wang, "Cretaceous Age for the Feathered Dinosaurs of Lianoing, China," *Nature* 400 (July 1, 1999): 58–61.
94. Zhexi Luo, "A Refugium for Relicts," *Nature* 400 (July 1, 1999): 23.
95. Shipman, *Taking Wing: Archaeopteryx and the Evolution of Bird Flight*, 155.
96. Alan Feduccia, *The Origin and Evolution of Birds*, 2d ed. (New Haven, CT: Yale University Press, 1999), 396.
97. Ibid., 382–85, 405.
98. Ibid., 405.

99. Edward B. Daeschler, Neil H. Shubin, and Farish A. Jenkins, "A Devonian Tetrapod-like Fish and the Evolution of the Tetrapod Body Plan," *Nature* 440 (April 6, 2006): 757–63.
100. For example, see John Roach, "Fossil Find Is Missing Link in Human Evolution, Scientists Say," *National Geographic News* (April 13, 2006), at news.nationalgeographic.com/news/2006/04/0413_060413_evolution.
101. Tim D. White et al., "Asa Issie, Aramis and the Origin of Australopithecus," *Nature* 440 (April 13, 2006): 883–89, emphasis added.
102. "'Lucy's baby' found in Ethiopia," BBC News (September 20, 2006), at news.bbc.co.uk/2/hi/science/nature/5363328.
103. Mark Henderson, ed., "Meet the Relatives: Little Lucy, the Half-ape Half-human," *London Times* (September 21, 2006), at timesonline.co .uk/article/0,,3-2367940,00.
104. Lenore Pipes, "Child Fossil Discovery Sparks Debate, Bridges Gaps," *The Phoenix* (September 28, 2006), at phoenix.swarthmore.edu/2006 -09-28/opinions/16372.
105. David McAlary, "Prehuman Skeleton Offers Clues to Evolution," *Voice of America News* (September 21, 2006), at voanews.com/english/2006-09 -21-voa4.cfm; David McAlary, "Scientists Find Ape-Man Skeleton Leading to Clues on Evolution," *Digital Journal* (September 25, 2006), at digitaljournal.com/article/37570/Scientists_Find_Ape_Man_Skeleton_ Leading_to_Clues_on_Evolution.
106. Jennifer A. Clack and Per Erik Ahlberg, "A Firm Step from Water to Land," *Nature* 440 (April 6, 2006): 747–49.
107. Ibid.
108. See Neil H. Shubin, Edward B. Daeschler, and Farish A. Jenkins Jr., "The Pectoral Fin of *Tiktaalik Roseae* and the Origin of the Tetrapod Limb," *Nature* 440 (April 6, 2006): 764–71.
109. White et al., "Asa Issie, Aramis and the Origin of Australopithecus," 883– 89, emphasis added.
110. See discovery.org/scripts/viewDB/filesDB-download.php?command= download&id=754, a picture of the actual "intermediate" teeth from the *Nature* article.
111. Seth Borenstein, "Fossil Discovery Fills Gap in Human Evolution," Associated Press (April 12, 2006), at msnbc.msn.com/id/12286206/.
112. McAlary, "Scientists Find Ape-Man Skeleton."
113. Henderson, "Meet the Relatives."
114. Ibid.
115. Ibid.
116. University of Michigan, "New Study Suggests Big Bang Theory of Human Evolution."
117. Bernard Wood and Mark Collard, "The Human Genus," *Science* 284.5411 (April 2, 1999): 65–71.

118. Robin Dennell and Wil Roebroeks, "An Asian Perspective on Early Human Dispersal from Africa," *Nature* 438 (December 22/29, 2005): 1099–1104, emphasis added.

119. For more on the lack of fossils documenting a transition between *Australopithecus* and *Homo*, see Casey Luskin, "Human Origins and Intelligent Design," *Progress in Complexity, Information, and Design* 4.1 (July 2005), at iscid.org/pcid/2005/4/1/luskin_human_origins.pkf.

120. Stephen Jay Gould, "Evolution as Fact and Theory," *Discover* (May 1981); reprinted in Stephen Jay Gould, *Hen's Teeth and Horse's Toes* (New York: W. W. Norton, 1994), 260.

121. Stephen Jay Gould, "The Return of Hopeful Monsters," *Natural History* 86 (June–July 1977): 22–24.

122. Niles Eldredge, *Macroevolutionary Dynamics: Species, Niches, and Adaptive Peaks* (New York: McGraw-Hill, 1989), 22.

123. Niles Eldredge, *The Monkey Business: A Scientist Looks at Creationism* (New York: Washington Square, 1982), 65–66.

124. Niles Eldredge, *Reinventing Darwin: The Great Debate at the High Table of Evolutionary Theory* (New York: Wiley & Sons, 1995), 95.

125. Robert L. Carroll, *Patterns and Processes of Vertebrate Evolution* (Cambridge, U.K.: Cambridge University Press, 1997), 9.

126. Mark Pagel, "Happy Accidents?" *Nature* 397 (February 25, 1999): 665.

127. Ernst Mayr, *What Evolution Is* (New York: Basic Books, 2001), 189.

128. National Academy of Sciences, *Teaching About Evolution and the Nature of Science* (Washington, DC: National Academy Press, 1998), 57.

129. Darwin, *The Origin of Species*, 209–10.

130. See Niles Eldredge and Stephen Jay Gould, "Punctuated Equilibria: An Alternative to Phyletic Gradualism," in *Models in Paleobiology*, ed. Thomas J. M. Schopf (San Francisco: Freeman Cooper & Co., 1972), 82–115.

131. B. Charlesworth, R. Lande, and M. Slatkin, "A Neo-Darwinian Commentary on Macroevolution," *Evolution* 36.3 (1982): 474–98.

132. Stephen Jay Gould and Niles Eldredge, "Punctuated Equilibrium Comes of Age," *Nature* 366 (November 18, 1993): 223–27.

133. Ibid.

134. J. Madeleine Nash, "Where Do Toes Come From?" *Time* 146.5 (July 31, 1995), at time.com/time/magazine/article/0,9171,983240,00.

135. Michael Denton, *Evolution: A Theory in Crisis*, 3d rev. ed., trans. (Bethesda, MD: Adler & Adler, 1986), 193.

136. Meyer, Ross, Nelson, and Chien, "Cambrian Explosion," 386.

137. Lönnig, "Dynamic Genomes, Morphological Stasis," 101–19.

138. There are numerous examples of leading scientific organizations rejecting intelligent design because they have been misled to believe that it is an untestable supernatural explanation. For example, the National Academy

of Sciences rejects intelligent design because they wrongly claim that it "argue[s] that the various types of organisms . . . could only have come about with supernatural intervention. . . ." National Academy of Sciences, *Science and Creationism: A View from the National Academy of Sciences*, 2d ed. (Washington, DC: National Academy Press, 1999), 7. Similarly, in September 2005, thirty-eight Nobel laureates wrote a letter to the Kansas State Board of Education urging the rejecting intelligent design because they wrongly believed "intelligent design is fundamentally unscientific; it cannot be tested as scientific theory because its central conclusion is based on belief in the intervention of a supernatural agent." Letter at media .ljworld.com/pdf/2005/09/15/nobel_letter.

139. Quoted in Brumfiel, "Outrageous Fortune," 10–12.

Chapter 4: Darwin's Black Box

1. Joseph Schwarcz, "The Right Chemistry," *The Gazette* (Montreal), C4.
2. Richard Dawkins, quoted in G. Easterbrook, "Science and God: A Warming Trend?" *Science* 277 (1997): 890–93.
3. Joseph Ratzinger, *In the Beginning: A Catholic Understanding of the Story of Creation and the Fall* (Grand Rapids: Eerdmans, 1986), 56–57.
4. Ibid.
5. Charles Darwin, *The Origin of Species* (1859; repr. ed., New York: Bantam Classics, 1999), 151.
6. "Calvin and Hobbes" by Bill Watterson is syndicated through Universal Press Syndicate.
7. Darwin, *The Origin of Species*, 158.
8. "The Far Side," by Gary Larson is syndicated through Farworks, Inc.
9. William A. Dembski, *The Design Inference: Eliminating Chance Through Small Probabilities* (New York: Cambridge University Press, 1998).
10. Michael Behe, *Darwin's Black Box: The Biochemical Challenge to Evolution* (New York: Free Press, 1996).
11. Franklin M. Harold, *The Way of the Cell* (New York: Oxford University Press, 2001), 205.
12. R. F. Doolittle, "A Delicate Balance," *Boston Review* (February–March 1997): 28–29.
13. Ibid.
14. T. H. Bugge et al., "Loss of Fibrinogen Rescues Mice from the Pleiotropic Effects of Plasminogen Deficiency," *Cell* 87.4 (November 15, 1996): 709–15.
15. Michael Ruse, "Answering the Creationists: Where They Go Wrong and What They're Afraid Of," *Free Inquiry* (March 22, 1998): 28.
16. Neil S. Greenspan, "Not-So-Intelligent Design," *The Scientist* (March 4, 2002): 12.
17. Ibid.

Chapter 5: Why Are We Here?

1. Phillip Johnson, *Darwin on Trial* (Downers Grove, IL: InterVarsity Press, 1991).
2. Charles Hodge, *Systematic Theology* (repr., Grand Rapids: Eerdmans, 1995), 1:19.
3. The photographs appear on a number of Web sites. See, e.g., nasa.gov/vision/universe/starsgalaxies/dotf-20061101.
4. Carl Sagan, *Pale Blue Dot* (New York: Ballantine Books, 1994), 7.
5. Peter Ward and Don Brownlee, *Rare Earth: Why Complex Life Is Uncommon in the Universe* (New York: Springer-Verlag, 2000).
6. Don Brownlee, script writer, "The Privileged Planet," visual media (La Habra, CA: Illustra Media, 2004).
7. Guillermo Gonzalez and Jay W. Richards, *The Privileged Planet: How Our Place in the Cosmos Is Designed for Discovery* (Washington, DC: Regnery, 2004). In this book we argue specifically for design. Phil Johnson has a story about how hard it was to get *Darwin on Trial* published, which only critiqued Darwinism. I learned that it is very difficult to get a book published that argues explicitly for design and purpose and claims that the history of science has been mistold. But we eventually succeeded.

Chapter 6: Philosophical Implications of Neo-Darwinism and Intelligent Design

1. The full title is *The Origin of Species by Means of Natural Selection, or the Preservation of Favoured Races in the Struggle for Life*.
2. Thomas Woodward, *Doubts About Darwin: A History of Intelligent Design* (Grand Rapids: Baker, 2003), 33–34.
3. Sir Julian Huxley, *Evolution After Darwin*, ed. Sol Tex, vol. 3 (Chicago: University of Chicago Press, 1960), in "The Centennial Celebration of *The Origin of Species*."
4. Although evolution, Darwinism, and neo-Darwinism (ND) are distinct terms, I sometimes use them interchangeably in regard to their philosophical implications or practical consequences. This is partly due to the various citations I have used as examples. Implicit in these citations regarding these evolutionary terms is that all living organisms are ultimately the result of random, nondirected, mindless, naturalistic processes consistent with the materialism in strong-ND.
5. Richard Lewontin, review of *The Demon-Haunted World*, by Carl Sagan, *The New York Review of Books*, January 9, 1997, 28–31.
6. Richard Weikart discusses the issue that some Darwinians did not embrace naturalism in his introduction of *From Darwin to Hitler: Evolutionary Ethics, Eugenics, and Racism in Germany* (New York: Palgrave MacMillan, 2004).

7. For more information regarding intelligent design, bioethics, and related issues, see Discovery Institute Web site, discovery.org.
8. Mark Hartwig, "Frequently Asked Questions About Intelligent Design" (Access Research Network, 2001), at arn.org.
9. William Lane Craig, *Reasonable Faith: Christian Truth and Apologetics*, rev. ed. (Wheaton, IL: Crossway, 1994), 63.
10. Dallas Willard, *Renovation of the Heart: Putting on the Character of Christ* (Colorado Springs, CO: Navpress, 2002), 106.
11. "What should be taught? Teachers and students explore creation and evolution," *The Bull's Eye* 3.3 (March 2005): 8–9. Those quoted were students at Rancho Buena Vista High School, Vista, California.
12. *Webster's Encyclopedic Unabridged Dictionary* (New York: Portland House, 1989): s.v., "Science."
13. J. P. Moreland, *Christianity and the Nature of Science: A Philosophical Investigation* (Grand Rapids: Baker, 1994), chap. 3, 106–8.
14. Ibid.
15. Ibid., 108–33.
16. J. P. Moreland and William Lane Craig, *Philosophical Foundations for a Christian Worldview* (Downers Grove, IL: InterVarsity Press, 2003), 353–66.
17. William A. Dembski, *Intelligent Design: The Bridge Between Science and Theology* (Downers Grove, IL: InterVarsity Press, 1999), 119.
18. Ibid.
19. Francis J. Beckwith, "Science and Religion Twenty Years After *Mclean v. Arkansas*: Evolution, Public Education, and the New Challenge of Intelligent Design," *Harvard Journal of Law Public Policy* 26, no. 2 (Spring 2003): 477–78.
20. Dembski, *Intelligent Design*, 120.
21. The scientific difference between ID and any form of scientific creationism is partly articulated by Behe:

> The most important difference [between modern intelligent design theory and Paley's arguments] is that [intelligent design] is limited to design itself; I strongly emphasize that it is not an argument for the existence of a benevolent God, as Paley's was. I hasten to add that I myself do believe in a benevolent God, and I recognize that philosophy and theology may be able to extend the argument. But a scientific argument for design in biology does not reach that far. Thus while I argue for design, the question of the identity of the designer is left open. Possible candidates for the role of designer include: the God of Christianity; an angel—fallen or not; Plato's demi-urge; some mystical new age force; space aliens from Alpha Centauri; time travelers; or some utterly unknown intelligent being. Of course, some of these possibilities may seem more plausible than others based on information from fields other than science.

Nonetheless, as regards the identity of the designer, modern ID theory happily echoes Isaac Newton's phrase *hypothesis non fingo*.

Michael Behe, "The Modern Intelligent Design Hypothesis," *Philosophia Christi* 2.3.1 (2001): 165, emphasis added.

22. Richard Dawkins, *The Blind Watchmaker: Why the Evidence of Evolution Reveals a Universe Without Design* (New York: W. W. Norton, 1996), 1.
23. Stephen C. Meyer, "DNA and Other Designs," *First Things* (April 1, 2000), at arn.org/docs/meyer/sm_dnaotherdesigns.
24. Dawkins, *The Blind Watchmaker*, 6.
25. William B. Provine, *Evolution: Free will and punishment and meaning in life*, Darwin Day address, University of Tennessee, Knoxville, February 12, 1998, at eeb.bio.utk.edu/darwin/DarwinDayProvineAddress.
26. Stephen Jay Gould, "The Meaning of Life," *Life*, December 1988, 84.
27. George Gaylord Simpson, *The Meaning of Evolution*, rev. ed. (New Haven, CT: Yale University Press, 1967), 345.
28. Edward O. Wilson, "The Meaning of Life," ed. David Friend et al., *Sunset* (1991): 94.
29. D. J. Futuyma, *Evolutionary Biology* (Sunderland, MA: Sinauer Associates, 1998), 5.
30. J. P. Moreland, "Philosophical Apologetics, the Church, and Contemporary Culture," *Journal of the Evangelical Theological Society* 39.1 (March 1996): 129–30.
31. Paul M. Churchland, *Matter and Consciousness*, rev. ed. (Cambridge, MA: MIT Press, 1993), 21.
32. As an undergraduate at UC San Diego in the 1990s, I heard Professor Churchland assert this proposition in his classroom more than once.
33. J. P. Moreland and Scott Rae, *Body and Soul: Human Nature and the Crisis in Ethics* (Downers Grove, IL: InterVarsity Press, 2000).
34. J. P. Moreland, "Humanness, Personhood, and the Right to Die," *Faith and Philosophy* 12.1 (January 1995): 95–112.
35. Ibid.
36. Ibid.
37. Hadley Arkes, *First Things: An Inquiry into the First Principles of Morals and Justice* (Princeton, NJ: Princeton University Press, 1986), 377.
38. See Francis J. Beckwith, "Defending Abortion Philosophically: A Review of David Boonan's *A Defense of Abortion*," *Journal of Medicine and Philosophy* 31.2 (April 2006): 177–203. Also see Patrick Lee, *Abortion and the Unborn Human Life* (Washington, DC: Catholic University of America Press, 1997).
39. Moreland, "Philosophical Apologetics," 137.
40. Michael Ruse and E. O. Wilson, "The Evolution of Ethics," in *Religion and the Natural Sciences: The Range of Engagement*, comp. James E. Huchingson (Fort Worth, TX: Harcourt Brace, 1993).

41. Benjamin Wiker, *Moral Darwinism: How We Became Hedonists* (Downers Grove, IL: InterVarsity Press, 2002), 18.
42. Ibid., 19.
43. Robery Audi, ed., *The Cambridge Dictionary of Philosophy* (Cambridge: Cambridge University Press, 1996), 231.
44. Ibid.
45. Ibid.
46. Wiker, *Moral Darwinism*, 304.
47. Ibid.
48. Ibid.
49. Ibid.
50. Richard Weikart, *From Darwin to Hitler: Evolutionary Ethics, Eugenics, and Racism in Germany* (New York: Palgrave MacMillan, 2004), 229–30.
51. Ibid., 233.
52. Joseph S. Levine and Kenneth R. Miller, *Biology: Discovering Life* (Lexington, MA: D. C. Heath, 1992), 152, emphases in original.
53. Armand M. Nicholi Jr., *The Question of God: C. S. Lewis and Sigmund Freud Debate God, Love, Sex, and the Meaning of Life* (New York: Free Press, 2003), 242.
54. Antony Flew and Gary Habermas, "My Pilgrimage from Atheism to Theism: A Discussion Between Antony Flew and Gary Habermas," *Philosophia Christi* 6.2 (2004): 200.
55. Ibid., 201.

Chapter 7: Darwinism and the Law

1. The bill reads as follows:

> BE IT ENACTED BY THE GENERAL ASSEMBLY OF THE STATE OF TENNESSEE:
>
> SECTION 1. Tennessee Code Annotated, Section 49-2008, is amended by adding the following paragraph:
>
> Any biology textbook used for teaching in the public schools, which expresses an opinion of, or relates to a theory about origins or creation of man and his world shall be prohibited from being used as a textbook in such system unless it specifically states that it is a theory as to the origin and creation of man and his world and is not represented to be scientific fact. Any textbook so used in the public education system which expresses an opinion or relates to a theory or theories shall give in the same textbook and under the same subject commensurate attention to, and an equal amount of emphasis on, the origins and creation of man and his world as the same is recorded in other theories, including, but not limited to, the Genesis account in the Bible. The provisions

of this Act shall not apply to use of any textbook now legally in use, until the beginning of the school year of 1925–1926; Provided, however, that the textbook requirements stated above shall in no way diminish the duty of the state textbook commission to prepare a list of approved standard editions of textbooks for use in the public schools of the state as provided in this section. Each local school board may use textbooks or supplementary material as approved by the State Board of Education to carry out the provisions of this section. The teaching of all occult or satanical beliefs of human origin is expressly excluded from this act.

SECTION 2. Provided however that the Holy Bible shall not be defined as a textbook, but is hereby declared to be a reference work, and shall not be required to carry the disclaimer above provided for textbooks.

This act shall take effect upon becoming a law, the public welfare requiring it.

Tennessee "Genesis" Law, TENN. CODE ANN. § 49-2008 (1973).

"In the five years following the Scopes trial, state legislatures considered twenty anti-evolution bills and passed two into law." Richard M Cornelius, "The Trial That Made Monkeys Out of the World," *USA Today*, November 1990, 90. The Tennessee legislature repealed this act in 1967. Joyce F. Francis, "Creationism v. Evolution: The Legal History and Tennessee's Role in That History," *Tenn. Law Review* 63 (1996): 757n. 53.

2. *Scopes v. State*, 289 S.W. at 363n. 1; see also law.umkc.edu/faculty/projects/ftrials/scopes/tennstat.
3. The actual ad as it appeared in the Chattanooga *Daily Times*, May 4, 1925, read, "We are looking for a Tennessee teacher who is willing to accept our services in testing this law in the courts," the New York–based American Civil Liberties Union announced soon after the antievolution statute passed. "Our lawyers think a friendly test can be arranged without costing a teacher his or her job. Distinguished counsel have volunteered their services. All we need now is willing client." Several newspapers were used in this campaign. The Interactive Bible, "Textbook Fraud: Inherit the Wind: Intellectual Pornography!" at bible.ca/tracks/textbook-fraud-scopes-trial-inherit-wind (accessed March 23, 2001).
4. L. Sprague de Camp, quoted in David N. Menton, "A Hollywood History of the 1925 Scopes 'Monkey' Trial," 432, at bible.ca/tracks/textbook-fraud-scopes-trial-inherit-wind.htm#overview.
5. Ibid.
6. See Jonathan Wells for examples of intentional fraud and cover-up of discovered fraud occurring to promote evolutionary theory. *Icons of Evolu-*

tion: Science or Myth? Why Much of What We Teach About Evolution Is Wrong (Lanham, MD: Regnery, 2000).

7. George W. Hunter, *Civil Biology* (New York: American Book, 1914), 196.

8. Charles Darwin, *On the Origin of Species by Means of Natural Selection, or The Preservation of Favoured Races in the Struggle for Life*, with introduction by Ernst Mayr (London, U.K.: John Murray, 1859; from a facsimile of the 1st ed., Cambridge, Mass.: Harvard University Press, n.d.).

9. John Thomas Scopes, *The World's Most Famous Court Trial: Tennessee Evolution Case*, 2d ed. (1925; Dayton, TN: Bryan College, 1990), 300.

10. Ibid., 285.

11. Ibid., 288, 293.

12. Ibid., 298–99, 302–3.

13. Ibid., 236–37; for discussion of past mistakes by evolutionists and creationists, see *Teaching Science in a Climate of Controversy: A View from the American Scientific Affiliation* (Ipswich, MA: Committee for Integrity in Science Education, American Scientific Affiliation, 1986), 18–21.

14. Scopes, *World's Most Famous Court Trial*, 245.

15. Ibid., 247. Also see discussions of these kinds of mischaracterizations of human fossils and other scientific data in contemporary science texts in Wells, *Icons of Evolution*.

16. Scopes, *World's Most Famous Court Trial*, 273.

17. R. M. Cornelius, "William Jennings Bryan: The Scopes Trial and Inherit the Wind," at bryan.edu/scopes/inherit.

18. Ibid.

19. See Francis, "Creationism v. Evolution," 757.

20. Wendell Bird, "Resolution for Balanced Presentation of Evolution and Scientific Creationism," *Impact Series* (Acts and Facts), icr.org/article/153/ (accessed March 2, 2007).

21. The author has in his possession a few of the actual bills from the following state legislatures: Georgia, HB 690 (date unknown); Missouri, HB 480 (1980); Oklahoma, HB 1158 (1981–1982); South Dakota, H. 1224 (1981); Texas, HB [bill number unknown], (1981).Washington, H. 234 (1981).

22. The commonality of the legislation was recognized by scientist Wayne Moyer: "The bills introduced in four states were virtually identical, evidently based on a model reportedly written by Wendell Bird, a Georgia law clerk, and distributed by the ICR." Wayne Moyer, "The Challenge of Creationism," *American Laboratory* 12 (1980): 14. Wendell Bird is a member of the Georgia bar and formerly was a law clerk on the Fourth Circuit Court of Appeals, and then the Fifth Circuit. He was a graduate of Yale Law School, a former editor of *Yale Law Journal*, and received the Egger Prize for outstanding legal scholarship for his Note published in that journal. He was attorney for the Institute for Creation Research and argued *Edwards v. Aguillard* for the state of Louisiana. See Bird's biography

at Wendell R. Bird, "Freedom from Establishment and Unneutrality in Public School Instruction and Religious School Regulation," *Harvard Journal of Law and Public Policy* (1979): 125.

23. Note, "Freedom of Religion and Science Instruction in Public Schools," *Yale Law Journal* 87 (1978): 515.

24. *McLean v. Arkansas Board of Education*, 529 F. Supp. 1255 (1982).

25. Marcel Chotkowski La Follette, ed., *Creationism, Science, and the Law: The Arkansas Case* (Cambridge, MA: MIT Press, 1983), 16.

26. *McLean v. Arkansas Board of Education*, 529 F. Supp. 1255 (1982).

27. See *Edwards v. Aguillard*, 482 U.S. 578 (1987).

28. For a complete transcript of the Scopes trial and additional important historical information, see Scopes, *World's Most Famous Court Trial*.

29. This was largely through the introduction of antievolution bills in Tennessee and the model creation bills in the early 1980s.

30. See, for example, *Epperson v. Arkansas*, 393 U.S. 97 (1968); 37 U.S. Law Week 4017, 89 S.Ct. 266, 21 L. Ed. 228, appealed from *State v. Epperson* (242 Ark. 922 (1967), 416 S.W. 2d 322.

31. Among other cases that have concerned the creation/evolution controversy is *Smith v. State of Mississippi and State Board of Education*, 242 So. 2d 692, 698 (1970). This is a case similar to Epperson and is mentioned by the Epperson court in its opinion, *Epperson v. Arkansas*, 393 U.S. 97 (1968); 37 U.S. Law Week 4017, 89 S.Ct. 266, 21 L. Ed. 228, appealed from *State v. Epperson*, 242 Ark. 922 (1967), 416 S.W. 2d 322, at 109. In *Smith*, the court held that §§ 6798 and 6799 of Mississippi code prohibiting teaching that mankind descended or ascended from a lower form of animal were in violation of freedom of religion mandate of First Amendment. *Wright v. Houston Independent School District* et al., 366 F. Supp. 1208, 1212–13 (1972) regards a complaint from students who desired to enjoin the school district and State Board of Education from teaching evolution as part of the academic curriculum and from adopting textbooks that exclusively taught evolution. Plaintiffs argued that this state action established a religion of secularism and violated neutrality. The court held that students failed to state a cause of action upon which relief could be granted since there was no state action denying them equal protection or free exercise of religion and since they were free to exempt themselves from the classroom during the instruction in evolution. *Moore v. Gaston County Board of Education*, 357 F. Supp. 1037, 1043 (1973) dealt with an unpaid student teacher, who was discharged for having revealed, upon questioning by students, his approval of Darwinism, indicating personal agnosticism, and questioning the literal interpretation of the Bible. His summary dismissal because his views were different from his students' parents violated the Establishment Clause of the First Amendment. The court reasoned that to allow the teacher to respond in a manner that comports with those who "complain the loudest" establishes the religion of those complainants. Ibid. This reasoning seems to

affirm the undemocratic perspective of the courts, and disenfranchisement of religious believers involved in self-governing. Hal Culbertson, "Religion in the Political Process: A Critique of Lemon's Purpose Test," *University of Illinois Law Review* (1990): 936n. 201. *Steele v. Waters*, 527 S.W. 2d 72, 74 (1975), is a case involving textbooks, similar to *Daniel v. Waters*, 515 F.2d 485 (6th Cir. 1975). Daniel was decided by the Sixth Circuit a few months before the state supreme court decided its case, and served as a precedent. In agreement with the Sixth Circuit, this court found the state statute to be in violation of the federal and state constitutions. In *Seagraves v. State of California*, Sacramento Superior Court #278978 (1981), the California Superior Court held that the California State Board of Education Science Framework, as written and as qualified by its antidogmatism policy, provided sufficient accommodation to the perspectives of Seagraves, in contrast to his argument that class discussion of evolution deprived him and his children of freedom of religion. The policy declared that class discussions of origins would center on "how" and not "ultimate cause"; speculative statements concerning origins should be presented conditionally, not dogmatically. Molleen Matsumura, *Seven Significant Court Decisions* 1, at ncseweb.org/resources/articles/620_seven_significant_court_decisi_12_7_2000. *Rodney LeVake v. Independent School District* 656 et al., is a recent decision in which District Court Judge Bernard E. Borne dismissed the case of *Rodney LeVake v. Independent School District* 656 et al. "Order Granting Defendants' Motion for Summary Judgment and Memorandum," Court File Nr. CX-99-793, District Court for the Third Judicial District of the State of Minnesota (2000). LeVake, a high school biology teacher, argued for his free speech right to teach "evidence both for and against the theory" of evolution in the classroom. The school district, after having examined his teaching content, concluded that it did not match the curriculum, which required the teaching of evolution. After examining the case law concerning the requirement of teachers to teach the curriculum of the school district employing the teacher, the judge held that LeVake did not have a free speech right to override the curriculum, nor was the school district guilty of religious discrimination. Molleen Matsumura, *Background: Eight Significant Court Decisions Regarding Evolution/Creation Issues*, 1, at ncseweb.org/resources/ articles/5445_eight_significant_court_decisi_2_15_2001.

32. Initiated Act No. 1, Ark. Acts 1929; Ark. Stat. Ann. §80-1627, quoted in 393 U.S. 97, 99, 89 S.Ct. 266 , 267 (1968).

33. 393 U.S. at 100. The opinion of the Chancery Court is not officially reported. See 393 U.S. at 101n. 4.

34. Ibid., 100; U.S. Const. amend. I.

35. Ibid., 109; U.S. Const. amend XIV.

36. Ibid.

37. *State v. Epperson*, 242 Ark. 922 (1967), 416 S.W. 2d 322.

38. 393 U.S. at 109. *Epperson v. Arkansas*, 393 U.S. 97 (1968); 37 U.S. Law Week 4017, 89 S.Ct. 266, 21 L. Ed. 228, appealed from *State v. Epperson*, 242 Ark. 922 (1967), 416 S.W. 2d 322.

39. See Harold P. Green, "Constitutional Implications of Federal Restrictions on Scientific Research and Communication," *University of Missouri-Kansas City Law Review* 60 (1992): 621.

40. Ibid., 103. The Court identifies this religious group later in the opinion: "It is clear that fundamentalist sectarian conviction was and is the law's reason for existence." Ibid., 107–8. Repeatedly the courts, as here, mention "fundamentalists" as seeking to enforce their view of religion on the body politic. The Epperson opinion characteristically avers, "It is clear that fundamentalist sectarian conviction was and is the law's reason for existence." Ibid.

41. This case is before the full development of what is known as the Lemon test. *Lemon v. Kurtzman*, 403 U.S. 602 (1971), declared a three-prong test to govern establishment clause jurisprudence. Recently this test's influence has diminished. "Under this tri-part test, the Establishment Clause allegedly takes a 'neutral' stand toward religion, promoting government activity in extending general benefits to nonreligious and religious interests alike." H. Wayne House, "A Tale of Two Kingdoms: Can There Be Peaceful Coexistence of Religion with the Secular State?" *Brigham Young University Journal of Public Law* 13 (1999): 270. Also see Bird, "Freedom from Establishment and Unneutrality," 143–54. See also Ned Fuller, "The Alienation of Americans from Their Public Schools," *B.Y.U. Journal of Public Law* (1994): 96.

42. For a discussion of the problem of defining religion, see House, "A Tale of Two Kingdoms," 252–55 and notes.

43. Ibid., 108–9. The court's statements are confusing in light of its own acknowledgement that a court cannot inquire into a legislature's motives: "It is not for the court to invalidate a statute because of the court's belief that the 'motives' behind its passage were improper; it is simply too difficult to determine what those motives were." *State v. Epperson*, 393 U.S. at 113. The court also in *Edwards v. Aguillard* doubted the honesty of the legislature in their stated purpose. Norman Geisler discusses the relevant facts regarding legislative intent. Norman L. Geisler, *The Creator in the Courtroom, "Scopes II": The 1981 Arkansas Creation-Evolution Trial* (Fenton, MI: Mott Media, 1982), 49.

44. Daniel Yves Hall, "Stripping Away First Amendment Protection," *Missouri Law Review* 57 (1992): 653n. 225. Also see Morell E. Mullins, "Creation Science and McLean v. Arkansas Board of Education: The Hazards of Judicial Inquiry into Legislative Purpose and Motive," *University of Arkansas-Little Rock Law Journal* 5 (1982): 345.

45. John Hart Ely, "Legislative and Administrative Motive in Constitutional Law," *Yale Law Journal* 79 (1970): 1211–12.

46. For discussion of legislative purpose or intent, see Laurence H. Tribe, *American Constitutional Law*, 2d ed. (Mineola, NY: Foundation Press, 1988), §12-6; and for a discussion of secular purpose, see ibid., § 1-7, 12n. 7.
47. Culbertson, "Religion in the Political Process," 936n. 201. Some commentators have expressed the view that *Epperson* could also have been decided on secular effects grounds (see ibid., 935). Others, such as Jesse Choper, believe *Epperson* was wrongly decided because the effects of the statute were valid. Jesse Choper, "The Religion Clauses of the First Amendment: Reconciling the Conflict," *University of Pittsburgh Law Review* 41 (1980): 687.
48. Culbertson, "Religion in the Political Process," 936–37.
49. *Epperson*, 393 U.S. at 104.
50. Ibid., 109.
51. Ibid.
52. Meyer v. Nebraska, 262 U.S. 390.
53. Epperson v. Arkansas, 393 U.S. at 106.
54. SB 394, chap. 377; substituted for HB 597.
55. See Francis, "Creationism v. Evolution," 767, for a discussion of the background to the legal challenge.
56. The court was clear in its judgment that the legislation under appeal was contrary to the constitution:

> We have examined with interest the order entered by the Supreme Court, along with the jurisdictional statement filed by Tennessee in the Supreme Court and the response thereto filed by the plaintiffs. We believe that the order can properly be interpreted as indication that no three-judge District Court was necessary in this action under 28 U.S.C. s 2281 (1970) because, as we have determined above, this state statute is patently unconstitutional.

   See *Bailey v. Patterson*, 369 U.S. 31, 82 S.Ct. 549, 7 L.Ed.2d 512 (1962); and *Turner v. City of Memphis*, 369 U.S. 350, 82 S.Ct. 805, 7 L.Ed.2d 762 (1962).
57. See *Lemon v. Kurtzman*, 403 U.S. 602 (1971). "Under this tri-part test, the Establishment Clause allegedly takes a 'neutral' stand toward religion, promoting government activity in extending general benefits to nonreligious and religious interests alike." House, "A Tale of Two Kingdoms," 270. Also see Bird, "Freedom from Establishment and Unneutrality," 143–54.
58. *Lemon v. Kurtzman*, 403 U.S. at 612–13.
59. *Daniel v. Waters*, 515 F.2d at 489.
60. Ibid., 491.
61. Ibid., 485.
62. *McLean v. Arkansas Board of Education*, 529 F. Supp. at 1255.
63. *Edwards v. Aguillard*, 482 U.S. at 578.
64. *Daniel v. Waters*, 515 F.2d at 491. See *Lemon v. Kurtzman*, 403 U.S. at 612–13.

65. Francis, "Creationism v. Evolution," 772.
66. *McLean v. Arkansas Board of Education*, 529 F. Supp. at 1255.
67. Act 590 required that "public schools within this State shall give balanced treatment to creation-science and to evolution-science." Ark. Stat. Ann. § 80-1663 et seq. (1981 Supp.). See Clifford P. Hooker, "Creation Science Has No Legitimate Educational Purpose: *McLean v. the Arkansas Board of Education*," *Education Law Reporter* 1 (1982): 1069.
68. There are concerns about the objectivity of the judge in this trial. See Geisler, *The Creator in the Courtroom*, 24–25. *McLean v. Arkansas Board of Education*, 529 F. Supp. at 1257.
69. *McLean v. Arkansas Board of Education*, 529 F. Supp. at 1258–59. The judge incorrectly sets forth the fundamentals as stated by Geisler. See Geisler, *The Creator in the Courtroom*, 49, for a correction of the testimony and clarification of the judge's statements on this. Also, Geisler offers a number of corrections here to factual and logical errors made by the judge in his opinion. Ibid., 26–32.
70. *McLean v. Arkansas Board of Education*, 529 F. Supp. at 1258.
71. Ibid., 1255.
72. See the various attempts during the trial to impose a particular view, including on the witnesses in Geisler, *The Creator in the Courtroom*, 24–25.
73. See ibid., 25.
74. Geisler, a defense expert in the trial, gives a personal account:

> I would say that the media almost totally distorted what really went on there and here's how they did it. First, they quoted irrelevant things rather than essential things. Second, they used headlines which tended to color everything else that was said. Even if some things were accurately said in the story, the headlines colored it. Third, some particular newspapers created their own stories. They reported things that didn't occur at all. Fourth, they really took things out of the context in which they were presented. Basically they wrote their own stories using a few facts here and there that they got from the trial.

"The Arkansas Creation Trial," *Dallas Today* (c. 1982 radio broadcast transcript on file with author), 7. For a more thorough account by Geisler, see Geisler, *The Creator in the Courtroom*, 222.
Geisler gives several of the misrepresentations about Act 590:
1. It mandates teaching the biblical account of creation. It actually forbids that.
2. It is opposed to teaching evolution. It actually mandates teaching evolution alongside other views.
3. It refers to God or religious concepts. There is no reference to God, and it forbids teaching religion.

    4. It forces teachers who are opposed to creation to teach it anyway. Actually, the teacher doesn't have to teach anything about origins and/or they can have someone else teach the lectures they do not want to teach.

    5. "It is a 'Fundamentalist' Act. Actually, the 'Fundamentalists' of the 1920s were categorically opposed to teaching evolution and for teaching only the Genesis account of creation. This Act is contrary to both of these stands of the 1920s 'Fundamentalists.'" Geisler, *The Creator in the Courtroom*, 222.

75. "The Arkansas Creation Trial," 2.

76. "Although this case was in some ways superseded by the subsequent ruling of the U.S. Supreme Court in *Edwards v. Aguillard*, . . . the *McLean* case, and the philosophy of science that underwrites it, pose an implied challenge to the scientific status of all theories of origins (including design theory) that invoke singular, intelligent causes as opposed to strictly material causes." David K. DeWolf, Stephen C. Meyer, and Mark E. DeForrest, *Intelligent Design in Public School Science Curricula: A Legal Guidebook* (Richardson, TX: Foundation for Thought and Ethics, 1999), 10.

77. *McLean v. Arkansas Board of Education*, 529 F. Supp. at 1265. Evolutionist theologian William G. Most argues against such an understanding:

> My professional opinion is that creation-science is not religious. It appears to me to be scientific. . . .
>
> . . . The concept of creation is not inherently religious and is non-religious when defined as abrupt appearance in complex form. The concept of a creator is also not inherently religious, although it can be stated in religious terms; and it is not religious in its relation to creation-science. Creation-science is no more supportive of religious concepts of a creator or other religious doctrines than evolution is in its theistic evolutionist formulations.

William G. Most, "Affidavit of W. Most," at 2, *Edwards v. Aguillard*, 482 U.S., 96 L. Ed. 2d 510 (1987) (R.D. 77 Ex. 4, R. 544), quoted in Wendell R. Bird, *The Origin of Species Revisited: The Theories of Evolution and of Abrupt Appearance*, vol. 2, *Philosophy of Science, Philosophy of Religion, and History, Education, and Constitutional Issues* (New York: Philosophical Library, 1989), 447.

Responding to Judge Overton, cosmologist and atheist Frank Tipler says:

> The sections of the opinion on cosmology make amusing reading for cosmologists. The 1981 Arkansas equal time law defined "creation-science" as "science" that involved, among other things, "Sudden creation of the universe, energy, and life from nothing." . . . The judge thought such an idea inherently unscientific. . . .

> ... The problem with this is that ... the standard big bang theory has the Universe coming into existence out of nothing, and cosmologists use the phrase "creation of the universe" to describe this phenomenon. Thus if we accepted Judge Overton's idea that creation out of nothing is inherently religious, and his ruling that inherently religious ideas cannot be taught in public educational institutions, it would be illegal to teach the big bang theory at state universities. ...

Frank J. Tipler, "How to Construct a Falsifiable Theory in Which the Universe Came into Being Several Thousand Years Ago," *Philosophy of Science Association* 2 (1984): 893–94, quoted in Bird, *The Origin of Species Revisited*, 2:464.

78. *McLean v. Arkansas Board of Education*, 529 F. Supp. at 1265. For Geisler's argument, see Geisler, *The Creator in the Courtroom*, 114–18.
79. *McLean v. Arkansas Board of Education*, 529 F. Supp. at 1267.
80. *Seeger v. United States*, 380 U.S. 163, 176, 187, 85 S.Ct 850, 13 L.Ed.2d 733 (1964). If mention of a deity were a necessary infringement on the First Amendment Establishment Clause, then a great number of the documents of this republic and acts of government would be in violation of the clause. See the discussion by Bird, *The Origin of Species Revisited*.
81. See examples in Geisler, *The Creator in the Courtroom*, 116–17.
82. Bird, *The Origin of Species Revisited*, 2:21.
83. Larry Laudan, "Commentary: Science at the Bar—Causes for Concern," *Science, Technology and Human Values* (1982): 19, quoted in Bird, *The Origin of Species Revisited*, 2:23.
84. Ibid.
85. Philip Quinn, "The Philosopher of Science as Expert Witness," in *Science and Reality: Recent Work in the Philosophy of Science*, ed. J. Cushing, C. Delaney, and G. Gutting (Notre Dame, IN: University of Notre Dame Press, 1984), 42, quoted in Bird, *The Origin of Species Revisited*, 2:23.
86. *Edwards v. Aguillard*, 482 U.S. at 578. DeWolf, Meyer, and DeForrest, *Intelligent Design in Public School Science Curricula*, 20.
87. For a thorough interaction with, and record of, the Louisiana statute, see the majority opinion in *Aguillard v. Treen*, 440 So. 2d 704, 14 Ed. Law Rep. 844 (1983).
88. Arkansas Act 590 required that "public schools within this State shall give balanced treatment to creation-science and to evolution-science." Ark. Stat. Ann. § 80-1663 et seq. (1981 Supp.). See Hooker, "Creation Science Has No Legitimate Educational Purpose: *McLean v. the Arkansas Board of Education*," 1069.
89. *Edwards v. Treen*, 440 So. 2d at 704.
90. *Aguillard v. Treen*, 634 F. Supp. 426 (ED La. 1985).

91. *Aguillard v. Edwards*, 765 F.2d 1251 (1985). The original decision was 2–1 and then consideration was made to hear the case en banc, which was denied 8–7. The seven justice minority wrote a dissenting opinion, chiding the majority for failure to hear the case en banc. See appendix 1 for the forceful dissent.

92. *Edwards v. Aguillard*, 482 U.S. at 578.

93. Ibid., 583, quoting *Lemon v. Kurtzman*, 403 U.S. at 602. Regarding this test, see House, "A Tale of Two Kingdoms," 270–71.

94. Ibid., 585, quoting *Lynch v. Donnelly*, 465 U.S. 668, 690, 104 S.Ct. 1355, 1368, 79 L.Ed.2d 604 (1984), Justice Sandra Day O'Connor concurring.

95. *Edwards v. Aguillard*, 482 U.S. at 585, quoting *Wallace v. Jaffree*, 472 U.S. 38, 56, 105 S.Ct. 2479, 2489, 86 L.Ed.2d 29 (1985)

96. Ibid., 586.

97. Ibid., 588–89, quoting *Aguillard v. Edwards*, 765 F.2d at 1257.

98. 482 U.S. at 593–94, citing *Stone v. Graham*, 449 U.S. 39, 42, 101 S.Ct. 192, 194, 66 L.Ed.2d 199 (1980).

99. Ibid., 611. Justice Antonin Scalia, dissenting, also criticizes the definitions of Justice Powell (598–99; Justice Lewis Powell concurring) and rehearses the manner in which the Court had handled the issue of secular purpose. Ibid., 613–36.

100. Ibid., 612.

101. Letter, June 19, 1987, Creation Science Legal Defense Fund. Emphasis in original.

102. Ibid. Emphasis in original.

103. Though the majority in *Edwards v. Aguillard* found the statute in violation of the Establishment Clause, under *Lemon's* first prong of a primary secular purpose (403 U.S at 612), it did not hold that creation is inherently religious and expressly stated that teachers may present other scientific theories besides evolution: "[T]eaching a variety of scientific theories about the origins of humankind to schoolchildren might be validly done with the clear secular intent of enhancing the effectiveness of science instruction" (482 U.S. at 96). Nadeen Strossen acknowledges that creation could be presented as a valid scientific alternative to evolution: "Absent the statute, nothing would have prevented any school teacher who so chose from discussing any scientific shortcomings in evolutionary theory or any scientific evidence supporting a different theory of origins, including a creation theory." Nadeen Strossen, "'Secular Humanism' and 'Scientific Creationism': Proposed Standards for Reviewing Curricular Decisions Affecting Students' Religious Freedom," *Ohio State Law Journal* 47 (1986): 403–4.

104. See *Edwards v. Aguillard*, 482 U.S. 578, 107 S.Ct. 2573, 96 L.Ed.2d 510 (1987).

105. *Mozert v. Hawkins County Board of Education*, 827 F.2d 1058 (6th Cir. 1987).

106. Other concerns expressed were the subjects of mental telepathy (ibid., 1060), secular humanism, "futuristic supernaturalism," pacifism, and false views of death. Ibid., 1062.
107. Ibid., 1061.
108. Ibid.
109. Ibid., quoting *Epperson v. Arkansas,* 393 U.S. 97, 106, 89 S.Ct. 266, 271, 21 L.Ed. 2d 228 (1968).
110. Ibid., 1064.
111. Ibid., quoting *Grove v. Mead School Dist. No.* 354, 753 F.2d 1528, 1533 (9th Cir. 1985), cert. Denied, 474 U.S. 826, 106 S.Ct. 85, L. Ed. 2d 70 (1986).
112. *Webster v. New Lenox School District No.* 122, 917 F. 2d 1004 (1990).
113. "Mr. Webster said the discussion of religious issues in his class was only for the purpose of developing an open mind in his students. For example, Mr. Webster explained that he taught nonevolutionary theories of creation to rebut a statement in his social studies textbook indicating that the world is over four billion years old." Ibid., 1006.
114. The First Amendment reads: "Congress shall make no law respecting an establishment of religion or prohibiting the free exercise therefore." U.S. Const. Amend. I.
115. *Webster v. New Lenox School District,* 917 F.2d at 1004.
116. Ibid., 1005.
117. Ibid., 1004.
118. Ibid., 1006.
119. Ibid., 1007.
120. Ned Fuller, "The Alienation off Americans from Their Public Schools," *Brigham Young University Education and Law Journal* (1994): 102–3.
121. *Bishop v. Aronov,* 926 F.2d 1066, 59 USLW 2583, 65 Ed. Law Rep. 1109 (1991).
122. Ibid.
123. *Hazelwood School Dist. V. Kuhlmeier,* 484 U.S. 260, 271, 108 S.Ct. 562, 569, 98 L.Ed. 2d 592 (1988); see *Bethel School District v. Fraser,* 478 U.S. 675, 685 (1986), stating that rights of students in public schools are not as broad as rights of adults in other forums.
124. *Wisconsin v. Yoder,* 406 U.S. 205 (1972).
125. *Bishop v. Aronov,* 1566.
126. *Widmer v. Vincent,* 454 U.S. 263, 102 S.Ct. 269, 70 L.Ed. 2d 440 (1981).
127. *Bishop v. Aronov,* 1567.
128. Ibid., 1066.
129. Ibid., 1071.
130. See the analysis of the Eleventh Circuit's reasoning by John W. Hamilton, "Bishop v. Aronov: Religion-Tainted Viewpoints Are Banned from the Marketplace of Ideas," *Washington and Lee Law Review* 49 (1992): 1558–59.

131. Ibid., 1562–68.
132. Ibid., 1568–78.
133. Ibid., 1571.
134. Ibid., 1579.
135. *Freiler v. Tangipahoa Parish Board of Education*, 185 F.3d, 337, 137 Ed. Law Rep. 195 (*reh'g en banc* requested, *Freiler v. Tangipahoa Parish Board of Education*, 201 F.3d 602, 141 Ed. Law Rep. 458 [2000] petition denied).
136. *Freiler v. Tangipahoa Board of Education*, 975 F. Supp. at 819. The disclaimer read:

> Whenever, in classes of elementary or high school, the scientific theory of evolution is to be presented, whether from textbook, workbook, pamphlet, other written material, or oral presentation, the following statement shall be quoted immediately before the unit of study begins as a disclaimer from endorsement of such theory. It is hereby recognized by the Tangipahoa Board of Education, that the lesson to be presented, regarding the origin of life and matter, is known as the Scientific Theory of Evolution and should be presented to inform students of the scientific concept and not intended to influence or dissuade the Biblical version of Creation or any other concept. It is further recognized by the Board of Education that it is the basic right and privilege of each student to form his/her own opinion or maintain beliefs taught by parents on this very important matter of the origin of life and matter. Students are urged to exercise critical thinking and gather all information possible and closely examine each alternative toward forming an opinion.

Freiler v. Tangipahoa Parish School Board of Education, 975 F. Supp. at 821.
137. Ibid. Also see Andrea Ahlskog Mittleider, "*Freiler v. Tangipahoa Parish Board of Education*: Ignoring the Flaws in the Establishment Clause," *Loyota Law Review* 46 (2000): 467. Mittleider argues that the Fifth Circuit Court should have brought a better standard of Establishment Clause interpretation than the confusing and diminishing Lemon tests.
138. *Freiler v. Tangipahoa Parish School Board of Education*, 975 F. Supp. 819, 121 Ed. Law Rep. 614 (1997).
139. Ibid., 826–29.
140. Ibid., 831.
141. *Freiler v. Tangipahoa Parish School Board of Education*, 185 F.3d, at 337, 344–48. Also see Mittleider, "*Freiler v. Tangipahoa Parish Board of Education*," 478–82.
142. See *Freiler v. Tangipahoa Parish Board of Education*, 975 F. Supp., 821. Molleen Matsumura, "Background: Eight Significant Court Decisions Regarding Evolution/Creation Issues," 1, at ncseweb.org/resources/

articles/5445_eight_significant_court_decisi_2_15_2001. The Court, however, merely assumed the interchangeability of the theories of creation science and intelligent design without evaluating the facts regarding them.

143. Antony Flew and Gary Habermas, "Atheist Becomes Theist: Exclusive Interview with Former Atheist Anthony Flew," available at http://biola .edu/antonyflew/.

144. *The Compact Edition of the Oxford English Dictionary*, P–Z (Oxford, U.K.: Clarendon, 1987), 2:2668.

145. J. P. Moreland, ed., *The Creation Hypothesis* (Downers Grove, IL: Inter-Varsity Press, 1994), 17. See the presentation by John W. Klotz on the reliability of sense impressions and logic in scientific investigations. John W. Klotz, *Genes, Genesis and Evolution*, 2d rev. ed. (1955; St. Louis: Concordia, 1970), 4–6.

146. Quoted in Donald F. Calbreath, "The Challenge of Creationism: Another Point of View," *American Laboratory* 12 (1980): 10. See the evaluation by John L. Wiester of the way in which the modern scientific establishment equates the term *evolution* with the "Blind Watchmaker." John L. Wiester, "The Real Meaning of Evolution," *Communications* 45 (1993): 1–4.

147. Moreland, *Creation Hypothesis*, 14.

148. Ibid., 15–17.

149. Bird, *The Origin of Species Revisited*, 2:21. Bird provides evidence that Overton's definition is fallacious. Ibid., 2:20–78. Philosopher of science Philip Quinn says of Ruse's definition in *McLean*:

> If the expert's views are not representative of a settled consensus of opinion in the relevant community of scholars, then policy based on those views will lack credibility within that community, and the members of that community are likely to regard such lack of credibility as discrediting the policy in question. This was the major problem in *McLean v. Arkansas*. Ruse's views do not represent a settled consensus of opinion among philosophers of science. Worse still, some of them are clearly false and some are based on obviously fallacious arguments. . . .

Philip Quinn, "The Philosopher of Science as Expert Witness," 32, 51; quoted in Bird, *The Origin of Species Revisited*, 2:23. See additional arguments regarding modern scientific perspectives on demarcation of what is science and what is not in DeWolf, Meyer, and DeForrest, *Intelligent Design in Public School Science Curricula*, 11–15.

150. Judge Overton refers to natural law in two of his five requirements for science: "it is guided by natural law" and "it has to be explanatory by reference to natural law." This definition excludes creation science and many other areas of scientific investigation. This use of natural law is ironic in that natural law came into science from theology. See Larry Laudan,

"Commentary: Science at the Bar—Causes for Concern," *Science, Technology, and Human Values* (Fall 1982): 16, 19; quoted in Bird, *The Origin of Species Revisited*, 2:23.

151. Laudan, "Commentary: Science at the Bar," 17–18, quoted in Bird, *The Origin of Species Revisited*, 2:25. Bird cites a number of cosmologists and other scientists who contend that often the known laws of physics do not apply. Ibid., 27–28.

152. *McLean v. Arkansas Board of Education*, 529 F. Supp. at 1265.

153. *Peloza v. Capistrano Unified School District*, 782 F. Supp. 1412, 1416, 1418 (C.D. Cal. 1992), *aff'd in part*, 37 F.3d 517 (9th Cir. 1994).

154. Responding to the assertion of Judge Overton that creation from nothing requires a supernatural deity, comes the comment of cosmologist and atheist Tipler:

> The sections of the opinion on cosmology make amusing reading for cosmologists. The 1981 Arkansas equal time law defined "creation-science" as "science" that involved, among other things, "Sudden creation of the universe, energy, and life from nothing." . . . The judge thought such an idea inherently unscientific. . . .
>
> The problem with this is that . . . the standard big bang theory has the Universe coming into existence out of nothing, and cosmologists use the phrase "creation of the universe" to describe this phenomenon. Thus if we accepted Judge Overton's idea that creation out of nothing is inherently religious, and his ruling that inherently religious ideas cannot be taught in public educational institutions, it would be illegal to teach the big bang theory at state universities. . . .

Tipler, "How to Construct a Falsifiable Theory," 893–94; quoted in Bird, *The Origin of Species Revisited*, 2:464.

155. See Bird, *The Origin of Species Revisited*, 2:447, for examples of references to creation. See Bird's discussion of the steady state theory. Ibid., 199–200. See also George Mulfinger, "Theories of the Origin of the Universe," in *Why Not Creation?* ed. Walter E. Lammerts (Nutley, NJ: Presbyterian & Reformed, 1970), 54–58, for discussion of steady state theory, and pages 39–66 in the same publication, for a look at a number of theories regarding the origin of the universe. The steady state theory of origins from radiation, rather than out of nothing, parallels ancient cosmology.

156. See William Paley, *Natural Theology: or, Evidence of the Existence and Attributes of the Deity Collected from the Appearances of Nature* (1802; rev. ed., Hallowell, England: Glazier, 1839), 5–7. A contrasting view to design can be observed in Richard Dawkins, *The Blind Watchmaker* (New York: Norton, 1996), 1: "Biology is the study of complicated things that give the appearance of having been designed for a purpose." His point is that

evolution is blind in its selection. If the universe looks like it is designed, that is only because it works. This seems to be less than forthright.

157. Dean Kenyon and Percival Davis, *Of Pandas and People* (Dallas, TX: Haughton, 1993), 126–27.

158. William Dembski, *No Free Lunch: Why Specified Complexity Cannot Be Purchased Without Intelligence* (Lanham, MD: Rowman & Littlefield, 2002), 314.

159. *McLean v. Arkansas Board of Education*, 529 F. Supp. at 1255, 1266. See Geisler, *Creator in the Courtroom*, 114–17, for refutation that the concepts of creation or a creator are necessarily religious. Also see John Zingarelli, "Is 'Creation' a Religious Concept?" *Regent University Law Review* 8 (1997): 35. Zingarelli argues that no established criteria can be given to identify a concept as religious or scientific.

160. See Bird, *The Origin of Species Revisited*, 2:451.

161. *McLean v. Arkansas Board of Education*, 529 F. Supp. at 1265, 1266.

162. Gerhard Hasel indicates that the Genesis account of the creation of man differs considerably from the general Mesopotamian view:

> The similarities and differences between the purpose of man's creation in Sumero-Akkadian mythology and Gen. 1:26–28 afford another point which requires our attention. Sumerian mythology is in complete accord with the Babylonian Atrahasis Epic and Enuma elish in depicting the need of the creation of man to result from the attempt to relieve the gods from laboring for their sustenance. This mythological picture, which views the creation of man as an afterthought to provide the gods with food and to satisfy their physical needs is contradicted in Gen. 1. The first chapter of the Bible depicts man as the "pinnacle of creation." Man is not made as a kind of afterthought in order to take care of the needs of the gods. He appears as the only one "blessed" by God (1:28); he is "the ruler of the animal and vegetable king-doms." All seed bearing plants and fruit trees are his for food (1:20). Here the divine concern and the divine care for man's physical needs come to expression in antithesis to man's purpose to care for the physical needs of the gods in Sumero-Akkadian mythology. It is obvious that when it comes to defining the pur-pose of man's creation. [*sic*] Gen. 1 combats pagan mythological notions while at the same time, the man-centered orientation of Gen. 1 and man's glory and freedom to rule the earth for his own needs is conveyed. We may suggest that the different idea with regard to the purpose of the creation of man in Gen. 1 rests upon the Hebrew anthropology and understanding of reality.

Gerhard Hasel, "The Polemic Nature of Genesis Cosmology," *Evangelical Quarterly* 46 (1974): 89–90.

Stanley Jaki says, "All ancient cultures were pantheistic. By contrast, the Christian concept of God [and historic Judaism] has for its essence the belief that He is truly a Creator, that is, a being absolutely transcendental to the world. He exists whether He creates a universe or not." Stanley L. Jaki, "Science: Western or What?" *Intercollegiate Review* 26 (1990): 9.

163. See Bird, *The Origin of Species Revisited*, 2:136, 193–94.
164. See Geisler, *The Creator in the Courtroom*, 114.
165. Justice Antonin Scalia dissent in *Edwards v. Aguillard*, 482 U.S., 629–30.
166. Bird, *The Origin of Species Revisited*, 2:187.
167. See Bird, *The Origin of Species Revisited*, 2:275–77; John W. Whitehead and John Conlan, "The Establishment of the Religion of Secular Humanism and Its First Amendment Implications," *Texas Tech Law Review* 10 (1978): 1, 47.
168. See, e.g., *Peloza v. Capistrano Unified School District*, 782 F. Supp, 521.
169. Even with disclaimers that scientific creationism or creation science is only built on scientific evidence and without reference to religious materials or texts, the McLean court continued to speak of the position as biblical creationism. See *Mclean v. Arkansas Board of Education*, 529 F. Supp. at 1255, 1258–59, 1264.
170. Jay D. Wexler, "Of Pandas, People, and the First Amendment: The Constitutionality of Teaching Intelligent Design in the Public Schools," *Stanford Law Review* 49 (1997): 439.
171. DeWolf, Meyer, and DeForrest, *Intelligent Design in Public School Science Curricula*, 10.
172. Laurence H. Tribe, *American Constitutional Law* (West Conshohocken, PA: Foundation, 1978), 827–28, quoted in DeWolf, Meyer, and DeForrest, *Intelligent Design in Public School Science Curricula*, 16.
173. See H. Wayne House, "A Tale of Two Kingdoms," 249–62.
174. *Alvarado v. City of San Jose*, 94 F.3d 1128 (9th Cir. 1996); quoted in DeWolf, Meyer, and DeForrest, *Intelligent Design in Public School Science Curricula*, 16.
175. Ibid., 17.
176. Justice Lewis Powell concurring, *Edwards v. Aguillard*, U.S. 605, quoting *McGowan v. Maryland*, 366 U.S. 420, 442 (1961).
177. DeWolf, Meyer, and DeForrest, *Intelligent Design in Public School Science Curricula*, 17.
178. The disclaimer text used this language:

The Pennsylvania Academic Standards require students to learn about Darwin's Theory of Evolution and eventually to take a standardized test of which evolution is a part.

Because Darwin's Theory is a theory, it continues to be tested as new evidence is discovered. The Theory is not a fact. Gaps in the Theory exist for which there is no evidence. A theory is defined as a well-tested explanation that unifies a broad range of observations.

> Intelligent Design is an explanation of the origin of life that differs from Darwin's view. The reference book, *Of Pandas and People*, is available for students who might be interested in gaining an understanding of what Intelligent Design actually involves.

> With respect to any theory, students are encouraged to keep an open mind. The school leaves the discussion of the Origins of Life to individual students and their families. As a Standards-driven district, class instruction focuses upon preparing students to achieve proficiency on Standards-based assessments.

Kitzmiller v. Dover, 400 F. Supp. 2d 707, 708–9 (M.D.Pa. 2005).

179. For a prointelligent design view, see David K. Dewolf, John West, Casey Luskin, and Jonathan Witt, *Traipsing into Evolution: Intelligent Design and the* Kitzmiller v. Dover *Decision* (Seattle, WA: Discovery Institute, 2006). For an anti-intelligent design view, see Jay Wexler, "Judging Intelligent Design: Should the Courts Decide What Counts as Science or Religion?" at bc.edu/bc_org/research/rapl/events/abstract_wexler. Accessed September 28, 2006.

180. DeWolf, Meyer, and DeForrest, *Intelligent Design in Public School Science Curricula*, 30–37.

181. *Kitzmiller v. Dover*, 400 F. Supp. 2d 707, 735 (M.D.Pa. 2005).

182. Note the differences between the traditional arguments of creation science and those of intelligent design noted above. See also the presentation of differences between scientific creationism and intelligent design in DeWolf, Meyer, and DeForrest, *Intelligent Design in Public School Science Curricula*, 22–24:

> [T]he prepositional content of design theory differs significantly from that of scientific creationism. Scientific creationism is committed to the following propositions:
>
> 1. There was a sudden creation of the universe, energy, and life from nothing.
> 2. Mutations and natural selection are insufficient to bring about the development of all living kinds from a single organism.
> 3. Changes of the originally created kinds of plants and animals occur only within fixed limits.
> 4. There is separate ancestry for humans and apes.
> 5. The earth's geology can be explained via catastrophism, primarily by the occurrence of a worldwide flood.
> 6. The earth and living kinds had a relatively recent inception (on the order of ten thousand years).

These six tenets taken jointly define scientific creationism for legal purposes. The Court in *Edwards* ruled that taken jointly this group of propositions may not be taught in public school science classrooms. (Nevertheless, the Court left the door open to some of these tenets being discussed individually.)

Design theory, on the other hand, asserts the following:

1. High information content (or specified complexity) and irreducible complexity constitute strong indicators or hallmarks of past intelligent design.
2. Biological systems have a high information content (or specified complexity) and utilize subsystems that manifest irreducible complexity.
3. Naturalistic mechanisms or undirected causes do not suffice to explain the origin of information (specified complexity) or irreducible complexity.
4. Therefore, intelligent design constitutes the best explanation for the origin of information and irreducible complexity in biological systems.

A comparison of these two lists demonstrates clearly that design theory and scientific creationism differ markedly in content. Clearly, then, they do not derive from the same source. Thus, the Court's ruling in *Edwards* does not apply to design theory and can provide no grounds for excluding discussion of design from the public school science curriculum.

183. See Henry Morris, "Guiding Lamp or Simply Luster," *Acts and Facts* (April 2006): 7; John C. Whitcomb, "The History and Impact of the Book: The Genesis Flood," *Impact* (May 2006); Henry M. Morris, "Intelligent Design and/or Scientific Creationism," *Back to Genesis* (April 2006); and Henry M. Morris, "Insufficient Design," *Back to Genesis* (March 2006).
184. Those making these proposals must strongly disassociate any reference to the Bible, evolution as religion and scientific theories that seek to prove portions of the Bible, and major religious voices in the community should not take a significant part in the activities. The emphasis must be on greater and fairer science education.
185. An ideal scenario would be for a popular and peer respected public school teacher (preferably high school) who has faithfully avoided any biblical references or allusions in class, who has taught intelligent design and random chance to his students, to be prohibited from teaching these scientific theories. This would entail viewpoint discrimination in violation of the First Amendment. See DeWolf, Meyer, and DeForrest, *Intelligent Design in Public School Science Curricula*, 24–26, for discussion of viewpoint

discrimination in reference to teaching intelligent design. Questions of freedom of religion or establishment of religion should be avoided.

186. The errors of attention attracted by having church groups seek to influence legislation should be avoided. Sponsors should restrict themselves to concerns of better science education and academic freedom for students.

Appendix: A Reply to Francis Collins's Darwinian Arguments for Common Ancestry of Apes and Humans

1. Francis Collins, *The Language of God: A Scientist Presents Evidence for Belief* (New York: Free Press, 2006), 199.
2. For example, see David Van Biema, "God vs. Science," *Time* (November 13, 2006): 48–55; and David Van Biema, "The Discover Interview: Francis Collins," *Discover* (February 2007): 44–47.
3. Two reviews of Collins's book concur that Collins does a good job of explaining and supporting arguments for intelligent design in cosmology, but then inconsistently rejects intelligent design in biology. See Logan Paul Gage, "Best Explanations," *American Spectator* (October 1, 2006), at discovery.org/scripts/viewDB/index.php?command=view&id=3749. See also Jonathan Witt, "Book Review: Random Acts of Design: Francis Collins Sees Evidence That God Made the Cosmos—But Life Is Another Matter," *Touchstone* (November 9, 2006), at touchstonemag.com/archives/article.php?id=19-08-032-f.
4. See Michael J. Behe, *The Edge of Evolution: The Search for the Limits of Darwinism* (New York: Free Press, 2007).
5. See Jonathan Wells, "Darwin's Tree of Life," in *Icons of Evolution* (Washington, DC: Regnery, 2000).
6. W. Ford Doolittle, "Phylogenetic Classification and the Universal Tree," *Science* 284 (June 25, 1999): 2124–28.
7. W. Ford Doolittle, "Uprooting the Tree of Life," *Scientific American* (February 2000): 90–95.
8. Carl Woese, "The Universal Ancestor," *Proceedings of the National Academy of Sciences USA* 95 (June 1998): 6854–9859.
9. Antonis Rokas, Dirk Krüger, Sean B. Carroll, "Animal Evolution and the Molecular Signature of Radiations Compressed in Time," *Science* 310 (December 23, 2005): 1933–38.
10. Stephen C. Meyer, Marcus Ross, Paul Nelson, and Paul Chien, "The Cambrian Explosion: Biology's Big Bang," in *Darwinism, Design, and Public Education*, ed. John Angus Campbell and Stephen C. Meyer (East Lansing, MI: Michigan State University Press, 2003).
11. Collins, *The Language of God*, 134.
12. The original paper on this is Jorge J. Yunis, Jeffrey R. Sawyer, and Kelly Dunham, "The Striking Resemblance of High-Resolution G-banded Chromosomes of Man and Chimpanzee," *Science* 208 (1980): 1145–48. A

follow-up paper that is widely cited is: Jorge J. Yunis and Om Prakash, "The Origin of Man: A Chromosomal Pictorial Legacy," *Science* 215 (1982): 1525–30. Information from these papers is frequently found in textbooks. For example: Gerald J. Stine, *The New Human Genetics* (Dubuque, IA: Wm. C. Brown, 1989), 313.

13. Nearly all blueprints for houses include sketches of doors, walls, ventilation, etc. This does not mean that one blueprint was necessarily taken from another. Rather, the functional requirements of houses require that houses have ways to enter and exit, structural support, and ventilation.

14. Collins, *The Language of God*, 137.

15. Stephen C. Meyer, "The Cambrian Information Explosion," in *Debating Design*, ed. Michael Ruse and William Dembski (New York: Cambridge University Press, 2004).

16. William A. Dembski, *No Free Lunch* (Lanham, MD: Rowman & Littlefield, 2002), xiv.

17. Stephen C. Meyer, "The Origin of Biological Information and the Higher Taxonomic Categories," *Proceedings of the Biological Society of Washington* 117.2 (2004): 213–39.

18. Jonathan Marks, *What It Means to Be 98% Chimpanzee: Apes, People, and Their Genes* (Berkeley, CA: University of California Press, 2002), 34.

19. James A. Shapiro and Richard Sternberg, "Why Repetitive DNA Is Essential to Genome Function," *Biological Review* 80 (2005): 227–50.

20. Richard Dawkins, "The Information Challenge," *The Skeptic* 18.4 (December 1998), at simonyi.ox.ac.uk/dawkins/WorldOfDawkins-archive/Dawkins/Work/Articles/1998-12-04infochallange.

21. Collins, *The Language of God*, 136.

22. Ibid., 137.

23. Ibid., 136–37.

24. Richard Sternberg, "On the Roles of Repetitive DNA Elements in the Context of a Unified Genomic–Epigenetic System," *Annals of the New York Academy of Sciences* 981 (2002): 154–88.

25. Ibid.

26. Tammy A. Morrish et al., "DNA Repair Mediated by Endonuclease-independent LINE-1 Retrotransposition," *Nature Genetics* 31.2 (June 2002): 159–65.

27. Galit Lev-Maor, Rotem Sorek, Noam Shomron, and Gil Ast, "The Birth of an Alternatively Spliced Exon: 3' Splice-site Selection in Alu Exons," *Science* 300.5623 (May 23, 2003): 1288–91; and Wojciech Makalowski, "Not Junk After All," *Science* 300.5623 (May 23, 2003): 1246–47.

28. Richard Sternberg and James A. Shapiro, "How Repeated Retroelements Format Genome Function," *Cytogenetic and Genome Research* 110 (2005): 108–16.

29. W. Wayt Gibbs, "The Unseen Genome: Gems Among the Junk," *Scientific American* (November 2003): 46–53, emphasis added.

30. Ibid.
31. Ibid.
32. Sternberg, "On the Roles of Repetitive DNA Elements," 154–88.
33. Rick Weiss, "Intricate Toiling Found in Nooks of DNA Once Believed to Stand Idle," *Washington Post* (June 14, 2007), A01.
34. Collins, *The Language of God*, 139.
35. Yali Xue et al., "Spread of an Inactive Form of Caspase-12 in Humans Is Due to Recent Positive Selection," *American Journal of Human Genetics* 78 (April 2006): 659–70.
36. Shinji Hirotsune et al., "An Expressed Pseudogene Regulates the Messenger-RNA Stability of Its Homologous Coding Gene," *Nature* 423 (May 1, 2003): 91–96.
37. M. Lamkanfi, M. Kalai, and P. Vandenabeele, "Caspase-12: An Overview," *Cell Death and Differentiation* 11 (2004): 365–68.
38. Sug Hyung Lee, Christian Stehlik, and John C. Reed, "COP, a Caspase Recruitment Domain-containing Protein and Inhibitor of Caspase-1 Activation Processing," *Journal of Biological Chemistry* 276.37 (September 14, 2001): 34495–500.
39. Lamkanfi, Kalai, and Vandenabeele, "Caspase-12: An Overview," 365–68.
40. Collins, *The Language of God*, 134.
41. We recognize that Collins at certain points notes that little is known about "junk" DNA and claims it requires hubris to call it "junk" DNA. Collins, *The Language of God*, 111. Nonetheless, Collins ignores his own advice. He assumes that various types of DNA have no function.
42. Ibid., 129–30.
43. Michael D. Lemonick and Andrea Dorfman, "What Makes Us Different?" *Time* (October 1, 2006), at time.com/time/magazine/article/0,9171,1541283,00.
44. Ibid.
45. Erika Check, "It's the Junk That Makes Us Human," *Nature* 444 (November 9, 2006): 130.
46. Collins, *The Language of God*, 127.
47. Ibid.
48. Lemonick and Dorfman, "What Makes Us Different?"
49. Collins, *The Language of God*, 139.
50. Bernard Wood, quoted in Joseph B. Verrengia, "Gene Mutation Said Linked to Evolution," Associated Press, taken from the *San Diego Union Tribune*, March 24, 2004.
51. Ian Tattersal, *The Monkey In the Mirror: Essays on the Science of What Makes Us Human* (Orlando, FL: Harcourt, 2002) , 160.
52. See Collins, *The Language of God*, 139–41.
53. Lemonick and Dorfman, "What Makes Us Different?"

54. Charles T. Snowdon, "From Primate Communication to Human Language," 224, in *Tree of Origin: What Primate Behavior Can Tell Us About Human Social Evolution*, ed. Frans B. M. de Waal (Cambridge, MA: Harvard University Press, 2001).

55. Richard W. Byrne, "Social and Technical Forms of Primate Intelligence," in deWaal, ed., *Tree of Origin*, 148–49.

56. Tattersal, *The Monkey in the Mirror*, 158.

57. See Carl Zimmer, *Evolution: The Triumph of an Idea* (New York: Harper Collins, 2001), 288–89.

58. Elizabeth Bates quoted in Steven Pinker, *The Language Instinct: How the Mind Creates Language* (New York: Harper Perennial, 1994), 350.

59. Ibid., 377.

60. Tattersal, *The Monkey in the Mirror*, 160.

61. Ibid., 162.

62. Noam Chomsky's belief as described in Pinker, *The Language Instinct*, 341. Pinker rejects Chomsky's view and believes that language can evolve in a Darwinian fashion. Readers are referred to chapter 11 of Pinker's book for details.

Name Index

Subject Index